BASIC CRIMINAL PROCEDURES

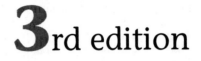

BASIC CRIMINAL PROCEDURES

EDWARD E. PEOPLES, DPA
Professor Emeritus
Administration of Justice Department
Santa Rosa College

PEARSON

Prentice
Hall

Upper Saddle River, New Jersey 07458

Library of Congress Cataloging-in-Publication Data

Peoples, Edward E.
   Basic criminal procedures / Edward E. Peoples. — 3rd ed.
      p. cm.
   Includes index.
   ISBN 0-13-173192-0
  1. Criminal procedure—United States.   I. Title.

   KF9619.P46 2007
   345.73′05—dc22   2006013258

Editor-in-Chief: Vernon R. Anthony
Executive Editor: Frank Mortimer, Jr.
Associate Editor: Sarah Holle
Marketing Manager: Adam Kloza
Editorial Assistant: Jillian Allison
Production Editor: Donna Leik, Techbooks
Production Liaison: Barbara Marttine Cappuccio
Director of Manufacturing and Production: Bruce Johnson
Managing Editor: Mary Carnis
Manufacturing Manager: Ilene Sanford
Manufacturing Buyer: Cathleen Petersen
Senior Design Coordinator: Mary Siener
Cover Designer: Allen Gold
Cover Image: Robert Shafer, Getty Images
Composition: Techbooks
Printing and Binding: Command Web

Pearson Education Ltd.
Pearson Education Singapore Pte. Ltd.
Pearson Education Canada, Ltd.
Pearson Education—Japan

Pearson Education Australia Pty. Limited
Pearson Education North Asia Ltd.
Pearson Educación de Mexico, S.A. de C.V.
Pearson Education Malaysia Pte. Ltd.

10 9 8 7 6 5 4 3 2
ISBN: 0-13-173192-0

Dedicated to my wife, Corinne,
for joining with me to share of life
in our process of loving and becoming.

BRIEF CONTENTS

CONTENTS

6

MIRANDA: ITS MEANING AND APPLICATION   86

7

BOOKING AND JAIL CUSTODY PROCEDURES 105

8

THE ADVERSARY SYSTEM: ROLES OF THE PROSECUTION AND DEFENSE 118

9

THE COURT STRUCTURE AND PRETRIAL PROCEDURES   134

10

TRIAL PROCEDURES   156

11

DEFENSE STRATEGIES AND TRIAL OUTCOMES   174

12

SENTENCING PROCEDURES AND ALTERNATIVES   183

13

POST-SENTENCING PROCEDURES   200

PREFACE

The purpose of this text is to explain and/or describe the procedural aspects of the criminal justice system in a way that can be applied within the context of any state's procedural laws. Although the federal court structure is described in brief, and federal court decisions are discussed, very little reference is otherwise made of federal laws, agencies, or procedures.

The book is designed to be the primary text in college courses entitled Criminal Procedures, Procedures in the Justice System, or some similar title. It is presented in a way that no prior knowledge of how or why the justice system operates is necessary. It is written with the student in mind. The writing style is direct and basic, yet the material is well-researched and current. However, it is not intended to be the definitive work on the subject. It is an introductory text, and there is ample opportunity for the instructor to include his or her own areas of emphasis.

Although the presentation is directed to the student new to this field, no study of criminal procedures can avoid the vocabulary used by those who work within the system: law enforcement, judges, lawyers, correctional officers, probation officers, parole agents, and related personnel. To the new student of criminal justice, the vocabulary might initially seem like a foreign language. In fact, it is. It is known as *legalese,* a language created by attorneys, grounded in our English common law heritage, with an overlay of French terms and Latin expressions.

It has been said that to understand criminal procedures, one needs only to know its vocabulary. It is almost that simple. And it is impossible to understand the procedures without knowing of its vocabulary. Consequently, the real job of the student is to gain a command of the words used to describe and explain the procedures. A list of key vocabulary terms and concepts is provided to help in this learning at the beginning of each chapter. Learning these will be useful in understanding the procedures and in preparing for exams. After that, the procedures will become self-evident.

The procedures we follow in criminal justice were not those created to deal with 20th-or 21st-century crime and society. Rather, they were devised to protect us from 18th-century England after we declared our independence. If you will excuse the paraphrasing of a relevant movie title, our system of justice, with its Bill of Rights, was designed to protect American citizens from the *Badness of King George*. Any frustrations one might feel about the deficiencies of our system come from that fact. Only recently have we had any concern for the victims of crimes or for the impact of violent crime on society.

In this third edition, the original 12 chapters are restructured into 13 chapters. Dividing the content of Chapter 5 into two chapters facilitates the teaching and learning experiences within a semester-length course.

Chapter 1 presents a descriptive history of how many of our procedures developed. Chapter 2 gives an array of the basic concepts that underpin the procedural aspects of our justice system. These chapters form the basis of much of the content to follow. A short discussion of the USA Patriot Act is included here as well.

Chapter 3 offers a detailed account of the development and current application of the Exclusionary Rule, one of the most significant procedural rules in all of criminal justice. This short chapter is devoted to its explanation because of its overriding influence on all police procedures and on the admissibility of evidence in court. The exceptions to the rule are detailed as well.

Chapter 4 presents a detailed examination of police procedures, from the point of first contact between a citizen and a law enforcement officer, through the first two of three primary elements of any police-citizen contact: consensual encounter and detention. Chapter 5 presents a full examination of the third aspect of police-citizen contacts, the arrest. Chapter 6 is a short chapter devoted exclusively to the *Miranda* decision and its meaning and application in interrogations of suspects by law enforcement officers. This chapter also includes a discussion of when the *Miranda* warning is not needed and how it should be applied in juvenile cases.

Chapter 7 explains the procedures and requirements necessary in a detention facility (jail) where arrested persons are booked and held pending some fashion of release and where sentenced misdemeanants might serve their sentences. Depending on the instructor's priorities, this chapter could very well be omitted or summarized in a course offering without affecting the continuity of the book's presentation.

Chapter 8 describes the nature and purpose of our adversary system of justice, including the roles of the prosecutor and the defense. Chapter 9 describes the structure of the court system, including the jurisdiction of each court and the procedures that occur in each court. The pretrial processes and procedures are described as well, including the initial court appearance for all defendants, the preliminary hearing in felony cases, the use of a grand jury, and selected pretrial motions by the attorneys. Plea bargaining, the primary method of settling most criminal matters, is also described.

In Chapter 10 we examine the trial, from the point of jury selection by both traditional and scientific methods, and the prosecutor's side of the case (the case-in-chief) through the presentation of evidence. The use of a jury of less than twelve persons is examined as well. The second half of the trial, the defendant's side of the case, is presented in Chapter 11 by a review of the common defense strategies used to counter the prosecution's version of the truth. We move from this to the conclusion of a trial by either a verdict or a hung jury and new trial. The use of a nonunanimous verdict is examined within the context of the trial's outcome.

The sentencing goals and procedures, along with sentencing alternatives, are presented in Chapter 12. This includes a detailed discussion of the Indeterminate and Determinate Sentence Laws, the role of the probation officer in preparing the presentence report, and an examination of probation as the primary alternative to sentencing. The uses and requirements of police searches of probationers also are described.

Chapter 13 offers a variety of postsentencing procedures, including county parole, state parole, with the requirements for police in making searches of parolees, the role of the Board of Prison Terms, sex offender registration requirements, and the new and controversial Sexually violent predator (SVP) laws. The four most common writs *(habeas corpus, Certiorari, Mandamus,* and *Prohibition)* are reviewed. The procedures used to implement the death penalty are presented in detail. Also included in this chapter is a discussion of four acts of executive clemency: pardon, reprieve, commutation, and amnesty. The chapter concludes with a summary of the indemnification procedures by which individuals who are wrongly convicted and imprisoned may receive financial compensation from the State.

A few selected appellate court decisions are summarized within the text's presentation because they serve as good examples of the thinking by which the courts create criminal procedures and because they offer additional meaning to the textual material. Many other appellate decisions are cited, merely to document the presented materials and to provide a direction for anyone who wants to expand their understanding of criminal procedures by individual research.

Throughout the book the word *police* is used when referring to law enforcement. There is no intention to slight any local, county, or state peace officers in using this term. It is merely done for convenience and because it is the generic nature of all law enforcement to police the community.

ACKNOWLEDGMENTS

The author gratefully acknowledges the help of the following who have contributed through their review of the manuscript: Richard J. Kelly, Georgia Military College, Troy University, Columbus, GA; Robert W. Lockwood, Portland Sate University, Portland, OR; Patricia Parke, East Carolina University, Greenville, NC.

Basic Criminal Procedures

chapter 1

CRIMINAL PROCEDURES IN PERSPECTIVE

KEY TERMS AND CONCEPTS

Adversary system	Misdemeanor
Atonement	Precedent
Bill of Rights	Probable cause
Common law	Recognizance
Doctrine of Precedent	Reeve
Eighth Amendment	Sheriff
Felony	Sixth Amendment
Fifth Amendment	*Stare decisis*
Fourteenth Amendment	U.S. Constitution
Fourth Amendment	U.S. Supreme Court
Magna Carta	

INTRODUCTION

Criminal procedures are founded upon a trilogy that includes two legal concepts and a body of law that is as old as our independence and as sacred as our freedom. First, we have an **adversary system** in which two sides (the prosecutor and the defense), having fair and equal access to the same resources and information, compete in open court to arrive at the legal truth. Secondly, we adhere to the idea that individuals are *innocent until proven guilty.* The notion that individuals are *innocent unless proven guilty* might be more appropriate. Regardless, we use the absolute maximum degree of proof that humans are capable of having for and against a person tried for a crime, **proof beyond a reasonable doubt**.

Within this same conceptual framework, we use lesser degrees of proof when less serious intrusions into a person's freedom occur, as discussed below. Third, we have a body of law derived from our British legal heritage called **common law**, a body of law that was not written, but that has evolved over time in Great Britain through custom, tradition, and court decisions (rather than statutes), to become recognized early in our history as the law of the land. This is not to say that we now have common law or practice the common law. Many states no longer recognize any common law.

Today our laws are written down in an array of books called **codes**, and are divided into categories, discussed below. If it is not written in some code, it is not the law. Nevertheless, the basis of the laws we follow today, as well as many appellate case decisions, comes from our common law heritage. However, our experiences with British law, both good and bad, strongly influenced what specific laws and legal safeguards our forefathers enacted. In fact, much of our procedural law, including the **Bill of Rights**, was created from our bad experiences with English law. It was a defense against the tyranny and legal abuses of the Crown's courts and the Crown's men.

The Founding Fathers wanted to be certain that similar abuses of the rights of our citizens did not occur under American criminal procedures. One could say that the due process guaranteed in the Bill of Rights, and the procedures that police, courts, and corrections must follow today, were created to protect us from the "Badness of King George," if you will pardon the play on words. Obviously, today's society is far different than colonial America and the problems of drugs, gangs, guns, and related violence are making it increasingly more difficult to maintain order under law.

The parts of this trilogy are bound together by a document that had become the ultimate source of all of our legal rights and wrongs, the **U.S. Constitution**. The reason that the Constitution is the ultimate source of our laws was summed up best in 1803 by Supreme Court Justice John Marshall when he stated, "Any nation created by a document, must hold that document supreme" (*Marbury v. Madison*, 1803).

It is that document that binds us together as a nation under law. Additional terms, concepts, and procedures are also found within this legal framework. We will examine a few more of these below—those that are necessary to know before we begin with the actual procedures themselves. Others will be integrated within the content of the remaining sections of this book. First, however, we will examine certain selected events in our history from which came the major procedures followed today.

A BRIEF HISTORY OF SELECTED PROCEDURES

The purpose here is not to provide an in-depth history lesson. Rather, it is to touch on the origins of selected procedures and processes that are used today and are important to know in appreciating why our current system operates as it does. Only those procedures that grew out of our British common law heritage are discussed. The focus is on certain aspects of procedural law and the court structure. Consequently, the history of law enforcement and police procedures is not addressed, other than that of the sheriff as his role relates to his court responsibilities.

Role of the Sheriff

After the fall of the Holy Roman Empire in 395 BC, various tribes from the continent of Europe began settling the country, primarily the Angles, Saxons, and Jutes. Their system of justice was tribal, had a high degree of citizen involvement, and emphasized restitution given directly to the victim of an offense. Eventually, these tribes merged into one super tribe, the Anglo-Saxons, and came to be ruled by Alfred the Great by about 870. For the first time, there was a king over the entire land and population, and he began the practice of the King (the State) moving from a tribal and restitutional approach to a state-run system in which the state is the victim.

One of his first acts was to divide England into 52 political subdivisions called **shires**. Then he appointed a knight to be his law enforcement agent in each shire. The term for "agent" was **reeve**. Consequently, by this early date, we have a chief law enforcement officer in each shire, the reeve. Now, if one were to say the two words together, faster and faster, while slurring slightly, it would come out as shire-reeve . . . shire-eeve . . . shireve . . . shirive . . . sheriff . . . sheriff . . . **sheriff**. The original responsibilities of the sheriff included enforcing the King's laws, arresting suspects, holding them for trial, and often acting as judge and executioner as well. Now, of course, other officials hold trial and carry out punishments, but the role has otherwise changed little in more than a thousand years. As an aside, it is interesting to note that in England the sheriff dropped his judicial role in favor of law enforcement, and now the role is just an honorary title. In Scotland today, however, the sheriff is the local judge but has no police powers.

Early Methods of Trial

Before the coming of the State under Alfred the Great, the Saxons and other tribes had a tribal court, described in our terms as a **Hundred Court**, that included representatives from the various tribes and kin-groups that lived on lands divided into hundreds. Each hundred could support approximately 100 kin-groups. As the State evolved, the sheriff came to head this court, and eventually headed the King's court, which he was responsible to form and direct.

Early trial methods were swift and rather brutal. One such method, known as **trial by ordeal**, required the accused to stand before the court and either hold his hands in a pot of boiling water or hold a hot iron for a few seconds. Then his hands would be wrapped for two days. On the third day, the wraps would be removed and he would show his hands. If burn or scar marks showed, he was found guilty and killed because God had not intervened, as he would with an innocent man, to remove the marks.

A similar method used if the court was near water was to have the accused swim with rocks tied to him or to tie him up, weighted down with rocks, and throw him into the water. If he managed to swim free, in the first example, or if he managed to undo the rocks and survive, he was guilty because the devil had helped to set him free. One can imagine that the recidivist rate (rate of return to crime) was very low with these methods.

A less severe method, known as **compurgation**, required the accused to purge himself by swearing his innocence, with the support of "**oath helpers**" to support his testimony. Interestingly enough, the number of "oath helpers" required was twelve. Another milder method was called **atonement**, which required the accused to pay compensation, or, as it was termed above, restitution to the victim. Initially, the amount atoned went to the victim. However, as the State assumed more control over the justice system, the amount was paid directly to the court.

This practice of atonement was also used extensively in the church courts, which were developing at a parallel with, and in support of, the King's courts. Atonement became a useful way of raising revenue for both. During this period, the sheriff presided over the courts and collected the compensation. Also, the Hundred Court gave way to the practice of the sheriff convening the court, with twelve men sitting to represent the Hundred, or the citizens.

The Norman Conquest

The next significant development occurred in 1066. From 1042 to 1066, St. Edward, the Aetheling (the Confessor), was King of England. As he neared the end of his reign, there were many disputes about who would succeed him. He promised the crown to William, Duke of Normandy (in France). However, just before dying, he changed his mind and appointed a local knight, Harold of Wessox, as king. He was crowned on January 6, 1066. Duke William (**William the Conqueror**) thought the crown was rightfully his, so he landed his troops at Hastings, in southern England, on September 27, defeated Harold, and declared all of England his. William was crowned king of England on Christmas day in Westminster Abbey.

One of his first efforts to control the citizens was to replace all the Anglo-Saxon reeves (sheriffs) with his own Norman knights. He also redistributed much of the land to his Norman knights. Consequently, his rule in general, and the Norman reeves in particular, were not well received. The people frequently hid men wanted by the sheriff or helped them to escape after arrest and before trial. In an effort to counter these reactions by the citizens, William initiated a procedure called **recognizance** (a French word), which required the accused or his family, friends, or townspeople to post something of value in order to gain the freedom of the accused pending trial. Then if they helped the accused escape, they would forfeit to the King what they had posted.

Today we call this procedure **posting bail**, posting an amount of money with the court to gain the freedom of the accused, pending trial. In fact, today we have gone beyond having the accused post money, and in many cases allow him or her to post their word, their promise to return to court when required. We call this procedure releasing the accused on his or her **own recognizance**, or **OR**. If the accused fails to appear, he or she can be charged with a new crime of failing to return, which can be either a felony or a misdemeanor, depending on the level of the original crime charged. Think of it—the word and procedure known as recognizance have been a vital part of our justice system for more than 930 years.

William also added **trial by battle** as a method of trial and settling disputes between individuals. However, the practice was limited to the knights. Commoners continued to perform ordeals or pay atonement. As the King's power grew, so did that of the Church, and the Church made increasing use of atonement as the preferred method for one to make up for violating church laws and other sins.

The State Becomes the Victim

Until the beginning of the 12th century, **victim restitution** played an important role in settling disputes. When a party was wronged during the commission of a crime, that injured party was considered the victim, deserving of compensation. That all changed when Henry I took the throne (1116–1132). He announced that from now on the **"King's Peace** shall be maintained throughout the kingdom," and anyone who disturbs that peace by committing a crime is committing a crime against the King. The King (State) became the victim of all crimes, and from that point until only recently, the real victim had been forgotten. The real victim suffered the loss from a crime, but the King reaped the rewards that came from a conviction: a fine or confiscation of property.

King Henry also created two crime categories. He said, "There will be certain crimes against the King's Peace that we will call **felonies.**" These were arson, robbery, false coinage, and all crimes of violence.

These felonies were punishable by death, and a person wanted for committing any of these crimes was declared an outlaw. Anyone could kill an outlaw and claim any reward that might be offered. In both cases, death or outlawry, the accused was considered to be *civilly dead*. They ceased to have any legal life, which meant that they could not own property, will or inherit property, or perform anything else that required a legal existence. Once they suffered civil death, the King assumed title of all their property. This practice of declaring convicted felons civilly dead and stripping them of their civil rights was practiced in many states as late as the 1970s.

All the lesser crimes were called **misdemeanors** (misbehaviors) and were punishable by atonement or corporal punishment. We no longer use corporal punishment, but we certainly use atonement, or a fine, for most misdemeanors, and the use of a fine is still a way for the State to raise money. Also consider the fact that the words to classify the two major crime categories we use today are nearly 900 years old and the basic behaviors of each category are about the same.

A Court Structure and Procedures Emerge

Under King Henry II (1154–1189), the King's court was centralized at Westminster, the country was divided into five **judicial districts**, and knights were appointed as **circuit-riding judges** to travel about the realm hearing cases. Initially, it was the sheriff's job to present the case in court. However, because the people had so long played a part in their own justice system, going clear back to the tribal days, and because they did not always trust the sheriff, pressure mounted from the people to have a more direct role. Consequently, by about 1176, when a person was accused of a crime, it became the sheriff's job to summon twelve knights from the shire and four from the town or village to hear a preliminary version of the case.

This group came to be known as the **grand jury**. The sheriff was responsible to present enough evidence to this grand jury to convince them that a crime really did occur and that the evidence showed that the accused probably did it. If the grand jury agreed, the accused was held for trial before the circuit-riding judge. Otherwise, the accused was allowed to go free. Consequently, when the judge arrived, he heard only those cases that had been screened by the grand jury in this preliminary type of hearing, which made better use of his time.

Today, every case that is prosecuted in federal court goes through the same process. An assistant attorney general in the district where the crime occurred summons a federal grand jury and presents sufficient evidence to convince them of the same issues: that a crime occurred and the accused probably did it. Therefore, the case should go to trial. The grand jury also is used on occasion at the state level, particularly in the eastern states. In other states, the prosecutor has the option of using the grand jury, or a similar procedure that is detailed in Chapter 9. Suffice it to say here that the way federal cases reach trial, and the way local cases may reach trial, is the same as it was more than 800 years ago.

Today, the phrase **probable cause** is used to describe these two aspects that the sheriff, and now the prosecutor, was/is required to prove:

- that a crime occurred
- that the accused probably did it

Today a **probable cause hearing** of some sort is required in every felony case before the accused can be held for trial. The details of this are described in Chapter 9.

Common Law

There was little, if any, written law controlling crime and punishment in England. Customs and traditions evolved out of the tribal practices and blended with the values of society at the time. Consequently, when judges arrived at a court, heard a case, and rendered a decision, they would follow the customs as much as possible and would write the decisions and their reasons for them in a book. Thus, over time, a body of law developed based on custom and tradition and the application of it to a variety of situations as determined by a judge. We call this **common law** because it was commonly understood as the tradition and practice within the community, and it was what judges commonly followed in deciding cases.

The Doctrine of Precedent

As the decisions of judges grew in number, they provided a basis for deciding future cases that were similar. Judges could look back to see how a similar situation had been judged in the past and could follow the same line of thinking. Today when a court reviews a case and makes a decision that can be used as an example for deciding future cases that are similar, the decision is called a **precedent**. The use of precedent-setting cases as a reference for deciding future cases is known by the Latin phrase *stare decisis*, or the **Doctrine of Precedent**.

Once an appellate court makes a case decision, it sets a precedent and establishes a procedural rule. It becomes the example against which procedures in future similar cases are decided.

As time passed, citizens clamored for an increasing role in their justice system, and the practice developed of using one group of citizens as the grand jury and a second group, composed of twelve citizens, as a *petite*, or **trial jury**. Initially, the trial jurors conducted their own investigations, as well as heard evidence and gave a verdict. This led to abuses in the fairness of trials because the jurors would listen to rumors and hearsay evidence during their investigations. Eventually, they were restricted to hearing the evidence in court, and the evidence was presented by the sheriff. Eventually, the practice was established whereby another knight (prosecutor) presented the evidence and the sheriff merely provided law enforcement and court security.

Defense Counsel

An accused knight could have the assistance of a fellow knight in presenting his defense, but only if the crime charged was a misdemeanor. The king had enough authority to prohibit the accused from having assistance in felony cases for many years. The king did not want an accused felon having help in his defense because he would have a better chance of not being convicted. Then the king would lose out on obtaining the felon's property. This practice is an early recognition that an accused person stands a better chance at trial with someone acting as counsel in presenting a defense.

The Magna Carta

Henry II, and the subsequent kings, did not completely support the use of jury trials and, when possible, encouraged the sheriff to act as judge, jury, and executioner. It made it easier for the kings to confiscate properties of convicted felons. One of the worst abusers was King John, who assumed the throne upon the death of his brother, Richard the Lion Hearted. He moved against commoner and noble alike.

The nobles did not seem too concerned when the king abused the rights of a commoner, but when John began abusing the rights of the nobles, they responded quickly to protect their interests. On June 15, 1215, they surrounded King John at a spot just north of Windsor Castle known as the Plains of Runnymead, placed their lances to his body, and offered him a deal he could not refuse. They told John that if he signed the document they laid before him, they would not run him through with their lances. John signed the document, known as the **Magna Carta**, or Great Charter, which listed 37 rights guaranteed to the citizens, which then were primarily to the nobles and the Church officials. Actually, much of the Magna Carta was copied from an earlier document of Henry I, titled the *Charter of Liberties*, but the Magna Carta is the document remembered and cited as the main source of our **Bill of Rights**.

One of the principle rights guaranteed in the Magna Carta stated that no free man would be seized or imprisoned, or deprived of his property, without first having the case reviewed and judged by his peers. At the time, that guarantee simply referred to those citizens (peers) to be chosen from the community to form the grand jury to review the evidence and determine if the case should go to trial. That initial guarantee was interpreted broadly to form the basis of our constitutional due process, and was expanded in our Constitution to include the right to both the grand jury and the trial jury of one's peers.

A Court Structure Is Completed

By the end of the 14th century, the use of the jury system was fairly well established. By about 1300, the role of **coroner** was created. A knight was appointed in each shire to view a dead body before burial and investigate suspicious deaths to determine the cause, to list all the property of a deceased, to record the names of those felons convicted or declared outlaws, and to list and confiscate their property for the King. A coroner performs very similar responsibilities today in each county.

By the 1400s society had grown more complex, with more population, more crime, and more cases to hear. The workload of the circuit-riding judges exceeded what the judges could hear. Consequently, England was divided into five judicial districts, with a Crown Court in each district where the judges sat and heard cases. The **Peace Knight Act** of 1361 authorized the appointments of Peace Knights in the various cities and towns to hear the misdemeanor cases, while the felony cases went to the district Crown Courts. However, the felony cases were first screened by the Peace Knight and grand jury at the local level, so that only those cases with sufficient evidence to show that a crime occurred and that the accused probably did it went to trial. In felony cases this amounted to a probable cause hearing before the Peace Knight in a lower court, after which the lower court judge, the Peace Knight, would either find that probable cause existed and refer the case to the district Crown Court for trial, or he would find probable cause lacking and dismiss the case.

If we keep the basic court structure and procedures in mind, we will see in Chapter 9 that the basic model has remained the same. Only now is it being modified in an increasing number of states to eliminate the two-tier structure. Suffice it to say at this point that the court system and primary roles of the justice system were well established by the end of the 14th century. By that time there was a chief law enforcement officer for each county, who also detained prisoners and provided court security; a coroner; a body of law; an adversary system; the use of both prosecution and defense; a two-tier court structure; a jury system; the basic crime categories of felony and misdemeanor; the State as the victim of all crime; the procedure of recognizance, or bail; and the principle of *stare decisis*, or precedent, which provides stability, predictability, and fairness in the application of the law.

This short history lesson shows that the foundation and structure of our current system of justice was established more than 600 years ago. What we have done beyond that has increased the complexity of justice, but in many ways that might be viewed as being more cosmetic than substantive.

Now we take a quantum leap from the 15th century to the present. First we need to bridge that 600-year gap with a look at the one essential link with the past that had the most significant impact on our procedural law, the Magna Carta. This document and its predecessor, the Charter of Liberties, hold for us the essence of the rights of all people and the guarantee of due process and equal protection that are found in the first ten amendments to the Constitution.

The Bill of Rights—1791

The federal document called the **Bill of Rights** contains the first ten amendments to the **U.S. Constitution**. By including these in the Constitution, the Founding Fathers intended to guarantee certain rights for all the people that they could not be deprived of by the government. They did this because they thought the English king and his agents frequently had abused their rights when America was a colony. They wanted to be certain that these rights had complete protection under the new form of government they were creating.

Additional amendments have been added to the Constitution over the years, and all of them are equally important. However, for our purposes in studying criminal procedures, only the following five amendments will be examined. They form the basis of most all criminal procedures that we will study.

Fourth Amendment   The right of the people to be secure in their persons, houses, papers, and effects, against unreasonable searches and seizures, shall not be violated, and no warrants shall issue, but upon probable cause, supported by Oath or affirmation, and particularly describing the place to be searched, and the persons or things to be seized.

Fifth Amendment   No person shall be held to answer for a capital, or otherwise infamous crime, unless on a presentment or indictment of a Grand Jury, except in cases arising in the land or naval forces, or in the militia, when in actual service in time of war or public danger; nor shall any person be subject for the same offense to be twice put in jeopardy of life or limb; nor shall be compelled in any criminal case to be a witness against himself, nor be deprived of life, liberty, or property, without due process of law; nor shall private property be taken for public use, without just compensation.

Sixth Amendment   In all criminal prosecutions, the accused shall enjoy the right to a speedy and public trial, by an impartial jury of the State and district wherein the crime shall have been committed, which district shall have been previously ascertained by law, and to be informed of the nature and cause of the accusation; to be confronted with the witnesses against him; to have compulsory process for obtaining witnesses in his favor, and to have the assistance of counsel for his defense.

Eighth Amendment   Excessive bail shall not be required, nor excessive fines imposed, nor cruel and unusual punishments inflicted.

Fourteenth Amendment   Section 1. All persons born or naturalized in the United States, and subject to the jurisdiction thereof, are citizens of the United States and of the State wherein they reside. No State shall make or enforce any law which shall abridge the privileges or immunities of citizens of the United States; nor shall any State deprive any person of life, liberty, or property, without due process of law; nor deny to any person within its jurisdiction the equal protection of the laws. (Added July 28, 1868)

Note that the Fourteenth Amendment was added 77 years after the original Bill of Rights was written. This addition was necessary to ensure that no one violated the other amendments. It often has been used by an appellate court as the basis for forcing states to comply with the other amendments because most states would not otherwise follow them, nor would they enact their own laws to insure those same rights.

SUMMARY

This chapter has introduced many of the practices that emerged from our history to provide a foundation for our criminal procedures. Their applications will be detailed in the appropriate portions of the chapters to follow.

The guarantees in the Fourth and Fifth Amendments serve as a springboard for the procedures that have been mandated for law enforcement officers, and they will be used as the basis for understanding the police procedures studied in Chapters 4, 5, and 6. The Fourth Amendment, protecting citizens against unreasonable search and seizure, was applied to police procedures through a series of **U.S. Supreme Court** cases that are detailed in Chapter 3.

The application of one guarantee in the Fifth Amendment, the protection against self-incrimination, and one guarantee from the Sixth Amendment, the right to an attorney, are examined in the presentation of the *Miranda* warning, detailed in Chapter 6. The application of the Eighth Amendment is a part of Chapter 12.

The fundamental concepts of law are introduced and defined in Chapter 2, which, when combined with those described in this introductory chapter, provide the conceptual foundation required to appreciate and apply the criminal procedures presented in the subsequent chapters.

ISSUES FOR DISCUSSION

1. Discuss the changes in the justice system implemented by King Henry I when he announced that "... from now on the King's Peace shall be maintained through the kingdom." How do these changes affect today's justice system?

2. How was the phrase "probable cause" used in early British justice?

3. Discuss the usefulness of adhering to the concept *stare decisis*, or the Doctrine of Precedent?

4. Discuss the various elements of each constitutional amendment mentioned in the chapter. Should the rights and protections contained in these amendments always be upheld? Why? Why not?

INTERNET REFERENCES

http://www.commonlaw.com/
http://en.wikipedia.org/wiki/Common_law
http://www.svpvril.com/OACL.html
http://wordiq.com/definition/Common_law
http://en.wikipedia.org/wiki/Magna_Carta
http://www.archives.gov/exhibits/featured_documents/magna_carta/

CASE DECISIONS

Marbury v. Madison, 5 U.S. 137 (1803)

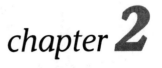

FUNDAMENTAL CONCEPTS OF LAW

KEY TERMS AND CONCEPTS

Accessory	Misdemeanor
Beyond a reasonable doubt	Preponderance of the evidence
Clear and convincing evidence	Principal
Corpus delicti	Probable cause
Crime	Procedural law
Degrees of proof	Reasonable suspicion
Elements of a crime	Retroactivity
Enhancement	Social contract
Ex post facto	Statutory law
Felony	Substantive law
Jurisdiction	USA Patriot Act of 2001
Mala en se	Venue
Mala prohibita	

INTRODUCTION

Chapter 1 provided a historical overview of how many of our basic criminal procedures developed, first out of English common law, then out of our American experience. This chapter complements that overview by explaining a number of basic legal concepts in the application of criminal procedures.

TYPES OF CRIMES

Crime

The terms *crime* and *public offense* often are used interchangeably because in the technical sense, today all crimes are offenses against the general public, or public will, just as they were against the King in early England. The public is always the legal victim.

Crime can be defined as

> any act committed or omitted in violation of a law forbidding or commanding it, and for which a penalty is proscribed following a conviction.

This means that some acts become crimes when they are committed, such as burglary or robbery, and some acts become crimes when they are omitted, such as not registering for the draft, or not filing an income tax return, or not stopping at the scene of an accident in which one was involved.

Obviously, the majority of crimes fall into the category of prohibited acts that are committed. While it is not within the scope of this text to spend much time with the laws of crime and punishment, it is appropriate at this point to define what crime is and how a crime may be divided into its elements.

Elements of a Crime

Three elements are found in the definition given above:

- the act
- the law prohibiting or requiring it
- the punishment

The criminal act is known by the Latin phrase ***actus resus***. Four additional elements are needed to complete the definition of crime:

- criminal intent (or negligence), which is the guilty mind, known by the Latin phrase as ***mens rea***
- the **concurrence** of the act with the intent
- **social harm** (harm to a victim)
- the fact that the **harm was caused by the act**

We can list these elements in order as follows:

1. Act, or *actus resus*
2. Intent, or *mens rea*
3. Law prohibiting the act
4. Concurrence between the act and intent
5. Social harm (to a victim)
6. The act caused the harm
7. Punishment follows conviction

When proving a crime in court, a prosecutor must show that the act occurred and that the act caused the harm. Criminal intent is either implied in the act or must be proven separately, depending on the specific crime charged. For example, burglary is the act of entering a place (house, barn, building, car, etc.) with the intent to commit theft or any felony.

A person can enter a house with the intent to steal, to assault, to kidnap, to murder, or any other felony, and the crime may be charged as a burglary. However, the intent is the key element that must be proven, and that is not always easy. Consequently, the police report submitted to the prosecutor to support the charge must be complete and accurate so that the prosecutor knows what elements are there for prosecution.

Degrees of Crime

There are three levels of crime; that is, three levels, or degrees of seriousness of the act:

1. Felony
2. **Misdemeanor**
3. Infraction

Actually, it is not the act itself that determines the level of crime. It is the seriousness of the punishment given for a conviction of the act that determines its level.

A **felony** is a crime which is **punishable by** execution or by imprisonment in the state prison. Some jurisdictions also have subgroups, such as Class A and Class B felonies. A misdemeanor is a crime **punishable by** a fine or a sentence of up to one year in jail, or both jail and fine. An infraction is a crime **punishable by** fine; one cannot lose his or her freedom as the result of an infraction conviction. In addition to these three basic degrees of seriousness, there is the category known as a **wobbler**, which is a crime that is **punishable** at the discretion of the court **by a term** either in prison or in jail.

No other crime categories are described officially in any penal codes, but there are two additional categories that exist, in fact, in some states. For lack of more creative titles, call these categories **special felonies (a)** and **special felonies (b)**.

Under the special felony (a) subcategory are those crimes which are misdemeanors, ordinarily, but when combined with a charge of having a prior conviction may be charged as felonies punishable by a term in state prison. For example, petty theft with a prior theft, a DUI (driving under the influence) with four prior DUI convictions, or carrying a concealable firearm without a license and with a prior felony conviction, may all be charged as felonies in some states, punishable by prison sentences in some states.

Special felonies (b) are those felonies that may come under what is termed the "three strikes" law, or a habitual offender law. If an offender is convicted of a felony and has had prior convictions of certain designated felonies, the sentence may be increased substantially. In some states, the additional penalty is mandatory, whereas in other states the sentencing judge has the discretion to strike (delete) one or more of the priors.

Enhancements

The phrase "to enhance" means to make better, as in value, desirability, or attractiveness. Ironically, several years ago, when various state legislatures were seeking ways to increase the severity of punishment for certain crimes, they adopted the term and created what are called **enhancements**. They are defined as

> some specific aspect of a crime, or of the criminal's role in the crime, or of the criminal's background (stated in the penal code) that may be added to a criminal complaint which, if proven, will add time to a felon's prison sentence if the felon is also convicted of the basic crime.

At the federal level, these are called *harms*, under the Federal Sentencing Guidelines. Examples of situations that may result in enhancements or harms include the offender who provides another with a firearm during a crime for the purpose of helping that person commit the crime, anyone who personally uses a firearm in the commission of a felony, anyone convicted of a felony and who has had a prior felony conviction, or anyone who commits a crime as a member of a street gang.

There are many other enhancements that are derived from the nature of the victim, such as a crime against a minor under the age of 14, or a pregnant woman, or that result in great bodily injury or a substantial financial loss to a victim. These enhancements usually must be charged and proved separately from the basic criminal charge that brings the accused before the court. Whether to charge them is a decision made by the prosecuting attorney. Also, the prosecutor may charge an enhancement initially then dismiss it later if warranted by the circumstances, such as a plea bargain agreement, discussed in a later chapter.

Mala En Se Versus Mala Prohibita Crimes

These are Latin phrases that represent two distinct categories of crime. **Mala en se** crimes are those that are inherently evil. They are, by their very nature, evil, bad, or wrong, such as most crimes against a person or property. Usually, there is wide agreement among the members of society that such acts as murder, rape, robbery, theft, arson, and assault are evil and must be prohibited by law.

Mala prohibita crimes are those acts that are not really evil, bad, or wrong, but they still pose a threat to society and need to be controlled. Most traffic offenses fall into this category.

Some crimes that lie somewhere between the two extremes of a continuum from totally evil to completely harmless have become crimes only because a sufficient majority thinks that legal control is necessary because harm results from those acts. However, others think that these behaviors pose no threat or harm and should not be controlled. These acts, usually called *victimless crimes*, fall within this category: gambling, drug use, prostitution, and related crimes of vice. Are these evil and wrong or just acts that need legal control?

TYPES OF LAWS

Laws can be put into one or more of several categories, depending on the point of view being considered. Several of the more commonly used categories are described below.

Substantive Law

This is the body of law that **defines crime and punishment**. It governs the behavior of the citizens within society and tells the citizens what they cannot do or what they must do to obey the law. And if one violates the substantive law, it is a crime. Substantive laws are found in the Penal Code, Health and Safety Code, Vehicle Code, Business and Professions Code, and Fish and Game Code, to name but a few. Their primary purpose is to protect society and protect the law-abiding citizens from the law breakers.

Procedural Law

This category of law, on the other hand, has nothing to do with regulating the behavior of citizens. It is the body of law that lays out the step-by-step procedures that must be followed by police officers, court personnel, correctional officers, and other officials in processing an accused person through the system. Procedural laws are the laws that must be obeyed by the officers and agents that work within the justice system to protect the constitutional rights and due process of every citizen at every level of involvement in the system, from the point of initial police contact, through arrest, booking, trial, and punishment.

Substantive law, then, protects society from the citizen who might threaten the social order and safety of others, whereas procedural law protects the citizen from any government effort to deprive him or her of any rights or freedoms, without due process.

Statutory Law

This refers to any law that originates in the Legislature. A law (bill) is introduced in the Senate or Assembly, referred to some appropriate committee for consideration, then voted in as law by the majorities in both Houses (the Senate and Assembly). It becomes **a law, a statute**.

Now we can mix two categories of law by saying that the vast majority of laws passed by the Legislature are laws to regulate some type of behavior by either criminalizing a behavior that threatens society or decriminalizing a behavior that is no longer viewed as a threat. Therefore, most statutory law is also substantive law.

Case Law

This is the body of law that results from a court case and is actually created by judges. In a typical case, a person is arrested, tried, and convicted of a crime. Either during or after this process, the person (or his or her attorney) believes that he or she has been denied some constitutional right or protection along the way and appeals the case to some higher court, either within the state or federal system. Judges on this higher court review the records of the case, read and listen to arguments by the attorneys representing the one who appealed and the one representing the state (prosecution), then decide who is right. This decision may result in clarifying or creating a procedure that must be followed by law enforcement officers or the lower courts in all future situations in order to ensure the constitutional rights of an accused person.

Procedural Versus Substantive Law

Again, we can mix two types of law categories by saying that most procedural law is created by case law decisions, and that rarely do case decisions affect the substantive law. When a person appeals his or her case from a trial court, he or she usually is not challenging the substantive law, only the procedural law. For example, if a person is arrested, accused, tried, convicted, and sent to prison for murder then appeals his case, he or she is not claiming that the substantive law prohibiting murder is wrong and should be changed. He or she is claiming that some procedures used by the police or the court violated his constitutional rights in some way, and therefore, his or her conviction was the result of some illegal activity by police or the court and should be reversed.

If the appellate court agrees, it will throw out the conviction either because some existing procedures had been violated or because the procedures violated some right protected by the Constitution but that is not yet controlled by an existing procedure. In this latter case, the court will create a new procedure to be certain that the constitutional right in question is protected in all future cases.

Many examples of this will be studied in subsequent chapters, and we will see that most of the procedures that exist today, which police, courts, and correctional officers must follow, were created by case decisions made within the past 35 years.

The Social Contract

The **Social Contract** refers to a theory that attempts to explain and/or describe the origin and maintenance of organized society and the legal relationship between the citizens and the government. In its simplest terms, the theory holds that the State, with its government and laws, was created, and is maintained through the mutual agreement entered into by all the citizens and the ruler (State) as a way of having social order, protection, and freedom.

The main principles are the equality of all citizens before the law, the merging of individual interests with those of the State, and the necessity of each individual surrendering certain rights for the good of all society. The citizens recognize that at times there is a conflict between having freedom and maintaining social order and safety, and that they cannot have both complete freedom and safety because they are sometimes in conflict with each other. Also, they cannot enjoy either one to the fullest because of the type of society that would result. Imagine what life would be like at either end of the following continuum:

The Social Contract Continuum

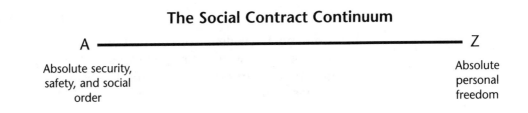

A ————————————————————————————— Z

Absolute security,
safety, and social
order

Absolute
personal
freedom

Establishing absolute order and security could severely limit what freedoms would be enjoyed by the individual. However, absolute freedom could lead to anarchy and a complete absence of social order and security. Consequently when entering this Social Contract, the citizens agree to give up some of their freedoms to the State to gain the desired level of safety and security. As an example, the citizens could have said to each other, "I won't steal from you and you don't steal from me, and we will all be protected from thieves." Or to put it in a contemporary legal framework, "I won't drive faster than 65 miles per hour and you don't drive faster than 65 miles per hour, and we will all be protected from speeders."

We all agree to give up the freedom to drive as fast as we want in order to be safe from the carnage on the freeway that would result. And in agreeing to give up some of their freedoms, the citizens also give consent to the State to take appropriate action against them if they break their end of the contract. On the other side, the State will not invade the privacy of the individual unless the State has some overriding interest, as defined by the rules of the contract, the law.

This Social Contract theory was primarily the work of the French philosopher, Jean Jacques Rousseau (*Le Contract Social*, 1762), supported by two English philosophers, Thomas Hobbes and John Locke, and John Stuart Mills's philosophy of utilitarianism, which had as its theme "the greatest happiness for the greatest number." For Rousseau, the State was the term used to mean the general will of the people, the common good. These two theories about the relationships between the individual and the State, the Social Contract and utilitarianism, embody principles underlying our current system of justice.

Without elaborating any further on the Social Contract, we can see how practical this approach is because it portrays exactly what we need and must deal with in today's society. The trick in applying it is knowing how to balance the two needs. How do we balance the needs of the State with those of the individual?

The Social Contract Teeter-Totter

A ——————————————————————————— Z

Absolute security,   Absolute
safety, and social   personal
order   freedom

The Balance
Point

How much freedom are you willing to give up to ensure your own safety? It probably would vary somewhat with each person who answered this question. Therefore, we use Mills's notion of the greatest good for the greatest number and build into the contract, laws, or procedures for determining that. As a reader, where would you place the balancing point? View closely the statue of the woman standing blindfolded, holding the scales of justice in her outstretched hand, and it will become obvious that she is trying to balance those same needs.

Read the decisions of the Supreme Court in any search and seizure case, or other right to privacy cases, and it will become equally obvious that the justices are trying to balance those needs, as well. Chapters 4, 5, and 6 deal with police procedures, including the authority to stop, detain, arrest, and interrogate. All of these steps in police procedures are controlled by case law that can be examined within the context of this safety-freedom continuum, or Social Contract teeter-totter.

We will see that as the Supreme Court became more involved in creating procedural law over the past 45 years, the balancing point has shifted back and forth, from a primary concern for individual freedom during the 1960s and 1970s to an increasing concern for public safety and social order in the 1980s and 1990s, from a Court concerned with due process to one more concerned with law enforcement and crime control.

The USA Patriot Act of 2001

One of the most controversial pieces of federal legislation to ever come out of Congress affecting criminal procedures is the act entitled Uniting and Strengthening America by Providing Appropriate Tools Required to Intercept and Obstruct Terrorism, otherwise know as the **USA Patriot Act of 2001**. This act is the result of legislative proposals introduced less than a week after the terrorist attacks of September 11, 2001. Attorney General Ashcroft warned Congress that new attacks were imminent and immediate action was needed to pass the legislation. President Bush signed the final bill into law on October 26, 2001.

Although much of this legislation primarily affects federal law enforcement procedures and the intelligence community, it does apply nationwide, and it serves as one of the most obvious applications of the Social Contract teeter-totter described previously. It is beyond the scope of this text to discuss the Patriot Act in detail. Suffice it to say, the Act significantly increased the surveillance and investigative powers of law enforcement agencies in the United States, particularly in the areas of monitoring (wire tapping) phone and Internet communications, and accessing student, medical, banking, library, Internet, phone, and credit records.

The Act provided for very limited judicial oversight and little justification for the use of monitoring and accessing procedures beyond the government authority certifying that the "information likely to be obtained by such installation and use is relevant to an ongoing criminal investigation." This gave the government rather broad authority and raised the concerns of millions of Americans over possible government intrusion into their privacy and the abuse of their civil liberties.

The Patriot Act had a sunset clause of four years, meaning that it automatically would expire on December 31, 2005. The debate over renewing the legislation began in mid-2005, both in Congress and in public venues. Ironically, the terrorist bombing attacks on the London transportation systems during July 2005 triggered knee-jerk reactions in the House and Senate, both of which passed versions of bills that extended the Patriot Act for up to 10 years. As of this writing, a reconciled version of the renewal legislation is being developed in Congress, between the House and Senate, and will be introduced and undoubtedly passed before the end of the year. No doubt, as well, President Bush will sign the bill. However, there is significant controversy over the extent of possible government intrusion allowed by the final version of the law, and there are mixed views among the legislators themselves (Kerr, 2004; Ziff, 2005).

This legislation again begs the question of the reader. How much of your privacy and civil liberties are you willing to give up in order for government to attempt to achieve its counterterrorist efforts?

PARTIES TO A CRIME

Individuals can become involved in a crime, be a party to a crime, in one of two ways:

- as a **principal**
- as an **accessory**

Principals are all the individuals involved in the commission of a crime, whether it be felony or misdemeanor, and whether they directly commit the crime or help (aid and abet) in its commission. It could also include those individuals who have advised and encouraged the commission of the crime; those individuals who advised, counseled, or encouraged others who are of a vulnerable age or are in a vulnerable condition, such as younger minors, people who are insane, or people who are mentally handicapped; those individuals who by fraud, contrivance, or force occasion the drunkenness of another for the purpose of causing him or her to commit any crime; or those individuals who by threats, menaces, command, or coercion compel another to commit any crime.

Accessories are individuals who, after a felony has been committed, knowingly and willingly harbor, conceal, or aid a principal in such felony with the intent of having the principal avoid or escape from arrest, trial, conviction, or punishment.

This definition of a principal is worded so as to include anyone who participates in the commission of any crime in any manner, either in planning it, committing it, or encouraging another to commit it. An accessory is not involved in the actual crime at all. Rather, after a crime has been committed, an accessory is the one who comes on the scene to knowingly assist the principal (felon) with the intent of letting the principal avoid arrest, prosecution, or punishment.

An example that might be familiar to the widest national audience comes from an early scene in the O.J. Simpson case in California. Simpson was wanted by the police as the principal in two murders. At one point before his arrest, his friend, Al Cowling, drove Simpson up and down the LA freeways at about 30 miles per hour, with the police swarming all around them, waiting for Simpson's Bronco to stop. Eventually, Simpson was arrested.

Authorities considered charging Cowling as an accessory because he certainly did provide some sort of assistance to Simpson by driving him around for so long. However, he was not charged, undoubtedly because it would not have been possible to prove the element of intent. If he had intended to help Simpson avoid arrest, he would have led the police in a far different type of chase.

In most states, the crime of being an accessory is a wobbler, punishable by a fine, jail, or prison. An accessory can be charged, tried, convicted, and punished regardless of whatever happens in the case of the principal. Think of the Simpson case. If Cowling had led police on some wild chase to help Simpson avoid arrest, he might now be sitting in some prison, while Simpson wanders about freely after being found not guilty by a jury.

DEGREES OF PROOF

Different **degrees of proof**, or standards of proof, are necessary at various steps in criminal procedures depending on the seriousness of the action taken against a citizen and the impact it has on the citizen's freedom from the point of police contact to conviction in court. The following continuum represents the points where we could place these proofs:

1	**2**	**3**	**4**	**5**	**6**

No legal
sufficiency

Complete
sufficiency

A police officer might have a hunch, a gut feeling, about some situation or some person, but that does not provide a basis for legal action. It should not be ignored, however, by the officer.

Reasonable Suspicion

An officer may be confronted with a situation or a person who arouses in the officer a **reasonable suspicion** that the person might be involved in some criminal activity that just occurred, is occurring, or is about to occur, based on some objective facts presented by the situation. This goes beyond a hunch, because there must be some factual basis for the officer's suspicion that the officer can explain in court, if necessary. Factors such as the time of day, location of the event, behavior of the person suspected, officer safety, or the officer's experience might combine to provide the factual basis.

There is no specific rule here that can be applied to every situation. Reasonableness is the guiding principal, and each situation must be judged by itself, considering the **totality of the circumstances**, a concept that will become a familiar benchmark when judging the legality of actions taken. The question to be answered is: Given any law enforcement situation, is it reasonable to conclude that an officer, any officer, would become suspicious? Here, the word *suspicion* provides an officer with the basis for investigation to determine if the suspicion is correct. In Chapter 4, reasonable suspicion is described in detail as the legal basis required in certain specific police procedures.

Probable Cause

Probable cause and reasonable cause are interchangeable terms and mean the same thing. Probable cause is a concept that comes into play in a variety of procedures. It is the basis of a valid search and seizure of evidence, of obtaining a valid arrest or search warrant, of making an arrest, or of a judge holding someone for trial. It consists of facts and trustworthy information, sufficient in themselves, to warrant a person of reasonable caution to believe that

- a crime has been committed or contraband has been concealed,
- the person under consideration has committed the crime or that some contraband does exist in the location to be searched.

Preponderance of Evidence

This is a degree of proof used in court and means a probability or sufficiency of belief 51 percent or greater to make a decision. It allows for some doubt or some evidence to the contrary. Consequently, it is used in various proceedings short of an actual criminal trial, in which a person's guilt would be established. For example, if a defendant challenges the legality of a confession used as evidence, the State would have to convince the judge by a **preponderance of the evidence** that the defendant was advised of his rights before questioning and freely and voluntarily waived them.

Clear and Convincing Evidence

This degree of proof lies somewhere between probable cause and reasonable doubt, but closer to the latter. It means that there is enough proof to show a high probability of belief to justify a conclusion. For example, it might be used in juvenile proceedings to determine whether a very young juvenile knew the wrongfulness of an act.

Beyond a Reasonable Doubt

This means that there is sufficient evidence to prove the case to the point of conclusive belief, beyond any conclusion reached by any other explanation. This is the degree of proof necessary to prove a defendant guilty of a crime. If two explanations seem reasonable and of similar comparison, a jury is instructed to believe that which favors the defendant. Therefore, a verdict represents a conclusion based on an explanation supported by the evidence that is far more reasonable to accept than any other explanation and conclusion. It is not absolute, but conclusive belief, so as to eliminate other explanations from consideration.

EX POST FACTO AND RETROACTIVE LAWS

The Latin phrase ***ex post facto*** means after the fact. It is a phrase that refers to a law that is passed, making some behavior a crime, aggravating or increasing the sentence for a crime, or lowering the degree of proof required for a conviction of a crime, and having that law apply to past cases. This is prohibited by the U.S. Constitution. However, if a law is passed, or a court decision made, that decriminalizes an act, lowers a sentence, or decreases some legal requirement, it may be applied **retroactively**, that is, to past cases.

If a law works to the advantage of the accused, it can be applied retroactively. It cannot be retroactive if it disadvantages the accused or adds a greater penalty. It would not be fair to punish a person for some past act. This does not apply when adding an extra penalty for some enhancement because of a prior conviction.

JURISDICTION AND VENUE

Jurisdiction always **refers to the authority** of some agent or agency to act in some capacity. Often that authority is limited by some political boundary. For example, a city police officer has jurisdiction (authority) to police within the city limits, a sheriff has authority to act within a county, a state police officer or trooper has authority to act statewide.

We will note in the discussions of the courts that each one has certain types of jurisdiction, their authority to act.

Venue always refers to either **the county in which the crime occurred or from which the jury is drawn**. A change of venue means a change in the location where the trial will be held and the jury drawn.

CORPUS DELICTI

The *corpus delicti* is the body of the crime, any crime. It consists of two elements:

- there was harm or loss to a victim
- the harm or loss was caused by some criminal means

This must be proved in the case of every crime, in addition to proving that the accused did it. This prevents a person from being convicted on his or her own confession alone, without proving that a criminal act occurred.

INDEPENDENT STATE GROUNDS

This phrase describes a legal concept by which a state, through its legislature, can enact laws that provide **greater procedural protection** for people accused of crimes than that required by the Constitution, but not less. In other words, the Constitution, and the U.S. Supreme Court's interpretations of what the rights in that document actually mean, set the minimum procedural standards that must be provided in any criminal proceeding. If a state wants an accused person to have more rights or greater protections, it can enact laws to provide them.

We will note examples of this in subsequent chapters, where some states provide greater protections for accused adults in many procedural areas than is required.

SUMMARY

This chapter defined a number of basic legal concepts that form the basis of today's criminal procedures. These are listed at the beginning of this chapter as a way of indicating the concepts and vocabulary that one should learn from the reading. Additional concepts and vocabulary are found throughout the text as we progress from the point of initial police contact with a suspect in Chapter 4 to the final forms of release from contact to the convicted person in Chapter 13.

The case decisions by appellate courts have created many procedural rules that have had the most profound effect on law enforcement and the efforts of police to solve crimes and provide sufficient evidence to the prosecutor that will lead to a criminal conviction. A majority of these rules have come from U.S. Supreme Court decisions within the past 40 years and, during the 1960s and 1970s, tipped the Social Contract balance in favor of individual freedom. That balancing point has been shifting back toward center, and even a little more toward public safety, in recent years by Court justices having a different orientation. That shift will probably continue in the years to come. One of the more moderate Supreme Court justices, Sandra Day O'Connor, resigned in July 2005, and President Bush initially selected a more conservative individual, John Roberts, to replace her. However, before the Senate confirmation hearings began on Roberts's appointment, Chief Justice Rehnquist died on September 3, 2005.

President Bush then withdrew his nomination of Roberts to replace O'Connor and appointed him to replace Rehnquist. There was some concern among senators over Roberts's lack of experience and lack of a track record on key issues, but his confirmation was easily approved, and Roberts took over the leadership of the Supreme Court on October 3, 2005, the first Monday in October. President Bush then appointed Harriet Ellen Miers, age 60, to replace O'Connor. Miers was a prominent trial attorney in Texas and a long-time associate of President Bush. More recently, she served as the legal assistant to President Bush and his deputy chief of staff.

In summarizing her qualifications, President Bush noted that Miers is a born-again evangelical Christian with conservative views. Apparently, the conservative right wing of the Republican party was not convinced of her stand on issues such as abortion and school prayer, the Democrats were not sure what to think, and both sides called it "cronyism." The conservative Republicans wanted a conservative justice, one with a record on abortion and other social issues that they could trust, and they put the pressure on Bush. Finally, on October 27, 2005, Harriet Miers asked the president to withdraw her nomination, and he did. On October 31, Bush nominated Samuel Alito, a veteran judge on the Third U.S. Circuit Court of Appeals located in Philadelphia, to the Supreme Court vacancy. Alito is considered to be a staunch conservative, opposed to abortion, and in favor of states' rights over federal control. He has received strong support from Senate Republicans, but the Democrats called him too radical for the American people, and they threatened a fight in the confirmation hearings and in the Senate. The confirmation hearings were held in January 2006, and as expected, the Democrats took him to task and the Republicans offered their encouragement. By the end of January, the political heat was spent and Alito received Senate confirmation and now sits on the highest court of the land. It will be interesting to watch his growth as a jurist.

As you continue your studies of the justice system, you will find a plethora of information available at your fingertips on the Internet, from discussions of the law to decisions of state and federal courts.

Several of these Internet addresses are given below, with the first two specifically for information on the USA Patriot Act and the others for general justice searches and court decisions.

Issues for Discussion

1. Refer to the concept known as *enhancement,* and discuss what types of enhancements are applied within your state.
2. Discuss the differences between *mala en se* and *mala prohibita* crimes. What types of acts would you list in each category?
3. Discuss the differences between substantive and procedural law.
4. Discuss the implications that the Social Contract has for relationships among individuals and between the individual and society.
5. Research and discuss the USA Patriot Act of 2001, relative to the Social Contract teeter-totter and the claims of government agencies about their need for antiterrorist legislation versus individual rights and freedom.
6. Discuss the differences between the concepts of *probable cause* and *reasonable suspicion*.

References

Ferdico, John N. *Criminal Procedure for the Criminal Justice Professional* (7th edition). Albany, New York: West/Wadsworth, 1999.

Friendly, Fred W., and Martha J. H. Elliott. *The Constitution: That Delicate Balance.* New York: Random House, 1984.

Kerr, Orin S. "The Fourth Amendment and New Technologies: Constitutional Myths and the Case for Caution," *Michigan Law Review,* Mar. 2004, v. 102, No. 5, p. 801.

Rothwax, Judge Harold J. *Guilty: The Collapse of Criminal Justice.* New York: Random House, 1996.

Rousseau, Jean Jacques. (Public Domain) *The Social Contract and the Discourses* (Everyman's Library), G.D.H. Cole, translator, New York: Knopf, 1993.

Samaha, Joel. *Criminal Procedure* (5th edition). Belmont, CA: Wadsworth, 2002.

Simon, James F. *The Center Holds: The Power Struggle Inside the Rehnquist Court.* New York: Simon & Schuster, 1995.

Ziff, David J. S. "Fourth Amendment Limitations on the Execution of Computer Searches Conducted Pursuant to a Warrant," *Columbia Law Review,* Apr. 2005, v. 105, No. 3, p. 841.

Internet References

http://www.epic.org/privacy/terrorism/hr3162.html

http://www.epic.org/privacy/terrorism/usapatriot/

http://www.bambooweb.com/articles/p/a/Patriot_Act.html

http://virlib.ncjrs.org/Courts.asp
http://www.findlaw.com/
http://supreme.lp.findlaw.com/
http://straylight.law.cornell.edu/supct/index.html
http://www.officer.com/
http://www.abanet.org/publiced/preview/briefs/home.html
http://www.ncjrs.org/
http://dir.yahoo.com/Government/Law/
http://www.statelocalgov.net/index.cfm

THE EXCLUSIONARY RULE

KEY TERMS AND CONCEPTS

Christian Burial Speech	Mapp decision
Exclusionary rule	Officer safety
Fourteenth Amendment	Public safety exception
Fourth Amendment	Silver Platter Doctrine
Fruit of the poison tree	Suppression of evidence
Good faith exception	Warren Court
Inevitable discovery exception	Weeks Doctrine

INTRODUCTION

To study police procedures in their proper legal context, it is necessary at this point to introduce one of the most important rules of law that law enforcement officers must obey, the **exclusionary rule**. It is a procedural rule that an officer must have on his or her mind in every investigative situation that might involve the collection of evidence. It also is a procedural rule that every defense attorney knows well and will use in an effort to exclude evidence in almost every criminal case.

In most instances, when a police officer is subpoenaed to testify in court, it is to testify as to how he or she obtained the evidence, not about the guilt of the accused. How this procedure was created, how it became a binding rule for every police officer to follow, and how exceptions to it have been allowed all make for an interesting story. Therefore, it will be presented in detail as a prelude to studying police procedures.

THE EXCLUSIONARY RULE

The exclusionary rule is a prime example of a procedural law created by case law; created by a decision of the U.S. Supreme Court. As was stated in Chapter 1, the role of the appellate courts, including the Supreme Court, is not to make law, but to interpret what existing law means. Specifically, the U.S. Supreme Court has the responsibility of interpreting what the U.S. Constitution means and whether any state or federal laws conflict with the rights therein guaranteed to the people.

Simply stated, the exclusionary rule is a rule of law that holds that

> evidence seized illegally by the government (law enforcement) is inadmissible in a court of law to prove guilt.

The reason that police need to follow this rule is obvious. If they do not follow it and seize evidence illegally, it cannot be used against the person arrested by the police and accused of the crime. It will result in the **suppression of evidence**. Without the evidence of a crime, the State cannot prove that a crime occurred, and the suspect will go free. One would think, then, that police would never seize evidence illegally because it would ruin their own case, and their efforts would be in vain.

The problem with this assumption, however, is the fact that whether police seize evidence illegally often is determined a long time after the fact by some appellate court sitting far away from the scene of the events that produced the evidence. Sometimes police do not realize they are not following the rule. Other times they do know but do not care.

True, there are certain guidelines for police to follow, but there is no absolute rule to govern every situation. Consequently, whether evidence is admitted or excluded from a trial depends on how judges interpret the general guidelines as applied to the situation before them. And sometimes a judge of a higher court will disagree with the trial judge, and a judge at an even higher court might disagree with the other judge, and so on.

Sometimes it takes two or three years in this appellate process for the police officer to know if the manner in which the evidence was seized was legal. Even when a case reaches the U.S. Supreme Court, where nine justices sit as the highest legal minds in the country, they might not agree with each other. However, their decision, possibly made by a vote of 5 to 4, will become the law of the land.

Three Supreme Court cases are discussed in the following section that demonstrate how and why the exclusionary rule was created and how it affects police procedures. Three more recent cases are then presented that explain certain basic exceptions to the rule made by the Court.

CASES LEADING TO THE EXCLUSIONARY RULE

Weeks v. United States, 1914

A man named Weeks was suspected by police of being involved in illegal lottery gambling. On December 21, 1911, in Kansas City, Missouri, local police went to his residence while Weeks was at work to search for evidence. After being told by a neighbor where the door key was hidden, they entered his home and searched his room and removed various papers and other personal property, which they turned over to the U.S. Marshal. Later that same day, the officers returned to Weeks's residence, accompanied by the marshal, where they were admitted by a roomer. They completed a more extensive search and took away many of Weeks's personal effects, including letters and lottery tickets showing his illegal activity.

Weeks was arrested at the express office where he worked at Union Station. He was charged in federal court with the use of the mails for the purpose of transporting illegal lottery tickets, in violation of §213 of the Federal Criminal Code. He petitioned the court for the return of all his effects, claiming they were illegally seized because police did not have a warrant. His petition was denied and he was convicted, fined, and imprisoned.

Weeks appealed to the U.S. Supreme Court, and his case was argued before it in December 1913, two years after his arrest and conviction. The Court announced its decision on February 24, 1914. Chief Justice Day wrote the opinion of the Court and stated:

> If letters and private documents can thus be seized and held and used in evidence against a citizen accused of an offense, the protection of the Fourth Amendment, declaring his right to be secure against such searches and seizures, is of no value, and, so far as those thus placed are concerned, might as well be stricken from the Constitution. . . .
>
> We therefore reach the conclusion that the letters in question were taken from the house of the accused by an official of the United States, acting under color of his office, in direct violation of the constitutional rights of the defendant. (*Weeks v. U.S.,* 1914)

The Supreme Court reversed Weeks's conviction and ruled that the evidence was seized illegally and could not be used in federal court. Consequently, he was not retried. The Court also discussed the seizure of documents by the local police, but declined to address the legality of that because, as Chief Justice Day stated, ". . . the Fourth Amendment is not directed to individual misconduct by such officials. Its limitations reach the Federal government and its agencies."

Although the Supreme Court did not mention the phrase *exclusionary rule*, its decision created the rule, and the phrase was created later. Notice, however, that in the words of Justice Day, the ruling applied only to federal courts because the Court believed that the Constitution applied only to federal procedures. In fact, the prevailing attitude was that all of the amendments of the Constitution applied only to federal procedures. Nevertheless, 20 states adopted the so-called **Weeks Doctrine** into their own body of procedural law.

Iowa had enacted their own version of an exclusionary rule even before Weeks. However, 27 states decided not to follow Weeks, and for a majority of local police and sheriffs, it was business as usual, making whatever illegal searches and seizures they wanted for the next 47 years. In fact, federal court allowed the admission of illegally seized evidence if it was seized by local police and not federal officers. Consequently, if federal agents suspected contraband located in a house and wanted to make a search but did not have sufficient probable cause to obtain a search warrant, they would have the local police make the search then give them the evidence. This practice came to be known as the **Silver Platter Doctrine** because the federal agents would be handed good evidence on a silver platter.

Wolf v. Colorado, 1949

In 1944, Dr. Julius A. Wolf, a Denver physician, was charged with conspiring to perform an illegal abortion. He and his co-conspirator pled not guilty. At their trial, the prosecutor introduced into evidence Dr. Wolf's appointment book, which would prove the charge that Mildred Cairo had obtained an illegal abortion from Dr. Wolf. Wolf moved to suppress the appointment book as evidence because it had been seized from his office without a warrant, in violation of Colorado's own version of the exclusionary rule. The trial judge denied his motion. He was convicted and sentenced to a term in prison from 15 months to five years. On appeal, his sentence was affirmed by the Iowa State Supreme Court. Finally, in 1948 the U.S. Supreme Court agreed to hear his case.

Supreme Court Justice Felix Frankfurter stated the issue clearly in the introduction to the Court's opinion, which was decided on June 27, 1949:

> The precise question for consideration is this: does a conviction by a State court for a State offense deny the "due process law" required by the Fourteenth Amendment, solely because evidence that was admitted at the trial was obtained under circumstances which would render it inadmissible in a prosecution for violation of a federal law in a court of the United Sates because there deemed to be an infraction of the Fourth Amendment as applied in *Weeks v. United States* 232 U.S. 383. (*Wolf v. Colorado,* 1949)

In a vote of 6 to 3, the Court answered with a resounding "No!" The Court suggested that an exclusionary rule was one remedy to illegal searches and seizures, but it was not the only remedy, and the federal court should not dictate to the states what sort of remedy to use. Justice Frankfurter also noted that if the defendant does not gain satisfaction in his criminal case, "The common law provides for damages against the searching officer . . . and against persons assisting in the execution of an illegal search." Consequently, in those states not having their own controls over search and seizure, the police were left to their own devices. For example, in New York police would stop and search people or places at will without ever obtaining a search warrant. The year following the decision in the next case, they obtained more than 800 warrants before searching.

Mapp v. Ohio, 1961

The **Mapp decision** stands as a watershed in the history of criminal due process. It established one of the most controversial procedures of our time, the exclusionary rule, as a **mandatory procedure in all states**. It is revered by defense attorneys and reviled by most law enforcement officers. The last three Republican administrations hoped to reload the U.S. Supreme Court by appointments of individuals who would reverse the vile thing that succeeded in letting the criminals go free. Needless to say, it did not work, that is, not completely. Just how this procedure came to be mandated on the states is a fascinating story.

Ohio was one of those states in which the courts had rejected the Weeks Doctrine (*State v. Lindusay*, 1930) as a part of its own criminal procedures in 1936. However, in 1955 the Ohio Legislature enacted an exclusionary rule, requiring police to obtain search warrants. And as it is in the case of any warrant, the officer must complete an affidavit stating the probable cause in support of a warrant request and convince a judge to issue the warrant.

At about 2:30 a.m. on May 20, 1957, a Cleveland police sergeant, Carl Delau, arrived home "a little drunk" from a party and went to bed. Shortly thereafter, he was awakened by a phone call from a man known to him as Don King, a reputed numbers racketeer (Rothwax, 1996). King told the sleepy Delau that someone had just bombed his house and wanted to know what to do. Delau asked how he knew it was actually a bomb, and King replied that his entire front porch and front wall had been blown off of his house. Apparently, Delau indicated that he would report it. Within a few minutes, however, the police dispatcher phoned Delau and told him to get out there to investigate a bombing.

Three days later, Sgt. Delau received a phone tip that the alleged bomber, Virgil Ogiltree, was hiding out at 14705 Milverton Road, Cleveland. That afternoon, Sgt. Delau and two other detectives went to the address, a two-story, two-family flat, identified Ogiltree's car parked near the residence, and staked it out. Finally, the officers got tired of waiting, so they went to the door of the flat occupied by a young black woman, Dollree Mapp, who was known to Delau from a prior arrest. They knocked on the door, and she called down from the upstairs window to inquire what they wanted. When they told her they wanted to search her house, she said she would call her attorney first, and disappeared from the window. She returned within a few minutes and told Delau that they could not search without a warrant.

Sgt. Delau and the two other detectives returned to their car and radioed in for a warrant and for some additional officers to help. Three hours later they returned to Miss Mapp's residence, along with six uniformed officers, and again asked Miss Mapp to search, claiming that they had a warrant. When she refused, one officer broke a door window pane, unlatched the door, and they all entered the hallway and moved toward her flat. She rushed down to meet them and demanded to see the warrant. When one officer held up a piece of paper, claiming it was the warrant, she grabbed it out of his hand and shoved it down inside the front of her sweater.

Stories about what occurred next vary. According to Sgt. Delau, the warrant was visible, protruding from her sweater, so he grabbed it back. She then became unruly and had to be restrained with handcuffs. According to Miss Mapp, the officers handcuffed her, held her in a corner, then reached in her bosom after the warrant.

Regardless of who is correct, the police obtained the piece of paper they claimed was the warrant, cuffed her, and thoroughly searched her residence, including drawers, closets, and cabinets. Ogiltree, the bombing suspect, was not found because he was not there. However, the police did find "pictures of both male and female nude models with all their organs totally undressed," and some pencil sketches of nudes, and four books: *London Stage Affair*, *Affairs of a Troubadour*, *Memoirs of a Hotel Man*, and *Little Darlings*.

Police also searched her basement and found illegal gambling material. She was arrested and charged with both possession of the betting material, a misdemeanor, and possession of obscene materials, a felony. On their way out, police also searched the other flat next to Mapp's, where they did find Ogiltree hiding, and arrested him for the bombing.

Miss Mapp was tried on the misdemeanor in Police Court and was acquitted. Her felony trial began in September 1958, and she was charged with "unlawfully and knowingly having in her possession certain lewd and lascivious books, pictures, and photographs." Her attorney questioned the legality of the search, and when police indicated that the so-called warrant had disappeared, he moved to suppress the evidence, claiming that the officers actually did not have a warrant. No one seemed to bring up the fact that if the police did have a real warrant, it would not have mentioned any "obscene" material anyway.

The trial judge denied the motion to suppress, and Mapp was convicted and sentenced to seven years in prison, seven years for possession of so-called obscene material in her own home. Her attorney appealed to the Ohio State Supreme Court on the basis that the Ohio obscenity statute violated the First Amendment and, therefore, was unconstitutional. Four of the Ohio justices agreed, but their votes were not enough to reverse her conviction. On further appeal, the U.S. Supreme Court agreed to hear the case in 1961.

The basis of the appeal by her attorney, and his written and oral arguments before the Court, centered on the constitutionality of Ohio's broadly worded obscenity statute and Mapp's First Amendment right to free expression and the right to possess any written materials or drawings in the privacy of her own home. Her attorney did not make this a Fourth Amendment search and seizure issue. And many of the questions raised by the justices during the oral argument by the State's attorney were about the fact that mere possession of obscenity in one's own home was a felony. That really concerned the justices.

When Mapp's attorney attempted to explain that the so-called obscene material did not even belong to her, but to a former roomer, Justice Felix Frankfurter interrupted to ask just exactly what was the issue before the court and asked if the legality of the search and seizure was before the Court. Her attorney seemed somewhat flustered by the mention of this new issue. Nevertheless, he did start to argue that it was illegal, when Justice Frankfurter interrupted him again to say, "Are you asking us to overrule the *Wolf* case in this Court? I notice it isn't cited in your brief." The attorney was not familiar with the *Wolf* case, and perhaps not even familiar with search and seizure issues, so he indicated no, that he was not asking the Court to reverse *Wolf*, and he let the issue of search and seizure drop.

Upon completion of the oral arguments by both sides, an unusual event occurred. For the first time in the Court's history, it allowed an oral argument to be presented by a representative of the American Civil Liberties Union (ACLU) who had submitted a written brief and requested to be heard as *amicus curiae*, a friend of the court. It was as if the ACLU attorney sensed that Justice Frankfurter wanted to make an issue out of the search and seizure by bringing it up himself, so the ACLU attorney began his address to the court by referring to the *Wolf* case and stated:

> The American Civil Liberties Union and its Ohio affiliate . . . [are] very clear as to the question directed toward the appellant that we are asking this court to reconsider *Wolf v. Colorado* and to find that evidence that is unlawfully and illegally obtained should not be permitted into a state proceeding and its production is a violation of the federal constitution's Fourth Amendment and the Fourteenth Amendment. We have no hesitancy in

asking the court to reconsider it because we think that it is a necessary part of due process.

After stating this, however, the attorney indicated that his primary purpose in addressing the Court was to urge them to declare the obscenity statute of Ohio unconstitutional, and he proceeded to address that statute as a First Amendment issue in the Mapp case.

Later, in the privacy of their chambers, the justices discussed the legality of Ohio's obscenity statute within the context of the First and Fourteenth Amendments, and they unanimously voted to reverse Mapp's conviction and declare the statute unconstitutional (Rothwax, p. 42). Justice Tom Clark was assigned to write the Court's opinion. However, the opinion he wrote focused on the Fourth Amendment and the exclusionary rule and did not address the obscenity issue or the Ohio statute at all.

When his opinion was circulated among the other justices to read and sign, Justice Potter Stewart was "shocked" by the change in the written opinion from that which had been accepted as the basis for reversal of Mapp's conviction. As Judge Harold J. Rothwax stated, Justice Clark's opinion ". . . was based on arguments that had never even been briefed, argued, or discussed before the Court" (Rothwax, p. 45). Justice Stewart later indicated that he believed the other justices met together to form a "rump caucus" and agreed to make the Mapp case a vehicle by which the Fourteenth Amendment could be used to make the Fourth Amendment and the exclusionary rule binding on the states.

Regardless of the objections of Justice Stewart and several other justices, the opinion written by Justice Clark was approved by a 5-to-4 majority (the **Warren Court**, with its due process orientation) and held that

> . . . the Fourth Amendment's right of privacy has been declared enforceable against the States through the Due Process Clause of the Fourteenth, it is enforceable against them by the same sanction of exclusion as is used against the Federal Government.
>
> Were it otherwise, then, just as without the Weeks rule the assurance against unreasonable federal searches and seizures would be "a form of words," valueless and undeserving of mention in a perpetual charter of inestimable human liberties, so too, without that rule, the freedom from state invasions of privacy would be so ephemeral and so neatly severed from its conceptual nexus with the freedom from all brutish means of coercing evidence as not to merit this Court's high regard as a freedom implicit in the concept of ordered liberty.

With this decision, the exclusionary rule was imposed on the states and on all state and local law enforcement officers as the primary procedural law that guides their actions. It is against this rule that much of the efforts by police are judged legal or illegal. Any evidence seized illegally, in violation of the Fourth Amendment, cannot be used in court to prove guilt. **The sole purpose of the rule is to police the police**; to deter police from violating the rights of citizens guaranteed by the Fourth Amendment.

The theory says that if the police know their evidence cannot be used if they seize it illegally, they will follow the law. It is a rule of procedural law that was railroaded through the Supreme Court by a majority of activist justices seeking to impose their version of due process on the rest of the legal community. It is also a rule of law that demonstrates just how delicate the balance is between individual freedom and social protection, and how a simple majority of the Court can decide where that balancing point will be.

One of the Supreme Court bailiffs in the Mapp case had agreed to phone Dollree Mapp when the justices reached their decision. He phoned her every Monday morning for 12 weeks after her case was argued to say that no decision had been made. But, finally, on the thirteenth Monday, he called her with the decision and, according to her, "that was the day that the Supreme Court washed my conviction down the drain." Dollree Mapp is all but forgotten by most people, but the rule that the justices created from her case remains on the mind of every law enforcement officer, every attorney, and every judge, every day.

As indicated in the beginning of the Mapp case presentation, how it developed makes for an interesting story. By way of conclusion, Dollree Mapp did not live happily ever after when her conviction was reversed. She was convicted of drug possession in New York in 1973 and was sentenced to a term of 20 years to life in state prison. After serving 9 years, 4 months, and 17 days in prison, her sentence was commuted to time served and she was paroled. She continued to maintain her innocence of the drug charge and has petitioned the governor for a full pardon. After her release, she went to work in Long Island as a legal aide for prison inmates.

As for Don King, who had his front porch and front wall blown away by the bomb, he went on to become one of the country's leading boxing promoters. Sgt. Delau eventually retired.

EXCEPTIONS TO THE RULE

As the saying goes, for every rule there are many exceptions. This is true for the exclusionary rule, and the Supreme Court has established three exceptions that affect the application of the rule by police in their collection of evidence:

- the **inevitable discovery exception**
- the **public safety exception**
- the **good faith exception**

Each was created from one or more of the following case decisions.

The Inevitable Discovery Exception

On Christmas Eve, 1968, a 10-year-old girl named Pamela Powers disappeared from a YMCA building in Des Moines, Iowa, where she had accompanied her parents to watch an athletic event. Shortly after she disappeared, a man later identified as Robert Williams was seen leaving the YMCA carrying a large bundle wrapped in a blanket. A 14-year-old boy who had helped Williams open his car door reported that he had seen "two legs in it and they were skinny and white."

Williams was a local man, known to police, and had recently been released from a mental institution. He became the immediate suspect. His car was found the next day 160 miles east of Des Moines in Davenport, Iowa. Later, several items of clothing belonging to the child, some of Williams's clothing, and an army blanket like the one used to bundle up the girl when Williams carried her out of the YMCA were found at a rest stop near Grinnell, a town between Des Moines and Davenport. A warrant was issued for Williams's arrest.

Police believed that Williams had left the girl or her body somewhere between Des Moines and the Grinnell rest stop where some of the young girl's clothing had been found. Consequently, on the day after Christmas, officers initiated a large-scale search, accompanied by more than 200 volunteers from the local community, who came forward out of concern for the child and her parents. They divided into teams and began the search. They were instructed to check all roads, abandoned farm buildings, ditches, culverts, and any other place in which the body of a small child could be hidden.

Meanwhile, Williams phoned his mother in Des Moines and learned from her that he was wanted by the police. She told him to surrender to the local police in Davenport and that she would obtain an attorney for him. Williams did surrender to local police, and he was detained on the warrant. The attorney, Henry McKnight, hired by Williams's parents in Des Moines, arranged for an attorney in Davenport to meet Williams at the Davenport police station. Des Moines police informed the attorney they would pick Williams up in Davenport and return him to Des Moines.

Police were advised by the attorney that his client would not waive his right to remain silent and that officers were not to question him. The officers acknowledged that they understood and agreed not to question Williams on their return trip.

Two Des Moines detectives then drove to Davenport, took Williams into custody, and drove back toward Des Moines. However, before they left the police station in Des Moines, they researched the file on Williams and learned that he was of low intelligence, mentally unstable, and a religious fanatic of fundamentalist beliefs. Like any good detectives, they wanted as much information as possible on their suspect to use to their advantage in dealing with him.

During the return trip, one of the policemen, Detective Leaming, addressed Williams as Reverend Williams and began a conversation saying:

I want to give you something to think about while we're traveling down the road. . . . They are predicting several inches of snow for tonight, and I feel that you yourself are the only person that knows where this little girl's body is . . . and if it gets snow on top of it, you yourself may be unable to find it. And since we will be going right past the area {where the body is] on the way into Des Moines, I feel that we could stop and locate the body, that the parents of this little girl should be entitled to a Christian burial for the little girl who was snatched away from them on Christmas Eve and murdered. . . . After a snow storm, we may not be able to find it at all. (*State v. Williams*, 1970)

This short speech became known as the **Christian Burial Speech**. Detective Leaming told Williams he knew that the girl was dead but not where the body was, and they needed to find her soon if she was to have a good Christian burial. He concluded the conversation by saying: "I do not want you to answer me. . . . Just think about it. . . ."

Later, as the police car approached Grinnell, Williams asked Leaming whether the police had found the young girl's shoes. After Leaming replied that he was unsure, Williams directed the police to a point near a service station where he said he had left the shoes. As they continued the drive to Des Moines, Williams asked whether the blanket had been found, and then directed the officers to a rest area in Grinnell where he said he had disposed of the blanket. After driving a short distance further, Williams, without any further conversation from Detective Leaming, directed the officers down a gravel road to where he had left the child's body, in a ditch next to a culvert. She had been sexually assaulted and strangled to death.

Williams was indicted for first-degree murder in February 1969. Before trial in the Iowa court, his attorney moved to suppress evidence of the body and all related evidence, including the condition of the body as shown by the autopsy. The grounds for the motion was that such evidence was the "fruit," or product, of Williams's statements made during the automobile ride from Davenport to Des Moines after Williams's attorney, McKnight, had told police not to interrogate his client without him being present. The motion to suppress was denied.

The jury found Williams guilty of first-degree murder; the judgment of conviction was affirmed by the Iowa Supreme Court (*State v. Williams*, 1970). Williams's attorney then appealed to the U.S. District Court for the Southern District of Iowa. That court concluded that the evidence in question had been wrongly admitted at Williams's trial (*Brewer v. Williams*, 1977). A divided panel of the Court of Appeals for the Eighth Circuit agreed, holding that Detective Leaming had obtained incriminating statements from Williams by what was viewed as interrogation in violation of his right to counsel, and Williams's conviction was reversed.

The court's opinion noted, however, that although Williams's incriminating statements could not be introduced into evidence at a second trial, evidence of the body's location and condition might well be admissible on the theory that the body would have been discovered in any event, even if police had not talked to Williams.

When a convicted person appeals his or her conviction on the basis of some procedural error and wins the appeal and has the conviction reversed, the person gives up his or her right not to be tried again. A retrial in this case is not considered double jeopardy. Williams's second trial in an Iowa court began in 1977. The prosecution did not introduce Williams's statements into evidence, nor did it seek to show that Williams had directed the police to the child's body. However, evidence of the condition of her body as it was found, articles and photographs of her clothing, and the results of postmortem medical and chemical tests on the body were admitted.

The trial court concluded that the State had proved by a preponderance of the evidence that if the search had not been suspended and Williams had not led the police to the victim, her body would have been discovered "within a short time" in essentially the same condition as it was actually found. The trial court also ruled that if the police had not located the body, the search would clearly have been taken up again where it left off, given the extreme circumstances of the case, and the body would have been found soon because the searchers were only two and one-half miles away from the culvert where Williams led them to the body, and they were heading in that direction.

In finding that the body would have been discovered in essentially the same condition as it was actually found, the court noted that freezing temperatures had prevailed and tissue deterioration would have been suspended. The challenged evidence was admitted, and the jury again found Williams guilty of first-degree murder. He was sentenced to life in prison.

Williams appealed his second conviction to the Supreme Court of Iowa, and again, his conviction was upheld. That court held that there was, in fact, a "hypothetical independent source" exception to the exclusionary rule and stated that:

> After the defendant has shown unlawful conduct on the part of the police, the State has the burden to show by a preponderance of the evidence that (1) the police did not act in bad faith for the purpose of hastening discovery of the evidence in question, and (2) that the evidence in question would have been discovered by lawful means.

The Iowa court then reviewed the evidence and concluded that the State had shown by a preponderance of the evidence that even if Williams had not guided police to the child's body, **it would inevitably have been found** by lawful activity of the search party before its condition had materially changed. Thus, the exception to the exclusionary rule, known as **inevitable discovery** was created, but the Williams case was not over yet.

Williams continued with his appeals. The U.S. District Court reviewed the case in 1980 and upheld his conviction. However, the Court of Appeals for the Eighth Circuit reversed the lower court's decision, holding that the prosecutor had not shown that ". . . the police did not act in bad faith for the purpose of hastening discovery of the evidence." Consequently, the case was reversed because of that procedural error, and therefore, the issue of inevitable discovery is of no importance. This left all the evidence tainted by the original illegal conduct of Detective Leaming, interrogating Williams by way of his Christian Burial Speech.

When an investigating police officer makes one procedural error, any other evidence discovered as a result of the first error becomes tainted and also is inadmissible. This is known as the **fruit of the poison tree** doctrine that originated from other appellate cases (*Silverthorne Lumber Co. v. United States*, 1920; *Wong Sun v. United States*, 1963). The first procedural error poisons the tree of evidence, causing all the fruit of that tree to become poisoned as well. And without the evidence, there is no basis for prosecution. We will note in Chapter 11 that questioning the legality of evidence seized is the heart of a defense strategy to have the charges dismissed.

Nix v. Williams, **1984**   Undoubtedly, Williams (or his attorney) thought he had finally won and that the case was over. However, the prosecutor, named Nix, was not to be denied. He appealed the case to the U.S. Supreme Court, and it was heard in January 1984. After much discussion about the Sixth Amendment right to have an attorney present during any police questioning, and about the exclusionary rule and Leaming's interrogation of Williams, the Court focused on the fact that the purpose of the exclusionary rule is to punish police for seizing evidence illegally by not admitting it into court. It is to control police misconduct and to uphold the Fourth Amendment protection against unreasonable search and seizure. Granted, the evidence obtained by Detective Leaming's conduct must be excluded. However, "exclusion of physical evidence that would inevitably have been discovered adds nothing to either the integrity or fairness of a criminal trial." The U.S. Supreme Court concluded that:

> . . . it is clear that the search parties were approaching the actual location of the body, and we are satisfied, along with three courts earlier, that the volunteer search teams would have resumed the search had Williams not earlier led the police to the body, and the body inevitably would have been found.

Williams's second conviction was upheld and, after 16 years in the appellate mill, his sentence could be carried out. **The inevitable discovery rule became a procedural law of the land**, binding on all the states. It is a rule that means, in essence, that if police obtain evidence in violation of the Fourth Amendment but they can prove by a preponderance of the evidence that their evidence would have been found in the same condition anyway, by some legal means or independent source, it is admissible in court, and the exclusionary rule does not apply. The complexity of the Williams case is exceeded only by the length of time necessary to complete it. Think how long it took for this case to bring closure for the girl's family.

The Public Safety Exception

Chief Justice Rehnquist described the circumstances of the case and delivered the opinion of the Supreme Court (*New York v. Quarles*, 1984). On September 11, 1980, at approximately 12:30 a.m., Officer Frank Kraft and Officer Sal Scarring were on road patrol in Queens, New York, when a young woman approached their car. She told them that she had just been raped by a black male, approximately six feet tall, who was wearing a black jacket with the name "Big Ben" printed in yellow letters on the back. She told the officers that the man had just entered an A & P supermarket located nearby and that the man was carrying a gun.

The officers drove the woman to the supermarket, and Officer Kraft entered the store while Officer Scarring radioed for assistance. Officer Kraft spotted the suspect, who matched the description given by the woman, approaching a checkout counter. He apparently saw the officer and turned and ran toward the rear of the store. Officer Kraft pursued him with a drawn gun but lost sight of him for several seconds. Upon locating the suspect again, the officer ordered him to stop and put his hands over his head.

Three other officers arrived on the scene by that time, but Officer Kraft was the first to reach the suspect. He patted him down for weapons and discovered that he was wearing a shoulder holster which was then empty. After handcuffing him, Officer Kraft asked him where the gun was, and the suspect nodded in the direction of some empty cartons and responded, "The gun is over there." Officer Kraft retrieved a loaded .38-caliber revolver from one of the cartons, formally placed the suspect under arrest, and read him his *Miranda* rights from a printed card. The suspect, identified as Benjamin Quarles, indicated that he would be willing to answer questions without an attorney present. Officer Kraft then asked Quarles if he owned the gun and where he had purchased it. Quarles answered that it was his gun and that he had purchased it in Miami, Florida.

Quarles was charged with criminal possession of a weapon, but the judge excluded the statement, "The gun is over there," and the gun, because the officer had not given Quarles the required *Miranda* warning before asking him where the gun was. The judge excluded the other statements as well because they were tainted by the initial procedural violation by the officer and became fruits of the poison tree of evidence. The Appellate Division of the Supreme Court of New York affirmed the trial judge's decision and rejected an argument by the State that the emergency nature of the situation justified Officer Kraft's failure to read Quarles his *Miranda* rights until after he had located the gun. The Appellate Court found no indication from Officer Kraft's testimony that his subjective motivation in asking the question was to protect his own safety or the safety of the public.

We will not go into any detail about the *Miranda* decision or warning at this point in the text. The specifics of that procedure are covered in Chapter 5. Nevertheless, the *Miranda* warning required by police is mentioned because it is a part of the Quarles case, and it is assumed that most any reader will have a general idea what it is. Suffice it to say, the State of New York appealed the lower court's decision to the U.S. Supreme Court, which agreed to hear the case. It was argued in January 1984 and decided in June 1984. In the Court's opinion, Justice Rehnquist stated that:

> The Fifth Amendment guarantees that "no person . . . shall be compelled in any criminal case to be a witness against himself." In *Miranda*, this Court for the first time extended the Fifth Amendment privilege against compulsory self-incrimination to individuals subjected to custodial interrogation by the police. . . . The only issue before us is whether Officer Kraft was justified in failing to make available to respondent (Quarles) the procedural safeguards associated with the privilege against compulsory self-incrimination since *Miranda*.

After a detailed review of all the facts and the relevant cases from previous decisions, the Court held

> . . . that, on these facts, there is a "public safety" exception to the requirement that *Miranda* warnings be given before a suspect's answers may be admitted into evidence . . . and that the availability of that exception does not depend upon the motivation of the individual officers involved. . . . Undoubtedly most police officers, if placed in Officer Kraft's position, would act out of a host of different, instinctive, and largely unverifiable motives— their own safety, the safety of others. . . .
>
> Whatever the motivation of individual officers in such a situation, we do not believe that the doctrinal underpinnings of *Miranda* require that it be applied in all its rigor to a situation in which police officers ask questions reasonably prompted by a concern for the public safety. . . . The police in this case, in the very act of apprehending a suspect, were confronted with the immediate necessity of ascertaining the whereabouts of a gun which they had every reason to believe the suspect had just removed from his empty holster and discarded in the supermarket. So long as the gun was concealed somewhere in the supermarket, with its actual whereabouts unknown, it obviously posed more than one danger to the **public safety**. . . .

We conclude that the need for answers to questions in a situation posing a threat to the public safety outweighs the need for the . . . rule protecting the Fifth Amendment's privilege against self-incrimination. We decline to place officers such as Officer Kraft in the untenable position of having to consider, often in a matter of seconds, whether it best serves society for them to ask the necessary questions without the *Miranda* warnings and render whatever probative evidence they uncover inadmissible, or for them to give the warnings in order to preserve the admissibility of evidence they might uncover but possibly damage or destroy their ability to obtain that evidence and neutralize the volatile situation confronting them.

From this abbreviated version of the Court's opinion, it is obvious that the justices were balancing the needs of society for safety with the rights of the individual, Quarles. This public safety exception to the exclusionary rule shows that in the Court's mind, public safety comes first. In fact, in situations like this, the Court leaves the balancing up to the police officer at the scene, who can best judge when the public safety is in jeopardy.

The wording of this opinion also captures a theme that will recur in many subsequent cases decided by the Supreme Court up through 1996, the subjective motivations of a police officer have absolutely no bearing on the legality of a situation. The only factors that count are the acts of the officer and the nature of the situation in which he or she is acting. What an officer thinks or feels is not relevant, only what the officer does. Public safety does not mean just the general public. It applies equally as well to **officer safety**, **victim safety**, and **suspect safety** (*United States v. Brady*, 1987; *United States v. DeSantis*, 1989; *United States v. Carrillo*, 1994), and particularly to the admissibility of statements taken without a *Miranda* admonition in an effort to ensure these safeties.

The Good Faith Exception

Supreme Court Justice White described the situation and delivered the opinion of the Court (*United States v. Leon*, 1984).

In August 1981 a confidential informant of unproven reliability informed an officer of the Burbank Police Department that two persons known to him as Armando and Patsy were selling large quantities of cocaine and methaqualone from their residence on Price Drive in Burbank. The informant also indicated that he had witnessed a sale of methaqualone by Patsy at the residence approximately five months earlier and had observed at that time a shoebox containing a large amount of cash that belonged to Patsy. He further declared that Armando and Patsy generally kept only small quantities of drugs at their residence and stored the remainder at another location in Burbank.

On the basis of this information, the Burbank police initiated an extensive investigation focusing first on the Price Drive residence and later on two other residences as well. Cars parked at the Price Drive residence were determined to belong to Armando Sanchez, who had previously been arrested for possession of marijuana, and Patsy Stewart, who had no criminal record. During the course of the investigation, officers observed an automobile belonging to a Ricardo Del Costello, who had previously been arrested for possession of 50 pounds of marijuana, arrive at the residence. The driver of that car entered the house, exited shortly thereafter carrying a small paper sack, and drove away. A check of Del Costello's probation records led the officers to a suspect, Alberto Leon, whose telephone number Del Costello had listed as his employer.

Leon had been arrested in 1980 on drug charges, and a companion had informed the police at that time that Leon was heavily involved in the importation of drugs into this country. Before the current investigation began, the Burbank officers had learned that an informant had told a Glendale police officer that Leon stored a large quantity of methaqualone at his residence in Glendale. During the course of this investigation, the Burbank officers learned that Leon was living at 716 South Sunset Canyon in Burbank.

Subsequently, the officers observed several persons, at least one of whom had prior drug involvement, arriving at the Price Drive residence and leaving with small packages; observed a variety of other material activity at the two residences as well as at a condominium at 7902 Via Magdalena; and witnessed a variety of relevant activity involving suspects' automobiles. The officers also observed suspects Sanchez and Stewart board separate flights for Miami. The pair later returned to Los Angeles together, consented to a search of their luggage that revealed only a small amount of marijuana, and left the airport. Based on these and other observations summarized in an affidavit, Officer Cyril Rombach of the Burbank Police Department, an experienced and well-trained narcotics investigator, prepared an application for a warrant to search 620 Price Drive, 716 South Sunset Canyon, 7902 Via Magdalena, and automobiles registered to each of the suspects for an extensive list of items believed to be related to the suspects' drug trafficking activities. Officer Rombach's extensive application was reviewed by several Deputy District Attorneys.

A facially valid search warrant was issued in September 1981 by a state superior court judge. The ensuing searches produced large quantities of drugs at the Via Magdalena and Sunset Canyon addresses and a small quantity at the Price Drive residence. Other evidence was discovered at each of the residences and in Stewart's and Del Costello's automobiles. The suspects were indicted by a grand jury in the District Court for the Central District of California and charged with conspiracy to possess and distribute cocaine and a variety of substantive counts.

The suspects then filed motions to suppress the evidence seized pursuant to the warrant. The District Court held an evidentiary hearing and, while recognizing that the case was a close one, granted the motions to suppress in part. It concluded that the affidavit was insufficient to establish probable cause, but the court made clear that Officer Rombach had **acted in good faith**. However, it rejected the Government's suggestion that the Fourth Amendment exclusionary rule should not apply where evidence is seized in reasonable, good faith reliance on a search warrant.

The District Court and a divided panel of the Court of Appeals for the Ninth Circuit agreed and concluded that Officer Rombach's affidavit could not establish probable cause to search the Price Drive residence, and the evidence retained was suppressed. On appeal by the U.S. Attorney General's office, the Supreme Court agreed to hear the State's case, that the officer should not be punished by having the evidence excluded when he acted in good faith and the error was made by someone else. It was the judge who found that probable cause existed and signed the search warrant. After a very lengthy discussion, the Court held that:

> This case presents the question whether the Fourth Amendment exclusionary rule should be modified so as not to bar the use in the prosecution's case-in-chief of evidence obtained by officers acting in reasonable reliance on a search warrant issued by a detached and neutral magistrate but ultimately found to be unsupported by probable cause. To resolve this question, we must consider once again the tension between the sometimes competing goals of, on the one hand, deterring official misconduct and removing inducements to unreasonable invasions of privacy and, on the other, establishing procedures under which criminal defendants are "acquitted . . . or convicted on the basis of all the evidence which exposes the truth."
>
> As yet, we have not recognized any form of good faith exception to the Fourth Amendment exclusionary rule. . . . But the balancing approach that has evolved during the years of experience with the rule provides strong support for the modification currently urged upon us. As we discuss below, our evaluation of the costs and benefits of suppressing reliable physical evidence seized by officers reasonably relying on a warrant issued by a detached and neutral magistrate leads to the conclusion that such evidence should be admissible in the prosecution's case . . . the officers' reliance on the magistrate's determination of probable cause was objectively reasonable, and application of the extreme sanction of exclusion is inappropriate. Accordingly, the judgment of the Court of Appeals is Reversed (and the evidence is admissible).

Thus, the third exception to the exclusionary rule, the good faith exception was created by case law by the Supreme Court with a majority of justices favoring public safety and law enforcement above the individual freedom of a suspected law violator. Their decision has been reaffirmed in many subsequent cases (*United States v. McLaughlin*, 1988; *Illinois v. Krull*, 1987; and *Arizona v. Evans*, 1996, to name but a few). Also, the pros and cons of the exclusionary rule and relevant case decisions have been discussed in many circles, from government to law enforcement to academia and by members of the bar (Bray, 2004; Colb, 2004).

SUMMARY

This chapter dealt exclusively with a procedural rule, the exclusionary rule, created by the Supreme Court in an effort to stop law enforcement officers from violating the Fourth Amendment rights of citizens who police might suspect of crimes. To repeat, it is a rule of law which holds that evidence seized by police illegally cannot be admitted in court to prove guilt.

The *Weeks* case actually created it, but applied it only in federal court cases. In the 1949 *Wolf* case, the Court specifically declined to extend that protection to state courts and make it binding on local law enforcement. Finally, in 1961, the *Mapp* case was used as a vehicle by the Supreme Court to apply the rule to all the states, and local law enforcement officers have had to comply with it in the collection of any evidence, whether that evidence is physical or testimonial. The *Mapp* case was decided by a due process–oriented court, headed by Chief Justice Earl Warren, whose concern for fairness and individual rights was paramount.

We have seen in recent years, through the *Williams*, *Quarles*, and *Leon* cases, that three exceptions to the rule also have been created. This is due primarily to the appointments of an increasing number of Supreme Court justices having a more law-and-order orientation than those before them. This includes Chief Justice Warren Burger followed by Chief Justice Rehnquist, both of whom hoped to lead the court back to the right and reverse the liberal due process–oriented procedures established under Chief Justice Earl Warren and, thereby, fulfill the plans of Presidents Nixon, Reagan, and Bush, whose appointments to the Court were to facilitate that reversal (Simon, 1995). Burger almost succeeded in convincing a majority of the justices to overturn *Mapp*, but his persuasive powers were just not quite enough (Woodward & Armstrong, 1979).

The full reversal has not occurred and probably will not. However, a number of decisions, like the three just covered, have chipped away at the foundations of both the Fourth and Fifth Amendments. The current body of the U.S. Supreme Court is in a delicate balance, with a slight moderate-to-liberal majority. Justice O'Connor often was the swing vote to the more liberal side. Now the new appointment of John Roberts to replace Rehnquist, and especially the appointment of Alito to replace Sandra Day O'Connor might tip the balance. It will be interesting to observe what new cases the new Supreme Court takes to hear and how their decisions are made.

ISSUES FOR DISCUSSION

1. Discuss how the exclusionary rule was created by the series of cases; then discuss how the exceptions to the rule were created.
2. Do you think that the exclusionary rule serves the ends of justice? Do you think that the rule might at times hinder law enforcement in their efforts? How should the exclusionary rule be applied?
3. Discuss the issues that were the basis of the original appeal in the *Mapp* case. How did these issues affect the Court's decision?

REFERENCES

Bray, Zack. "Appellate Review and the Exclusionary Rule," *Yale Law Review*, Mar. 2004, v. 113, No. 5, p. 1143.

Colb, Sherry. "A World without Privacy: Why Property Does Not Define the Limits of the Right Against Unreasonable Searches and Seizures," *Michigan Law Review*, Mar. 2004, v. 102, No. 5, p. 990.

Ferdico, John N. *Criminal Procedure for the Criminal Justice Professional* (7th edition). Albany, New York: West/Wadsworth, 1999.

Kamisar, Yale. "The Exclusionary Rule in Historical Perspective: The Struggle to Make the Fourth Amendment More Than an Empty Blessing," *Judicature*, Nov. 1978.

Rothwax, Judge Harold J. *Guilty: The Collapse of Criminal Justice*. New York: Random House, 1996.

Simon, James F. *The Center Holds: The Poser Struggle Inside the Rehnquist Court*. New York: Simon & Schuster, 1995.

Tushnet, Mark. *A Court Divided: The Rehnquist Court and the Future of Constitutional Law*. New York: W. W. Norton, 2005.

Woodward, Bob, and Scott Armstrong. *The Brethren: Inside the Supreme Court*. New York: Simon & Schuster, 1979.

Zalman, Marvin, and Larry Siegal. *Key Cases and Comments on Criminal Procedures* (1994 edition). St. Paul: West, 1994.

INTERNET REFERENCES

http://caselaw.lp.findlaw.com/data/constitution/amendment04/06.html

http://www.landmarkcases.org/mapp/exclusionary1.html

http://www.legal-definitions.com/exclusionary-rule.htm

http://www.kletc.org/DW_legal/exclusionary.html

http://www.landmarkcases.org/mapp/home.html

http://www.oyez.org/oyez/resource/case/223/audioresources=oral arguments

CASE DECISIONS

Arizona v. Evans, 514 U.S. 1 (1996)

Brewer v. Williams, 430 U.S. 387 (1977)

Illinois v. Krull, 480 U.S. 340 (1987)

Mapp v. Ohio, 367 U.S. 643 (1961)

New York v. Quarles, 467 U.S. 649 (1984)

Nix v. Williams, 467 U.S. 431 (1984)

Silverthorne Lumber Co. v. United States, 251 U.S. 385 392 (1920)

State v. Lindusay, 131 Ohio St. 166. 2 N. E. 2d 490 (1930)

State v. Williams, 182 N. W. 2d 396 (1970)

United States v. Brady, 819 F. 2d 884 (9th DCA 1987)

United States v. DeSantis, 870 F. 20 536 (9th DCA 1989)

United States v. Carrillo, 16 F. 3d 1046 (9th DCA 1994)

United States v. Leon, 468 U.S. 897 (1984)

United States v. McLaughlin, 1988

Weeks v. United States, 232 U.S. 383 (1914)

Wolf v. Colorado, 338 U.S. 25 (1949)

Wong Sun v. United States, 371 U.S. 471 (1963)

chapter 4

POLICE-CITIZEN CONTACTS
CONSENSUAL ENCOUNTERS
AND DETENTIONS

KEY TERMS AND CONCEPTS

Border checkpoints	Investigative car stops
Consensual encounter	Patsearch
Consent search	Pretext carstop
Detention	Racial profiling
Detention factors	Reasonable suspicion
Independent state grounds	Sobriety checkpoints
Individualized suspicion	Stop-and-frisk
Informational checkpoints	

INTRODUCTION

This chapter examines those procedures of primary concern to the street officer on patrol in a municipal police agency, state police, or county sheriff's department. It examines those police-citizen contacts that occur prior to, and often instead of, arrest: the consensual encounter and the police detention. Often, however, the procedures completed in either of these situations do lead to arrest. Arrest laws and procedures follow in the next chapter.

POLICE-CITIZEN TRANSACTIONS

In the appellate case *Florida v. Royer,* 1983, U.S. Supreme Court Justice White addressed the three different categories, or levels, of police-citizen contacts: consensual encounter, detention, and arrest. Subsequent cases have continued to uphold these distinctions as the relevant criteria by which to guide police in dealing with citizens. At each level, a peace officer has certain legal authority, which is limited by the nature of the particular level. A clear distinction of what is allowed at each level is crucial to effective policing.

Consensual Encounter

This is defined as *a voluntary exchange between an officer and a citizen, with no restraint of individual liberty*, because police do not have any objective justification to stop, detain, or arrest. The citizen is free to leave at any time and free not to cooperate and not to answer questions. And, according to Justice White, the citizen must have the perception that he or she is free to leave and is not under any legal restraint.

If an officer creates an atmosphere of intimidation or one in which a reasonable person would not feel that he or she is free to leave, it might move the transaction from consensual encounter to a detention without any legal basis. For example, if the officer tries to engage a person in casual conversation but blocks the person's exit or asks to see some identification then retains it during the entire conversation, the person might genuinely feel not free to leave.

A **consensual encounter** may occur in the field, as well as at a police station, if the subject voluntarily appears at the station and responds to questioning. For example, a 17-year-old was called in for an interview with a Los Angeles detective, then was questioned for nearly two hours about his efforts to help a friend try to steal a truck, during which the truck driver was shot to death. The boy's parents brought him to the police station and waited in the lobby while the boy was questioned. The detective made no pretense of arresting or detaining the boy and acted as if it were a consensual encounter, even asking the boy if he wanted to take a break during the questioning.

The boy finally admitted his involvement and described the events leading up to the shooting of the truck driver. After the interview was over, the boy was returned to his parents, who drove him home. The detective then obtained an arrest warrant, and the boy was arrested, tried, and convicted of murder and attempted robbery. On appeal, and in a 5-to-4 decision, the U.S. Supreme Court upheld the conviction and the fact that the encounter was consensual, and ruled that age and inexperience with the justice system are not factors to be considered with *Miranda* (*Yarborough v. Alvarado*, 2004).

Consent Search

At this level of consensual encounter, any search or seizure of property must be by the consent of the citizen. This so-called **consent search** is one of the most frequent types of encounters that police have with citizens, either independent of any other contact or immediately following contact for another purpose, such as after a traffic stop (Holcomb, 2004).

When an officer is talking to a citizen and has a hunch that something illegal might be going on, the officer can say: "Do you mind if I search your trunk?" Or, "Do you mind if I search your car?" When the officer asks for permission, he or she knows that he or she does not have the legal authority to demand access. If the citizen refuses to cooperate, that conduct does not give an officer any cause to detain or arrest, and the officer must allow the person to leave. Often, however, the citizen is not aware of this and thinks that he or she must submit to the officer's request. It is amazing how many individuals agree to let an officer search his or her car or backpack, knowing full well that it contains contraband.

If a peace officer elevates a consensual encounter into a detention without any legal cause, any evidence seized probably will be excluded from trial under the exclusionary rule. In addition to the evidence being excluded, the officer might face criminal prosecution for false imprisonment or he or she might face civil liability or criminal prosecution for a violation of civil rights. Once consent is given by a subject, it may also be revoked (Holcomb, 2005).

Detention

Detention is *a seizure of the citizen that is limited in duration, scope, and purpose.* A detention or stop occurs when a peace officer compels a person to stop, to stay in one place, or to perform an act.

Legal Basis for Detention　Any detention of a person by a peace officer must be based on **reasonable** (and articulable) **suspicion** by the officer that the person has committed, is committing, or is about to commit a crime. Reasonable suspicion is often known as **individualized suspicion** (see *United States v. Sokolow*, 1989). The person is not free to leave and has the perception that he or she is not free to leave, but the detention is only for the purpose of settling the issue raised by the suspicion of the officer.

Under ordinary circumstances, the officer does not have the authority to search the citizen during a detention. However, in the

Terry case, summarized below, the U.S. Supreme Court, created certain search procedures that allow a peace officer to **patsearch** the outside of a person's clothing if specific conditions described in *Terry* are present.

***Terry v. Ohio,* 1968**   A Cleveland police officer named McFadden was patrolling a downtown business area, on a beat that he had been patrolling for many years, when he observed two strangers, later identified as Terry and Chilton, standing on a street corner. He saw them take turns walking back and forth along the sidewalk, pausing to stare in the same store window for a total of about 24 times. After each one walked back from the store, they talked for a few minutes. Soon they were joined by a third man, identified as Katz, who came and left swiftly. Suspecting the two men of "casing a job, a stick-up," the officer followed them and saw them rejoin the third man two blocks away in front of the store. The officer approached the three, identified himself as a policeman, and asked their names. The men mumbled something, whereupon McFadden turned Terry around, patted down his outside clothing, and found a pistol jammed in his overcoat pocket, which McFadden was unable to remove at the scene.

McFadden ordered the three into the store. He removed Terry's overcoat, took out the revolver, and ordered the three to face the wall with their hands raised. He patted down the outer clothing of Chilton and Katz and felt a hard object in the pocket of Chilton. He reached in the pocket and removed a revolver. He did not find anything in the patsearch of Katz. All three were taken to the police station, and Terry and Chilton were charged with carrying concealed weapons. Katz was released.

At trial, the defense moved to suppress the weapons, claiming the exclusionary rule prohibited such a search. The prosecution claimed that the guns were seized after a lawful arrest. Though the trial court rejected the prosecution's theory that the guns had been seized during a search incident to a lawful arrest, the court denied the defense motion to suppress, and admitted the weapons into evidence on the grounds that the officer had cause to believe that Terry and Chilton were acting suspiciously, that their interrogation was warranted, and that the officer, for his own protection, had the right to pat down their outer clothing, having reasonable cause to believe that they might be armed.

The trial court distinguished between an investigatory "stop," a detention, and an arrest, and between a "frisk" of the outer clothing for weapons, and a full-blown search for evidence of crime. Terry and Chilton were found guilty, an intermediate appellate court affirmed, and the State Supreme Court dismissed the appeal on the ground that "no substantial constitutional question" was involved. Eventually, the case was appealed to the U.S. Supreme Court, where the arguments centered around the legality of Officer McFadden's patsearch within the context of the exclusionary rule. The Court's opinion, delivered by Chief Justice Earl Warren, held:

> Where a police officer observes unusual conduct which leads him reasonably to conclude in light of his experience that criminal activity may be afoot and that the persons with whom he is dealing may be armed and presently dangerous, where in the course of investigating this behavior he identifies himself as a policeman and makes reasonable inquiries, and where nothing in the initial stages of the encounter serves to dispel his reasonable fear for his own or others' safety, he is entitled for the protection of himself and others in the area to conduct a carefully limited search of the outer clothing of such persons in an attempt to discover weapons which might be used to assault him. (*Terry v. Ohio*, 1968)

The Court ruled that the revolver seized from Terry was properly admitted into evidence against him, since the search that led to its seizure was reasonable under the Fourth Amendment in this type of detention situation.

Stop-and-Frisk   Because of the *Terry* decision, this procedure, known as **stop-and-frisk**, gives the officer the authority to pat down the citizen for weapons if the officer has (articulable) reasonable suspicion to believe that the suspect might be armed. This is a patsearch outside the person's clothing for the sole purpose of looking for any weapons that the person might possess.

In a subsequent decision (*Adams v. Williams*, 1972), the Supreme Court extended this stop-and-frisk authority to situations in which the officer's reasonable suspicion is based on reliable information, rather than on personal observation.

One year later, the Court held that a full-body search is permitted after an officer makes an arrest, regardless of the offense and regardless of the apparent danger (*United States v. Robinson*, 1973).

In determining if an officer has reasonable suspicion to detain, the circumstances known or apparent to the officer must include

> specific and articulable facts causing him or her to suspect that some offense has taken place or is occurring or is about to occur and that the person he or she intends to detain is involved in that offense.

The circumstances must be such as would cause

> any reasonable peace officer in like position, drawing when appropriate on his or her training and experience, to suspect the same offense and the same involvement by the person in question.

Detention Factors

Reasonable suspicion justifies the detention and provides the officer with the basis for investigation to determine whether the suspicions are correct. These suspicions, however, must be based on objective facts, or factors, that can be stated and not on mere hunches. A detention is based on two elements:

- reasonable suspicion by the officer of criminal activity
- knowledge by the person stopped that or she is not free to leave

In addition, there are certain factors about any situation that an officer may consider in forming a legal and articulable basis for reasonable suspicion. It is important that the officer state all the relevant factors in his or her report to support the legality of the detention, and possibly a patsearch, and any evidence that might be seized as a result.

The following are three **detention factor** categories to consider:

- the appearance of the suspect
- the actions of the suspect
- the area in which the suspect is observed

Questions to consider about the appearance of the suspect include:

- Does he or she appear to be under the influence of drugs or alcohol?
- Does he or she resemble the description of an offender recently given by the victim?
- Does he or she resemble a wanted person?
- Does he or she appear to be casing a house, store, building, etc.?
- Is he or she injured?
- Is he or she parked in an unusual place, or parked or walking at an odd hour and/or in an odd manner?

Questions about the actions of the suspect include:

- Does he or she appear to be hiding?
- Does he or she appear to be trying to conceal something?
- Is he or she running from a crime scene?
- Did he or she throw something away upon seeing the officer?
- Did he or she just exchange some object that looked like contraband with another person?
- Did he or she change his or her driving pattern immediately upon seeing the officer?

Questions to consider about the area:

- Is it a high-crime area ? If so, consider the following:
  - (a) What types of crimes are committed in the area?
  - (b) What is the frequency and location of the crimes?
- Is it a residential, industrial, or business area?

These are more than just questions to answer or consider. They represent some of the factors that an officer might have to articulate (to explain) to a judge on the stand under cross-examination, to justify making the detention. If a detention cannot be justified by such factors, any evidence obtained might not be admissible in court.

Usually, no single factor would be sufficient, and the more factors available, the better. However, the U.S. Supreme Court held that in certain circumstances, the mere flight of a person from officers might be sufficient grounds to justify reasonable suspicion (*Illinois v. Wardlow*, 2000). However, the U.S. Supreme Court also ruled that an anonymous tip about a person carrying a gun, absent some independent corroboration, is not sufficient evidence to justify a detention or a patdown for the weapon (*Florida v. J.L.*, 2000). On the other hand, a tip about a person possessing a gun, given to police in a face-to-face situation from an individual in which the individual could lose his or her anonymity, could justify a detention and patsearch (*People v. Coulombe*, 2000).

There are no absolute guidelines, and each situation must be considered within the *totality of the circumstances*, a phrase one often finds as the basis for judging the legality of procedures used by police.

If one factor used by an officer to justify a detention is information provided the officer by some outside source, the officer needs to be prepared to describe the source and its reliability to the court as well. In every situation, an officer should be prepared to explain and/or describe the full array of factors derived from the existing scene that made the officer suspicious. In fact, after a situation has been resolved, the officer would be wise to note those factors present for later recall in court. Finally, all of these factors may be considered within the context of the police officer's knowledge, training, and experience.

Some states, such as Nevada, have laws that specifically require a subject to identify himself or herself if requested to do so by an officer during a detention. A 5-to-4 ruling by the U.S. Supreme Court in 2004 upheld just such a Nevada law, holding that in a state that has a *stop and identify law*, the detainee must provide identification or face arrest (*Hiibel v. Sixth Judicial Dist. Court of Nev.*, 2004; also see *Harvard Civil Rights-Civil Liberties Law Review*, 2005).

CONSENSUAL ENCOUNTER VERSUS DETENTION

Often the distinction between a consensual encounter and a legal detention is very slight and might depend on how a judge interprets the situation. On the other hand, the distinction is obvious in many cases. Selected case summaries are provided below to demonstrate the current interpretations of the Supreme Court justices, and they will be useful in learning how appellate courts distinguish between a legal detention based on reasonable suspicion and an illegal detention.

A traffic car stop is an example of a legal detention if the officer stops the car with the reasonable belief that the driver might have violated a traffic law. A recent Ohio case shows how an officer may use a traffic stop to move from a legal detention to a consensual encounter without the motorist being aware of the shift. This new decision, *Ohio v. Robinette*, 1996, would probably make Justice White turn over in his grave in view of the fact that he stated in the original *Royer* case that a citizen "must know he is free to leave and free not to respond to questions." That requirement has recently been changed by a case that came from the following set of facts.

An Ohio deputy sheriff stopped Robert D. Robinette for speeding, gave him a verbal warning, and returned his driver's license. Then, without indicating to Robinette that he was free to leave, the deputy asked whether he was carrying illegal contraband, weapons, or drugs in his car. Robinette answered "No" and consented to a search of the car, which revealed a small amount of marijuana and a pill. He was arrested and later charged with knowingly possessing a controlled substance when the pill turned out to be methylenedioxy methamphetamine.

Robinette made a motion to suppress the evidence, claiming that the search was the result of an unlawful detention, rather than a consensual encounter, because Robinette did not know he could go or refuse to cooperate. The trial court denied his suppression motion, and he was found guilty, but the Ohio Court of Appeals reversed his conviction on the grounds that the search did result from an unlawful detention because Robinette did not know he was free to leave (following the reasoning in *Royer*).

The Ohio State Supreme Court affirmed the decision, establishing a specific rule (bright-line prerequisite) for consensual interrogation under these circumstances, stating that after the officer has completed the traffic stop matter, the officer must tell the motorist he or she is ". . . legally free to go." Then, and only then, said the Ohio Court, can the officer ask for a consent search.

This Ohio decision was in line with the *Royer* requirements, that to truly be a consensual encounter, the citizen must know he or she is free to go then give consent. However, the prosecutor in Ohio appealed this decision to the U.S. Supreme Court, and it ruled that the Ohio Court erred in its decision because it used an interpretation of the U.S. Constitution as the basis for its decision, rather than using its own state's constitution.

The Supreme Court held that if Ohio wants to have a law requiring its officers to tell citizens they are "free to go" before they ask for consent, it may do so through its own laws (**independent state grounds**). However, that procedure is not required under the Constitution. Robinette's conviction was upheld, and the Court said that an officer does not have to tell a citizen that he or she is free to leave or otherwise indicate that the traffic stop is over.

CONSENT SEARCHES REVISITED

The *Robinette* decision is another example of the Supreme Court's shift toward law and order and away from due process. It opens up a whole new way for police to gain "consent" to search vehicles. Most citizens believe that they may not leave from a traffic stop until told they may. Therefore, they will not know that they are free to leave and might think that they must submit to a search.

Until recently, the laws in some states have allowed the police to go far beyond the *Robinette* type of consent search. In Iowa, for example, the code allows a police officer to arrest a motorist if the officer has cause to believe that the motorist has violated any traffic law or motor vehicle equipment law. In that case (after an arrest) a full search of the person and car would be legal.

The Iowa law also provides that the officer may cite the motorist instead of making the arrest, but the decision to cite rather than arrest "does not affect the officer's authority to conduct an otherwise lawful search." Apparently, the police in Iowa would routinely search motorists after issuing a citation. One motorist named Patrick Knowles was cited in Newton, Iowa, for driving 43 mph in a 25 mph zone, after which the officer searched his car and found a bag of marijuana and a pot pipe under the driver's seat. The officer admitted that he had no consent and no cause.

In court, Knowles's motion to suppress the evidence as a Fourth Amendment violation was denied, and he was convicted. His conviction and the search practice of the police were upheld by the Iowa Supreme Court. However, the case was appealed to the U.S. Supreme Court. The tenor of that Court's thinking was suggested during oral arguments on November 3, 1998, when one justice noted that a person who gets pulled over on a traffic stop and receives a ticket would hardly be prepared for such full-blown scrutiny, and another justice stated that the police practice sanctioned by Iowa law "does seem an enormous amount of authority to put into the hands of the police."

On December 14, 1998, the Court gave its unanimous decision (*Knowles v. Iowa*, 1998) that there is no justification for an officer to conduct a search of a person or a car during a routine traffic stop and citation. Knowles's conviction was reversed. The justices noted that if an officer requests the driver or passenger to exit the vehicle, the officer may still make a *Terry* patdown **if there is reason to believe** that officer safety requires it. This decision prohibits the police search incident to a routine traffic stop (LaFave, 2004). Consequently, the *Robinette* type of consent search is as far as the police may go.

INVESTIGATIVE CAR STOPS

An **investigative car stop** is not a routine traffic stop. It is a car stop (detention) made when an officer has reasonable (individualized) suspicion to believe that the driver is at the moment engaged in some sort of illegal activity. The driver might be in the process of smuggling or transporting illegal drugs, or any other illegal activity (*United States v. Arvizu*, 2001; also see Pelic, 2003).

PRETEXT CARSTOP DETENTIONS

In another recent U.S. Supreme Court decision, *Whren v. United States*, 1996, the Court added to this law enforcement emphasis by sanctioning the use of a **pretext carstop**, as long as it is based on probable cause to believe that the driver has violated some traffic law. The so-called pretext carstop is the use of some very minor traffic violation to stop a car when the officer's real purpose is to see who is in the car or to find a way to obtain a consent search of a car if the officer suspects some more serious illegal activity. Examples of a pretext violation include the officer finding a dirty license plate tag, a faulty taillight, or an unlit rear license plate.

WARRANT CHECKS DURING TRAFFIC STOPS

A traffic stop is a legal detention, and a peace officer is allowed to run a warrant check, in addition to a DMV check, without any cause or legal justification. Also, for officer safety, a law enforcement officer may order both the driver and the passengers out of the car during any carstop, pending completion of the detention (*Maryland v. Wilson*, 1997). However, if a warrant check is pending, the officer may not legally delay the motorist to wait for the results of the warrant check beyond the time needed to complete the traffic citation. It might constitute an illegal detention.

PROBABLE CAUSE SEARCHES DURING TRAFFIC STOPS

As you know, the U.S. Supreme Court has held that a warrantless search of a car is reasonable if police have probable cause to believe that it contains contraband (*Carroll v. United States*, 1925), as well as containers within the car (*United States v. Ross*, 1982). On April 5, 1999, the U.S. Supreme Court extended that thinking to include any containers that belong to passengers (*Wyoming v. Houghton*, 1999).

In that case, during a **routine traffic stop** a Wyoming Highway Patrol officer noticed a hypodermic syringe in the driver's pocket. The driver admitted using it to take drugs. The officer then began a search of the passenger compartment. Other officers arrived at the scene to assist, and two passengers were asked to step out of the car. One female passenger left her purse on the car seat, and an officer searched it. He found drug paraphernalia in the purse and arrested the passenger on a felony drug charge. At trial she moved to suppress the evidence as a fruit of a poison tree, an unlawful search of the passenger's property.

The trial court denied her motion, and she was convicted. However, the Wyoming Supreme Court reversed her conviction, stating that if the officer knew or should have known it was her property and there was no reasonable cause to suspect her of criminal activity, her property was outside the scope of any legal search. On appeal by the state, the U.S. Supreme Court reversed and held that if an officer has probable cause to search a car for contraband, the officer may search any containers capable of containing that contraband regardless of whose property it is. The vote was 6 to 3, which shows there is still a strong majority favoring public safety. However, there were three strong dissenters.

In most usual circumstances, police follow a **bright-line rule** (a standard) established by the U.S. Supreme Court in 1981 (*New York v. Belton*, 1981) that permits a law enforcement officer who has made a lawful custodial arrest of the occupant of a car to search the passenger compartment of that car as a contemporaneous incident of the arrest.

The U.S. Supreme Court issued a ruling along a similar line of thinking in *Illinois v. Caballes*, 2005. In this case one Illinois State Trooper walked his drug-sniffing dog around a vehicle while another state trooper completed a routine traffic stop and warning. The dog alerted officers to drugs in the vehicle's trunk. Officers found marijuana in the trunk and arrested the suspect. The suspect was convicted, but the Illinois Supreme Court reversed. On appeal, the U.S. Supreme Court held that the routine use of a drug-sniffing dog during a traffic stop does not violate the Fourth Amendment (Sanchez, 2004). The conviction was upheld.

SOBRIETY, BORDER, AND INFORMATIONAL CHECKPOINTS

The U.S. Supreme Court, mindful to assure the Fourth Amendment protection for each individual, has not allowed roadblocks or checkpoints for general enforcement purposes. However, it has allowed them for three specific purposes: **sobriety checkpoints, border checkpoints**, and more recently **informational checkpoints**.

The first ruling was a case that came on appeal in 1986, after the Michigan State Police Department created a sobriety checkpoint program aimed at reducing drunk driving within the state. The program included guidelines governing the location of roadblocks and the amount of publicity to be given to the operation. Before the first roadblock went into effect, a licensed Michigan driver challenged the constitutionality of the checkpoints. He thought they were an unlawful invasion of his privacy. The case eventually reached the U.S. Supreme Court on appeal. At issue was whether drunk driving checkpoints violate motorists' privacy protected by the Fourth Amendment.

In a 6-to-3 decision, the Court held that the checkpoint did not violate the Fourth Amendment. The Court noted that "no one can seriously dispute the magnitude of the drunken driving problem or the States' interest in eradicating it." The Court then found that "the weight bearing on the other scale—the measure of the intrusion on motorists stopped briefly at sobriety checkpoints—is slight." The Court also found that empirical evidence supported the effectiveness of the program and that individualized suspicion was not necessary (*Michigan Department of State Police v. Sitz*, 1990).

The second exception to the usual Fourth Amendment requirement came as a result of the Border Patrol's routine stopping of a vehicle at a permanent checkpoint located on a major highway away from the Mexican border for brief questioning of the vehicle's occupants. The issue again was whether the stops and questioning in the absence of any individualized suspicion that a particular vehicle contained illegal aliens violated the Fourth Amendment. The U.S. Supreme Court ruled that no, it did not (*United States v. Martinez-Fuerte*, 1976).

The Court held:

> To require that such stops always be based on reasonable suspicion would be impractical because the flow of traffic tends to be too heavy to allow the particularized study of a given car necessary to identify it as a possible carrier of illegal aliens. Such a requirement also would largely eliminate any deterrent to the conduct of well-disguised smuggling operations, even though smugglers are known to use these highways regularly.
>
> While the need to make routine checkpoint stops is great, the consequent intrusion on Fourth Amendment interests is quite limited, the interference with legitimate traffic being minimal and checkpoint operations involving less discretionary enforcement activity than roving-patrol stops.
>
> Under the circumstances of these checkpoint stops, which do not involve searches, the Government or public interest in making such stops outweighs the constitutionally protected interest of the private citizen.

The third exception was allowed in 2004 (*Illinois v. Lidster*, 2004). Police in Illinois set up a highway checkpoint to obtain information from motorists about a hit-and-run accident occurring about one week earlier at the same location and time of night. Officers stopped each vehicle for 10 to 15 seconds, asked the occupants whether they had seen anything happen there the previous weekend, and handed each driver a flyer describing and requesting information about the accident.

As a driver named Lidster approached, his minivan swerved, nearly hitting an officer. The officer smelled alcohol on Lidster's breath. Another officer administered a sobriety test and arrested Lidster for driving under the influence. He was convicted and challenged his arrest and conviction on the grounds that the government obtained evidence through use of a checkpoint stop that violated the Fourth Amendment. The trial court rejected that challenge, but the state appellate court reversed. The State Supreme Court agreed, holding that the stop was unconstitutional. The state appealed to the U.S. Supreme Court. The Court reasoned that individualized suspicion was not needed because in this case:

> . . . the stop's primary law enforcement purpose was *not* to determine whether a vehicle's occupants were committing a crime, but to ask the occupants, as members of the public, for help in providing information about a crime in all likelihood committed by others.
>
> Nor does the Fourth Amendment require courts to apply a standard rule of the automatic unconstitutionality to such stops. The fact that they normally lack individualized suspicion cannot by itself determine the constitutional outcome, as the Fourth Amendment does not treat a motorist's car as his castle, see, *e.g.*, *New York v. Class*, 475 U.S. 106, 112-113, and special law enforcement concerns will sometimes justify highway stops without individualized suspicion, see, *e.g.*, *Michigan Dept. of State Police v. Sitz*, 496 U.S. 444. Moreover, the context here (seeking information from the public) is one in which, by definition, the concept of individualized suspicion has little role to play, and an information-seeking stop is not the kind of event that involves suspicion, or lack thereof, of the relevant individual. In addition, information-seeking highway stops are less likely to provoke anxiety or to prove intrusive, since they are likely brief, the questions asked are not designed to elicit self-incriminating information, and citizens will often react positively when police ask for help. The law also ordinarily permits police to seek the public's voluntary cooperation in a criminal investigation.
>
> The checkpoint stop was constitutional. In judging its reasonableness, hence, its constitutionality, this Court looks to "the gravity of the public concerns served by the seizure, the degree to which the seizure advances the public interest, and

the severity of the interference with individual liberty. . . . The relevant public concern was grave, as the police were investigating a crime that had resulted in a human death, and the stop advanced this concern to a significant degree given its timing and location. Most importantly, the stops interfered only minimally with liberty of the sort the Fourth Amendment seeks to protect. Viewed objectively, each stop required only a brief wait in line and contact with police for only a few seconds. Viewed subjectively, the systematic contact provided little reason for anxiety or alarm, and there is no allegation that the police acted in a discriminatory or otherwise unlawful manner.

RACIAL PROFILING

A topical issue that deals with the practice of certain law enforcement agencies is **racial profiling**: singling out an individual to stop, detain, and/or arrest based on the subject's race or ethnic background. Recent studies show that not only are minority motorists stopped more frequently, but they are asked for (and they agree to) consent searches more often than do Caucasians. Racial profiling not only applies in traffic stop and pretext traffic stop situations, but also to individuals walking, traveling through airports, loitering about in shopping centers, and walking to or from a place of worship.

A 2001 Department of Justice report on citizen-police contacts in 1999 found that, although African Americans and Hispanics were more likely to be stopped and searched, they were less likely to be in possession of contraband. On average, searches and seizures of African American drivers yielded evidence only 8 percent of the time, searches and seizures of Hispanic drivers yielded evidence only 10 percent of the time, and searches and seizures of white drivers yielded evidence 17 percent of the time.

A 2000 General Accounting Office report on the activities of the U.S. Customs Service during fiscal year 1998 found that black women who were U.S. citizens were nine times more likely than white women who were U.S. citizens to be X-rayed after being frisked or patted down and, on the basis of X-ray results, black women who were U.S. citizens were less than half as likely as white women who were U.S. citizens to be found carrying contraband. In general, the report found that the patterns used to select passengers for more intrusive searches resulted in women and minorities being selected at rates that were not consistent with the rates of finding contraband.

In June 2003, the U.S. Department of Justice issued guidance rules forbidding racial profiling by federal law enforcement agencies, but these rules are actually advisory and not legally binding and do not specify punishment for anyone who violates them. The rules also do not cover profiling based on religion, religious appearance, or national origin. This latter type of profiling undoubtedly is more extensive now in border crossings, ports, and airports because of 9/11, and will probably continue as long as there is a perception of terrorism. Supporters do not see this as racial profiling but as a necessary bending of individual freedom justified by an extension of criminal profiling because of the sources of terrorist activities.

Critics of racial profiling believe that it harms those individuals subjected to it because they experience fear, anxiety, humiliation, anger, resentment, and cynicism when they are unjustifiably treated as criminal suspects. By discouraging individuals from traveling freely, racial profiling impairs both interstate and intrastate commerce. It also harms law enforcement agencies and local governments in the form of resentment by and loss of support from minority communities. Most critics state the obvious objection, that racial profiling is racist and violates the Fourth Amendment. Some critics also claim that its practice is a vestige of our heritage of slavery and violates the Thirteenth Amendment (Carter, 2004).

Most local agencies are now addressing the issue and are either in the process of examining the car stops and field stops of their officers or developing policies to control the practice of racial profiling.

SUMMARY

This chapter detailed the primary situations and activities that one finds in the contact of an individual by a law enforcement officer short of the actual arrest. Consensual encounters occur often and include consent searches. Police detention—the detaining of an individual for a limited time and purpose—occurs often as well and includes the procedures known as stop-and-frisk, traffic stops, pretext traffic stops, and warrant checks during traffic stops. The dynamics of racial profiling were discussed as well.

Frequently, the transaction between police and the citizen ends after one of these two brief encounters. The alternative action leads to a formal arrest, the subject of the following chapter.

ISSUES FOR DISCUSSION

1. Discuss the differences between the two levels of police-citizen transactions: consensual encounter and detention. What are the legal requirements for police in each situation?
2. Discuss the police procedure known as the *consent search*. How many of you have experienced, or know someone who has experienced, such a search? What consequences do you think would follow if the citizen refused to give consent?

3. Discuss the use of a pretext carstop by police. Should such a practice be allowed?
4. Discuss the issue of *racial profiling*. Research your local agencies via interviews or ride-alongs to determine the extent of it in your community. If it is true that police stop more minorities than Caucasians and request consent searches from minorities more often than Caucasians, what are some of the reasons for these practices?

REFERENCES

Carter, William M., Jr. "A Thirteenth Amendment Framework for Combating Racial Profiling," *Harvard Law Review*, Winter 2004, v. 39, No. 1, p. 17.

Harvard Civil Rights-Civil Liberties Law Review. Winter 2005, v. 40, No. 1, p. 13.

Holcomb, Jayme W. "Consent Searches Scope," *FBI Law Enforcement Bulletin*, Feb. 2004, v. 73, No. 2, p. 22.

Holcomb, Jayme W. "Revoking Consent to Search," *FBI Law Enforcement Bulletin*, Feb. 2005, v. 74, No. 2, p. 25.

LaFave, Wayne R. "The 'Routine Traffic Stop,' From Start to Finish: Too Much Routine, Not Enough Fourth Amendment," *Michigan Law Review*, Aug. 2004, v. 102, No. 8, p. 1843.

Pelic, Jennifer. "United States v. Arvizu: Investigatory Stops and the Fourth Amendment," *Journal of Criminal Law & Criminology*, Fall 2003, v. 93, No. 4, p. 1033.

Sanchez, Julian. "Search 'n' Sniff," *Reason*, July 2004, v. 36, No. 3, p. 10.

INTERNET REFERENCES

http://www.racialprofilinganalysis.neu.edu
http://www.racialprofilinganalysis.neu.edu/

CASE DECISIONS

Adams v. Williams, 407 U.S. 143 (1972)

Carroll v. United States 267 U.S. 132 (1925)

Florida v. J.L., 120 S.Ct.1375 (2000)

Florida v. Royer, 460 U.S. 491 (1983)

Hiibel v. Sixth Judicial Dist., Court of Nev. (2004) No. 03-5553

Illinois v. Caballes, No. 03-923 (2005)

Illinois v. Lidster, No. 02-1060 (2004)

Illinois v. Wardlow, 120 S.Ct. (2000)

Knowles v. Iowa, 525 U.S. 113 (1998)

Maryland v. Wilson, 519 U.S. 408 (1997)

Michigan Department of State Police v. Sitz, 496 U.S. 444 (1990)

New York v. Belton, 453 U.S. 454 (1981)

Ohio v. Robinette, 519 U.S. 33 (1996)

Terry v. Ohio, 392 U.S. 1 (1968)

United States v. Arvizu, 000 U.S. 00-1519 (2002)

United States v. Martinez-Fuerte, (with *Sifuentes v. United States*) 428 U.S. 543 (1976)

United States v. Robinson, 414 U.S. 218 (1973)

United States v. Ross, 456 U.S. 798 (1982)

United States v. Sokolow, 490 U.S. 1 (1989)

Welsh v. Wisconsin, 466 U.S. 138 (1984)

Whren v. United States, 517 U.S. 806 (1996)

Wyoming v. Houghton, 000 U.S. 97-7597 (1999)

Yarborough v. Alvarado, 000 U.S. 02-1684 (2004); also see a discussion of this case and its implications in the *Harvard Civil Rights-Civil Liberties Law Review*, Winter 2005, v. 40, No. 1, p. 13.

chapter 5

The Laws and Procedures of Arrest

Key Terms and Concepts

Abuse of authority	Knock-and-notice
Affidavit	*Posse comitatus*
Arrest	Private person arrest
Arrest warrant	Probable cause
Authority to arrest	Reasonable cause
Diplomatic immunity	Resisting arrest
Exigent circumstances	Stale misdemeanor rule
Fresh pursuit	Statute of limitations

INTRODUCTION

This chapter details the primary aspects of transactions between the police and the individual in arrest situations, including laws of arrest, the definition of arrest, the discretion an officer has in making an arrest, the limits on that discretion, the elements of an arrest, the different requirements in daytime and nighttime arrests, the differences between felony and misdemeanor arrests, the responsibilities of a police officer during and after arrest, exceptions to a peace officer's powers of arrest, and civil and criminal liabilities that might attach to an illegal arrest.

A discussion of arrests by private persons, and the responsibilities of police in those situations, also is included.

This chapter does not include any material on search and seizure or search warrants. That content is complex and is usually detailed in a separate course.

THE ARREST

The third level of police-citizen transactions is the **arrest**. This is defined as *taking a person into custody in some manner that is authorized by law* and (we could add) for the purpose of having the person charged with a crime. An arrest may be made by a peace officer or by a private party, although the laws that affect the arrest in either case vary in certain specific ways that are presented below.

An arrest is made by the actual physical restraint of the person, or by the submission of the person to the custody of an officer. And the person arrested may be subjected to whatever restraint is reasonable for his or her arrest and detention.

Peace Officer's Authority to Arrest

State laws are very specific as to when and under what circumstances a law enforcement officer has **authority to arrest**. These can be divided into three categories of authority:

- When the officer has **reasonable cause** (aka **probable cause**) to believe that the person to be arrested has committed an offense in the officer's presence. The officer's authority in these situations usually is the same in both felony and misdemeanor offenses.
- When the officer has reasonable (probable) cause to believe that the person to be arrested has committed a felony, whether or not in the officer's presence and whether or not a felony actually was committed. An officer lacks the authority to arrest a person on a misdemeanor offense based solely on probable cause (*In re Alonzo C.,* 1978). The misdemeanor must have been committed in the officer's presence. Any crime that is punishable by either prison or jail (a wobbler) is treated as a felony for purposes of arrest.
- On the basis of a warrant.

In most states, an arrest for the commission of a felony may be made on any day and at any time of the day or night. An arrest for the commission of a misdemeanor or an infraction often is limited to a certain time frame. For example, in some states, a misdemeanor arrest warrant cannot be served between the hours of 10 p.m. of any day and 6 a.m. of the succeeding day, unless the warrant is served and the arrest made in a public place, or is made when the person is in custody for some other lawful arrest, or the warrant specifically allows for nighttime service.

Reasonable/Probable Cause

When we examine these three circumstances, we find the concept, probable cause (PC) that was defined in Chapter 1, as "consisting of facts and trustworthy information, sufficient in themselves, to warrant a person of reasonable caution to believe:"

- that a crime has been committed
- the person to be arrested probably has committed it

Probable cause and reasonable cause are used interchangeably in this text. It is the word *cause* that provides an officer with the basis for action, whereas reasonable suspicion was a basis for investigation, as stated in Chapter 4. Probable cause always consists of the above two elements.

Exceptions to the Requirement of PC in Misdemeanor Arrests

There are several exceptions to the requirement that a misdemeanor must be committed in an officer's presence before an arrest can be made. States vary in these exceptions, but the following is a list of the most common exceptions found. The reader must check with his or her state's law to determine which, if any, apply.

- When a peace officer is responding to a call alleging a violation of a domestic violence protective order or restraining order and the peace officer has reasonable cause to believe that the person against whom the order is issued has notice of the order and has committed an act in violation of the order.
- When an officer, responding to a call, has probable cause to believe that the person to be arrested has committed assault or battery on a spouse or other person with whom he or she is cohabiting, or on the parent of his or her child.
- When the officer has reasonable cause to believe that a person has been driving under the influence of alcohol and was involved in an accident.
- When the officer has reasonable cause to believe that the person has committed assault or battery on school property during school hours.
- When the officer has reasonable cause to believe that the person is carrying a loaded firearm in a vehicle or in a public place within the city limits.

In addition, some court jurisdictions have ruled that with probable cause a police officer may arrest a person for misdemeanor driving under the influence of alcohol or drugs not committed in the officer's presence, where evidence may be destroyed unless the person is immediately arrested (*People v. Schofield*, 2001).

Legally speaking, juveniles do not commit crimes; they commit delinquent acts. The law in most states gives a peace officer the authority to take a minor into temporary custody (arrest) whenever the officer has reasonable cause to believe that the minor has committed any law violation. No distinction is made between felony and misdemeanor because they are all delinquent acts and are treated the same for arrest purposes.

Probable Cause Versus Reasonable Suspicion

These two phrases, or concepts, have distinctly different meanings and provide an officer with two differing bases for dealing with a citizen. Reasonable suspicion occurs either before, during, or after some sort of criminal activity is suspected by an officer and suggests that "maybe he or she is up to something."

This suspicion is derived from, and based on, articulable facts. Investigation clears up the suspicion one way or the other. Probable cause, however, always comes into play either during or after a crime has been committed and suggests that "he or she probably did it." It is derived from and based on more conclusive (and articulable) facts. Then the officer has the legal basis for making an arrest.

Even though these two concepts are different, the line dividing them often can be close and sometimes unclear, and their exact distinctions can be elusive. However, this should not be unsettling for an officer when he or she attempts to apply one or both because the real nature of each arises from the setting in which each occurs. Each situation must be evaluated on its own merits, using the totality of the circumstances as basis for review.

As Chief Justice Rehnquist explained (*Ornelas v. United States*, 1996):

> Articulating precisely what "reasonable suspicion" and "probable cause" mean is not possible. They are common sense, nontechnical conceptions that deal with "the factual and practical considerations of everyday life on which reasonable and prudent men, not legal technicians, act." As such, the standards are "not readily, or even usefully, reduced to a neat set of legal rules. . . ."
>
> We have cautioned that these two legal principles are not "finely-tuned standards," comparable to the standards of proof beyond a reasonable doubt or of proof by a preponderance of the evidence. . . . They are instead fluid concepts that take their substantive content from the particular contexts in which the

standards are being assessed. . . . The principal components of a determination of reasonable suspicion or probable cause will be the events which occurred leading up to . . . [them] . . . , and then the decision whether these historical facts, viewed from the standpoint of an objectively reasonable police officer, amount to reasonable suspicion or to probable cause.

If an officer does not have probable cause to make an arrest but sets into motion a sequence of events in which a suspect is taken to a police station, *Mirandized*, questioned, and confesses, the confessions might be inadmissible, regardless of the suspect's involvement in a crime, because the first step, the requirement of probable cause, was missing. A case like this turns on the Fourth Amendment rule that a confession "obtained by exploitation of an illegal arrest" may not be used against a criminal defendant (*Brown v. Illinois*, 1975).

A recent case like this serves as an example (*Kaupp v. Texas*, 2004). A 14-year-old girl disappeared in January 1999. The Harris County Sheriff's Department learned she had had a sexual relationship with her 19-year-old half brother, who had been in the company of suspect Robert Kaupp, then 17 years old, on the day of the girl's disappearance. On January 26, deputy sheriffs questioned the brother and Kaupp at headquarters. Kaupp was cooperative and was permitted to leave, but later the brother implicated Kaupp in the crime.

Detectives immediately tried but failed to obtain a warrant because probable cause was lacking. Detective Gregory Pinkins nevertheless decided (in his words) to "Get Kaupp in and confront him with what the brother had said."

In the company of two other plainclothes detectives and three uniformed officers, Pinkins went to Kaupp's house at approximately 3 a.m. on January 27. After Kaupp's father let them in, Pinkins, with at least two other officers, went to Kaupp's bedroom, awakened him with a flashlight, identified himself, and said, "We need to go and talk." Kaupp said "Okay." The two officers then handcuffed Kaupp and led him, shoeless and dressed only in boxer shorts and a T-shirt, out of his house and into a patrol car. The state points to nothing in the record indicating Kaupp was told that he was free to decline to go with the officers.

They stopped for five or 10 minutes where the victim's body had just been found, in anticipation of confronting Kaupp with the brother's confession, then went on to the sheriff's headquarters. There, they took Kaupp to an interview room, removed his handcuffs, and advised him of his rights under *Miranda*. Kaupp first denied any involvement in the victim's disappearance, but 10 or 15 minutes into the interrogation, when told of the brother's confession, he admitted having some part in the crime.

After moving unsuccessfully to suppress his confession as the fruit of an illegal arrest, Kaupp was convicted and sentenced to 55 years' imprisonment. The State Court of Appeals affirmed the conviction, concluding that no arrest had occurred until after the confession. The state court said that Kaupp consented to go with the officers when he answered "Okay" to Pinkins's statement that, "We need to go and talk."

On appeal to the U.S. Supreme Court, the court held that the seizure of the person within the meaning of the Fourth and Fourteenth Amendments occurs when:

> . . . taking into account all of the circumstances surrounding the encounter, the police conduct would have communicated to a reasonable person that he was not at liberty to ignore the police presence and go about his business.
>
> Although certain seizures may be justified on something less than probable cause, see, *e.g.*, *Terry v. Ohio*, 392 U.S. 1 (1968), we have never sustained against Fourth Amendment challenge the involuntary removal of a suspect from his home to a police station and his detention there for investigative purposes . . . absent probable cause or judicial authorization. The police can stop and briefly detain a person for investigative purposes if the officer has a reasonable suspicion supported by articulable facts that criminal activity 'may be afoot,' even if the officer lacks probable cause" (quoting *Terry*, *supra*, at 30). Such involuntary transport to a police station for questioning is "sufficiently like arrest to invoke the traditional rule that arrests may constitutionally be made only on probable cause.
>
> The state does not claim to have had probable cause here, and a straightforward application of the test just mentioned shows beyond cavil that Kaupp was arrested within the meaning of the Fourth Amendment. . . ."

The Court ruled the confession inadmissible, and the conviction was reversed (for a discussion of the case see Robinson, 2004).

Once an officer does have probable cause to arrest, he or she does not need to effect an arrest at that point. Other options are available. However, once probable cause has been established, the officer immediately may search the person for dangerous weapons "whenever he has reasonable cause to believe that the person possesses a dangerous weapon." If weapons are found on the suspect, then he or she shall either return it or arrest the person. If the suspect is in possession of the weapon(s) illegally, then he or she may be arrested for that, as well as the original charge that gave rise to the probable cause.

Arrests by Warrant

An **arrest warrant** is *a legal order signed and issued by a magistrate (judge) directed to any peace officer commanding that the person named* *in the warrant be arrested and brought before the court*, usually to answer to some charge. The warrant is issued at the request of a peace officer or deputy district attorney, who completes a sworn statement, known as an **affidavit**, in which the officer or deputy explains the probable cause in support of the warrant (refer to the wording in the Fourth Amendment). If the magistrate is convinced that probable cause exists, he or she will sign the warrant.

As soon as an arrest warrant is issued, the clock stops running on what is called the **statute of limitations**, the legal time within which a person must be charged with a crime. For a misdemeanor, the time in most states is one year, and for most felonies it varies from three to five years. In many states, there is no time limit on prosecuting a person for embezzling public funds or for any crime punishable by execution or life in prison.

To be valid, an arrest warrant must contain the following information:

- name of the person to be arrested
- legal description of the charge(s)
- amount of bail, or no bail
- date issued and the judge's signature
- court issuing the warrant

Only a peace officer can make an arrest pursuant to a warrant. Obviously, a private person does not have access to warrants. The officer need not have personal possession of the warrant at the time of the arrest. However, before arresting a person on the basis of a warrant, the officer must verify that it is still valid. An officer on patrol will have this verification completed by a dispatcher prior to making the arrest.

As soon as it is practicable, the officer must show a copy of the warrant to the arrested party if that person requests it. In most situations, such as during a routine traffic stop, if a patrol officer makes an arrest on a warrant, the dispatcher will be certain that a copy of the warrant is waiting for the officer at the jail where the subject is booked.

When a person is arrested by a peace officer on the basis of a warrant, the officer must proceed with the person arrested as commanded by the warrant or as provided by law.

If the person is arrested on a misdemeanor warrant, however, the person may be issued a citation instead of being physically arrested, in most cases. States often limit the officer's discretion in situations in which the offense involves violence or a firearm, the person resists arrest or gives false information or identification, the person is a danger to self or others, the person is under the influence of alcohol or narcotics, or the person refuses to sign the citation. Other limitations might also apply in a particular state, such as an offense that involves domestic violence.

Private Person Arrest

Thus far, the discussion of arrest has focused on the authority and procedures of law enforcement officers. However, any person may make an arrest if the conditions are legal. The phrase "citizen's arrest" is not really appropriate because someone might think that it is limited to actual citizens as opposed to noncitizens. The preferred phrase is "arrest by **private persons**," which is enough to distinguish it from an arrest by a peace officer.

Situations in which a private person may arrest another person can be divided into two basic categories of authority:

- a public offense committed or attempted in the person's presence
- a felony has been in fact committed, and the private person has reasonable cause for believing the person arrested committed it

There are two distinctions between the authority of a peace officer and a private person in making an arrest: (1) the peace officer is the only one who may serve a warrant; and (2), when a private person makes an arrest for a felony, based on probable cause, a felony must have been committed, whereas in an arrest by a peace officer, the officer needs only believe that one has occurred. A private person faces liability for false arrest or false imprisonment if he or she makes an arrest and no felony actually occurred.

Private person arrests occur frequently in two types of misdemeanor situations:

- When a security officer of a store detains a shoplifter and calls the police. The security officer must make the arrest (unless the suspect is a juvenile) because it did not occur in the presence of the peace officer.
- When a misdemeanor is committed in which a victim summons a peace officer to the scene of the crime and wants the suspect arrested. Again, the offense did not occur in the officer's presence.

In-Field Showup or Drive-by

The second situation described above in which a private person must make the arrest often includes a common police procedure known as an **in-field showup**, or **drive-by**.

This is a procedure used when an officer arrives at the scene of a misdemeanor crime shortly after it occurs, obtains a description of the suspect, and puts it out over the radio. A second officer, on patrol in the general area where the crime occurred, sees a person who matches the description of the suspect given over the radio. That officer has the reasonable suspicion to stop and detain the person. In order to clear up the suspicion, the officer at the crime scene has the victim accompany him or her in the police car, and they drive by the location where the suspect is detained. The victim is told that a person is being detained just to see if the victim can identify him or her.

The officer must be careful not to suggest to the victim that the real offender is in custody. If the victim does identify the suspect, the victim will accompany the officer to the police station, and the officer detaining the suspect also will take the suspect to the police station. There, the victim will tell the suspect he or she is under arrest and will sign a private party arrest form. In some jurisdictions, the officer will merely ask the victim if he or she wants the suspect arrested. If so, the victim signs the form and the officer takes custody of the suspect without the victim ever having to face the person.

Requesting Help When Arresting

If a peace officer or a private person needs assistance to complete an arrest, he or she may exercise an old common law procedure called *posse comitatus*, or power of the county (in effect, to form a posse). Consequently, a peace officer and a private person may request help from anyone over age 18 and not in military uniform to help them effect an arrest. And in most states it is a misdemeanor offense for a person to refuse to come to the aid of a peace officer who requests help.

When a private person comes to the aid of a peace officer, at the request of the officer, that person has the same authority, rights, and privileges as the officer. And as long as that person is acting in good faith, he or she is protected from any civil or criminal liability, even if the officer is acting illegally.

Acceptance by Police of Private Person Arrest

After a private person makes an arrest, a peace officer is required by law in many states to assume custody of the person. If the officer thinks that the arrest is unlawful, he or she may advise the person making the arrest, but if that person insists, the officer must take custody. If the officer refuses to take custody, he or she may be charged with a crime, usually a felony.

A peace officer assumes no civil liability in accepting custody from an unlawful arrest by a private person. After taking custody, the officer has whatever discretion he or she would have in a regular peace officer arrest. That is, the officer may release the person, give a citation, or book the person in jail.

Informing the Person Arrested

State laws require that anyone making an arrest must provide the arrested person certain information. The officer (or private person) must inform the person to be arrested of the intention to arrest him or her, of the legal reason for the arrest, and the authority to a make it, except when the person making the arrest has reasonable cause to believe that the person to be arrested is then actually engaged in the commission of or an attempt to commit an offense, or the person to be arrested is pursued immediately after its commission, or after an escape from some form of custody.

Effecting an Arrest with Force

When an officer has the legal authority to make an arrest, he or she may use reasonable force to effect the arrest, to prevent escape, or to overcome resistance.

A peace officer who makes or attempts to make an arrest need not retreat or stop his or her efforts because of the resistance or threatened resistance of the person being arrested. However, the officer may use only reasonable force, which is the amount of force necessary to overcome the resistance posed by the person being arrested. Excessive force is illegal.

Abuse of Authority by a Peace Officer

The behavior of peace officers is rigorously controlled by law. Not only is his or her authority to act in any situation dictated every step of the way in the state code sections, but the **abuse of authority** is spelled out in various laws as well.

State laws usually include two areas of behavior by peace officers that are illegal:

- Acting under color of authority (which means using one's peace officer powers to gain a desired result) without actually having legal cause in two procedural aspects:
  - detaining a person against his or her will without having reasonable suspicion
  - arresting a person without having probable cause, or other legal cause
- Acting under color of authority, but without having legal need, to assault or beat any person.

Along with these areas that are controlled by state laws, Title 18, United States Code, describes circumstances under which a local law enforcement officer may violate Federal law:

§241: Conspiracy against rights. If two or more persons conspire to injure, oppress, threaten, or intimidate any person in any State, Territory, or District in the free exercise or enjoyment of any right or privilege secured to him (or her) by the Constitution or law of the United States, or because of his having so exercised the same; or if two or more persons go in disguise on the highway, or on the premises of another, with intent to prevent or hinder his free exercise or enjoyment of any right or privilege so secured. They shall be fined under this title or imprisoned not more than ten years, or both; and, if death results from the acts committed in violation of this section or if such acts include kidnapping or an attempt to kidnap, aggravated sexual abuse or an attempt to commit aggravated sexual abuse, or an attempt to kill, they shall be fined under this title or imprisoned for any term of years, or for life, or both, or may be sentenced to death.

§242: Deprivation of rights under color of law. Whoever, under color of any law, statute, ordinance, regulation, or custom, willfully subjects any person in any State, Territory, or District to the deprivation of any rights, privileges, or immunities secured or protected by the Constitution, or law of the United States, or to different punishments, pains, or penalties, on account of such person being an alien, or by reason of his color, or race, than are prescribed for punishment of citizens, shall be fined under this title or imprisoned not more than one year, or both; and if such acts include the use, attempted use, or threatened use of a dangerous weapon, explosives, or fire, shall be fined under this title or imprisoned not more than ten years, or both; and if death results from the acts committed in violation of this section or if such acts include kidnapping or an attempt to kidnap, aggravated sexual abuse, or an attempt to commit aggravated sexual abuse, or an attempt to kill, shall be fined under this title, or imprisoned for any term of years or for life, or both; or may be sentenced to death.

Fortunately, there are very few incidents in which a peace officer violates the rights of a citizen or abuses a citizen, under the color of his or her authority. Unfortunately, it only takes a few situations in which flagrant abuses do occur to taint the reputation of all police. This is particularly true in those situations in which the media gets involved and reports the facts before they are even known.

Entry for an Arrest: Knock-and-Notice Requirements

Under common law, if a peace officer had legal authority to arrest a person, the officer also had the authority to break in and/or enter a dwelling to look for that person as long as the officer had reasonable cause to believe that the person was inside. However, that common law procedure is no longer recognized as legal (*Wilson v. Arkansas*, 1995).

Today the Fourth Amendment guarantees that a person has the reasonable expectation of privacy in his or her own dwelling and other possessions. Unless officers have consent, or some **exigent** (emergency) **circumstances** exist, they must have an arrest warrant (*People v. Ramey*, 1976, *Payton v. New York*, 1980). Police also may not enter the dwelling of some third party to arrest a person, whether or not they have an arrest warrant (*Steagald v. United States*, 1981). In that situation, they would need a search warrant as well.

When officers do want to arrest a person inside a dwelling with an arrest warrant, they must complete the procedure known as **knock-and-notice**. They must first knock on the door, or otherwise announce their presence, identify themselves as peace officers, state their purpose for being there and their authority to carry out that purpose (the warrant), demand entry, then wait a reasonable period of time for the resident to open the door. The phrase "reasonable period of time" means whatever time it normally would take the resident to answer the door. This leaves the officers with a great deal of discretion.

There are three exceptions to the knock-and-notice requirement:

- if the officers or any occupant would be placed at an increased peril or risk, such as those situations in which the suspect is known to use violence or to possess and/or use firearms
- if the officers have reasonable cause to believe that some evidence will be destroyed
- if the wanted person would attempt to flee

Officers need a strong factual basis to justify an entry under any of these situations.

In addition to consent, there are five exceptions to the warrant requirement in which exigent circumstances are created:

- When the situation presents danger and/or serious risk to an officer or to others. Within this context, the gravity of the underlying offense may be considered (*Welsh v. Wisconsin*, 1984; also see *Richards v. Wisconsin*, 1997, which did leave the door open for the possibility of "no-knock" search warrants).
- When an officer has reasonable cause to believe that evidence is being destroyed, based on reliable information or facts.
- To prevent the imminent escape of the suspect.
- When there is imminent danger of serious damage to property.
- When an officer is in hot pursuit or fresh pursuit.

The U.S. Supreme Court took up an interesting knock-and-notice case that originated in Oregon, *United States v. Ramirez*, during the 1998 session that might have affected police conduct nationwide. At issue, again, was when police must give the knock-and-notice warning before breaking into a home to serve a warrant or, do certain blanket exceptions exist.

In the Oregon case, it seems that in November 1994, state and federal authorities were looking for Alan Shelby, a fugitive who allegedly had assaulted a jail guard and escaped from the Tillamook County (Oregon) Courthouse on November 1. A few days later, an informant told police that he saw Shelby enter the home of a man named Ramirez, so several dozen state and federal law enforcement officers surrounded his house before dawn and prepared to serve a warrant to search for Shelby.

Without knocking, officers broke a window in the garage. Ramirez claimed he thought burglars were breaking in, so he grabbed a gun and fired several shots. One officer was slightly wounded. The police returned the fire then broke in. They yelled "police," whereupon Ramirez surrendered.

He was charged and convicted in federal court of being an ex-felon in possession of a gun. However, on appeal, U.S. District Judge Ancer L. Haggerty in Portland ruled the search unconstitutional because state and federal officers did not give a knock-and-notice before they entered. Based on precedent, the judge held that there is no blanket exception to the knock-and-notice requirement. He reasoned that if officers had complied by knocking and announcing who they were and their purpose, Ramirez would not have mistaken them for burglars and would not have had a reason for shooting at them. Therefore, the officers would not have been at risk.

Officers did not know for certain that Shelby was in the house or that, if he was, he planned an imminent escape, so they did not have sufficient cause to initiate the break-in, thus violating both the Fourth Amendment and §3109 U.S.C., a code section that requires exigent circumstances to justify the destruction of property in executing a warrant.

The U.S. Attorney appealed to the U.S. Supreme Court, and the case was decided on March 4, 1998. The Court ruled that

> . . . the Fourth Amendment does not hold officers to a higher standard when a no-knock entry results in the destruction of property . . . [and that] . . . under *Richards v. Wisconsin*, 1997, a no-knock entry is justified if police have a reasonable suspicion that knocking and announcing their presence before entering would "be dangerous or futile, or . . . inhibit the effective investigation of the crime."

Therefore, the Supreme Court held that the actions of the police were justified, and it reversed the lower federal court's decision to suppress the evidence. Ramirez's conviction in federal court stands, and the exigent circumstances justification, based on reasonable suspicion, was reaffirmed.

Shelby was not found in the house, nor were his whereabouts ever an issue in this case.

Fresh Pursuit

If officers had been chasing Shelby at the time and actually had seen him enter the home of Ramirez, they could have followed him in without knock-and-notice being an issue because their conduct would have been governed by a procedure known as **fresh pursuit**.

This is a situation in which an officer pursues a suspect from the scene of a crime, or from where the arrest is attempted, and the suspect flees to avoid arrest. Once in fresh pursuit, an officer need not stop just because a suspect enters some building to evade arrest, regardless of the nature of the offense.

Fresh pursuit is one in which an officer's pursuit efforts are **continuous and uninterrupted**. This pursuit may cross into other jurisdictions without affecting an officer's powers of arrest. In fact, most states participate in what is termed the Uniform Act of Fresh Pursuit, allowing officers to cross state boundaries and bring with them their state's authority to arrest. According to U.S. Supreme Court ruling (*County of Sacramento v. Lewis*, 1998), if injury or death results from a suspect being pursued in a vehicle high-speed chase, the officer is free from civil liability unless his or her actions "shocks the conscience," the motives of the officer are malicious, or the harm is intentional.

Resisting Arrest

If a person being arrested has knowledge or, by the exercise of reasonable judgment, should have knowledge that he or she is being arrested by a peace officer, it is the legal duty of that person to submit to arrest and not resist. However, the person may resist any excessive force used by an officer in effecting the arrest, such as a beating. In this situation, however, the person arrested has the burden of proving that the officer used excessive force.

Interfering with an Officer

A crime similar to that of resisting arrest is interfering with an officer in the performance of his or her duty. In fact, it is a crime (misdemeanor) in most jurisdictions to interfere with or disobey any public officers in the performance of their duties. This includes police officers, fire officers, ambulance personnel, or any other person authorized to act in public emergency situations.

If a person disarms, injures, or kills any officer during any act of resistance and interference, the punishment and/or crime becomes correspondingly more serious. The laws in most states have gone about as far as they can to provide emergency personnel with legal protection.

Exceptions to Peace Officer Powers of Arrest

There are two situations in which a peace officer does not have the authority to arrest a person whom the officer believes committed a crime.

Stale Misdemeanor Rule   An arrest for a misdemeanor committed in an officer's presence must be made right after it occurs, or "within a reasonable time thereafter." This means that the officer must immediately effect the arrest or, if the suspect flees, must pursue the suspect until he or she can make the arrest.

If an officer delays an arrest until a later time for the convenience of the officer, the offense becomes what is termed a stale misdemeanor, and the officer loses jurisdiction. If the officer observes the suspect in a public place at a later time, the officer may detain the person and make an identification but may not make an arrest. He or she must obtain a warrant to make the arrest.

Diplomatic Immunity   The second exception to an officer's powers of arrest occurs when the person claims, and is eligible to claim **diplomatic immunity**. By international and federal law, there are certain official representatives of foreign governments who are immune from arrest (http://www.state.gov/m/ds/immunities/c9127.htm). That is, they may not be arrested. Since they are here as official representatives of their country's government, they bring their country's soil with them. Wherever they go, they are walking on their soil, and police in this country do not have jurisdiction over any foreign soil. Any peace officer who violates the immunity status may be subject to federal felony arrest and prosecution (§22 U.S.C. 252, 253).

There are specific levels of immunity given to foreign representatives depending on the position and function they serve. Foreign ambassadors and United Nations' representatives are at the highest level and receive the most immunity. Both they and their families are completely immune from arrest and detention.

The next level is that of the consular officers: consul general, consul, and vice-consul. They perform most of the formal functions of their governments and are immune from arrest or detention (and civil liability) only when a criminal act occurs while performing the official duties assigned to them by their government. Their families do not have any immunity.

An exception to all of these guidelines includes the consular officers and their families from the Commonwealth of Independent States, China, Poland, Hungary, and the Philippines. They are granted ambassador-level immunity. Also, the employees and staff of Russian and Chinese consulates receive the same level of immunity as regular consular officers.

All foreign representatives have official identification cards issued by the U.S. Department of State's (DOS) Office of Foreign Missions (OFM).

These cards contain a photograph, identifying information, and a description of their immunity status. Their automobiles also are registered with DOS OFM, and display distinctive red, white, and blue license plates. These vehicles may not be impounded, stored, or searched, except by consent. An exception to these guidelines occurs whenever the public safety is jeopardized or police action is necessary to prevent a serious crime.

If a patrol officer stops a person who claims diplomatic immunity, the officer should call for a supervisor, document all the information available, initiate an investigation, and allow the subject to leave. Most states have an Office of Emergency Services (OES), which is responsible for the liaison between local police agencies and the U.S. State Department. In a serious crime such as a homicide, the State Department can ask a foreign government to recall its diplomat, and the foreign country may even prosecute its diplomat in its own country if it has a law prohibiting the same crime. Or the foreign country could revoke the diplomatic status of its representative and allow prosecution in this country.

Delivery of a Person after Arrest

State laws require that after a person has been arrested, he or she must be taken before a judge or magistrate without unnecessary delay. However, it is a rare occasion when the arresting officer actually delivers an arrested person to a judge after arrest. The arrested person is either cited to appear in court at some later date or is booked in a county jail, after which the case is referred to the local prosecuting attorney who determines whether to file charges against the arrested person.

If charges are filed, the person will be brought before the judge, magistrate, or in some states, the grand jury, within 48 hours to hear the charges. These alternative procedures satisfy the requirements of the law.

Release Procedures without a Charge after Arrest

Not all persons arrested are booked in jail. And some are not even charged with a criminal offense. If a crime is not serious and the peace officer believes that the person does not pose a threat to his or her own safety, or to the public safety, and that he or she will appear in court when required, the officer may give the person a **citation**, which is similar to a traffic ticket. It is a promise to appear, signed by the person.

The use of a citation as opposed to a full arrest is increasingly becoming the more common practice, particularly in states where the jails are overcrowded, and in those states where the local sheriffs, who run the jails, charge other police agencies booking fees that run as high as $200 per subject booked.

If the arresting officer believes that no charges are warranted, such as in cases of public intoxication or disturbing the public peace, he or she may follow the particular procedures provided in his or her state that provide for a direct release of the subject without further action. In these cases the record of the person is changed from an arrest to a detention and release.

SUMMARY

This chapter has presented the laws and behavioral elements of arrest from every aspect, including all the requirements and limitations of a peace officer and of a private person in the various arrest situations. The knock-and-notice requirement was detailed, along with a description of diplomatic immunity and fresh pursuit procedures, as well as procedures for police to follow after arrest for minor infractions.

ISSUES FOR DISCUSSION

1. Discuss the differences between an arrest by a peace officer and that by a private person.
2. Who is exempt from being arrested, and why are these exceptions allowed?
3. Define *fresh pursuit* and discuss the justification for it.
4. Discuss the differences between the concepts *probable cause* and *reasonable suspicion*. Refer to the Police-Citizen Transaction Matrix in your discussion.

Police-Citizen Transaction Matrix

Type of Encounter	Legal basis	Duration & Scope	Location	Privacy Invasion
Consensual	None	Limited by consent	On the spot	None
Stop & detention	Reasonable suspicion	Brief & focused	Usually on the spot	Identification & explanation of presence & patsearch
Arrest	Probable cause or warrant	Until booked or cited	On the spot or when located	Booking search & procedures, with jail or cite & release

REFERENCE

Robinson, Denise. "Kaupp v. Texas: Breathing Life into the Fourth Amendment," *Journal of Criminal Law & Criminology,* Spring 2004, v. 94, No. 3, p. 762.

INTERNET REFERENCES

http://en.wikipedia.org/wiki/Diplomatic_immunity offers an interesting history of diplomatic immunity.
http://www.state.gov/m/ds/immunities/c9127.htm details the U.S. State Department descriptions of the various levels of immunity.

CASE DECISIONS

Brown v. Illinois, 422 U.S. 590, 603 (1975)
County of Sacramento v. Lewis, 523 U.S. 833 (1998)
In re Alonzo C., 87 Cal.App.3d 707 (1978)
Kaupp v. Texas, 000 U.S. 02-5636 (2003)
Ornelas et al v. United States, 517 U.S. 960 (1996)
Payton v. New York, 455 U.S. 573 (1980)
People v. Coulombe, 86 Cal.App.4th 52 (2000)
People v. Ramey, 16 C 3d 263 (1976)
People v. Schofield, Cal.App.4th (2001)
Richards v. Wisconsin, 520 U.S. 385 (1997)
Steagald v. United States, 451 U.S. 204 (1981)
United States v. Ramirez, 523 U.S. 65 (1998)
United States v. Sokolow, 490 U.S. 1 (1989)
Welsh v. Wisconsin, 466 U.S. 138 (1984)
Wilson v. Arkansas, 133 l. Ed.2d 976 (1995)

chapter 6

MIRANDA

ITS MEANING AND APPLICATION

KEY TERMS AND CONCEPTS

Beheler Admonition	*Miranda* warning
Custodial interrogation	Prompt arraignment
Interested adult laws	Right to on-the-spot counsel

INTRODUCTION

This chapter deals exclusively with the *Miranda* decision and the effect that it has had on police procedures. The *Miranda* decision ranks alongside the *Mapp* and *Gideon* decisions as one of the three most significant precedent-setting cases in the history of procedural due process. Imagine what it must have been like before 1966, when police could take a suspect into custody, place him or her in an interrogation room at the police station, and question him or her at length without even considering that the suspect had any rights.

Imagine what it must have been like for the suspect. The police could create enormous pressures within that coercive environment for a person to confess. Then consider what one of those old-school detectives might think if he was told that he must advise the suspect of the right to remain silent. "How absurd," he might say. "Why should I tell him he has the right to remain silent when I want him to talk freely, to confess? That's the craziest idea I ever heard of."

Most people take it for granted today that police comply with the requirements of *Miranda*. However, it took many years and several appellate decisions to finally achieve the full due process that suspects now enjoy when being questioned by law enforcement. Consequently, before examining *Miranda*, it will be useful to review a summary of the important cases leading up to the 1966 decision. Later on in the chapter, the use of what is called the *Beheler* Admonition is presented as a current method used by police to avoid having to advise a suspect of any rights.

FORERUNNERS TO *MIRANDA*

Prior to the *Miranda* decision, the criteria for determining if a confession was admissible in court was whether it had been given *freely and voluntarily*. Those terms are rather vague and leave much to interpretation. There were many efforts to change that standard, and three cases stand out as forerunners to the current standard, as spelled out in *Miranda*. Two of these are examples of how the U.S. Supreme Court avoided dealing with the issue of confessions obtained by police interrogation, and one case shows the result of making a decision without including any method to enforce it.

Prompt Arraignment Cases

The first case is *McNabb v. United States*, 1943, in which two McNabb brothers were convicted of killing a federal revenue agent during a raid on their family's still in the mountains near Chattanooga, Tennessee. They were arrested during the raid, locked in a strip cell for more than 14 hours, then interrogated continuously over the next two days. They finally confessed, were convicted on the basis of their confession, and were sentenced to 45 years in prison. On appeal, the Supreme Court refused to address the legality of their confession and instead used the federal arraignment rule, Rule 5a of the Federal Rules of Criminal Procedures, to reverse the McNabbs' convictions. This Rule required **prompt arraignment** after arrest. The Court did not want to establish any precedent on custodial interrogation.

In the second case, *Mallory v. United States*, 1957, the 19-year-old Mallory, a man of limited intelligence (Robin, 1987, p. 171), was arrested by police in Washington, D.C., on a charge of rape, a capital offense at the time. He was interrogated at the police station by a polygraph operator and a detective for more than 10 hours. He finally confessed, was convicted on the basis of his confession, and was sentenced to be executed. On appeal, the Supreme Court again refused to deal with the legality of the confession. The Court again used Rule 5a to reverse his conviction, holding that Mallory had not been promptly arraigned.

The real significance of these two cases, aside from their requiring prompt arraignment, is the fact that no precedent was set in the area of illegal confessions. The Court had the opportunities to address the issue but declined to do so. There was a strong belief at the time that the Constitution was a federal document and the rights guaranteed therein applied only to federal proceedings. There was an equally strong belief that the states should be free to determine their own laws and justice system procedures. States rights was a popular, and almost sacred, theme throughout the nation.

The On-the-Spot Counsel Case

On the night of January 19, 1960, Danny Escobedo's brother-in-law was fatally shot, and Danny was the prime suspect. He was arrested without a warrant in the early hours of the next morning and was interrogated at police headquarters. He made no statement to the police and was released late that afternoon after his attorney obtained a writ of habeas corpus, an order stating that he was being held illegally.

On January 30, Benedict DiGerlando, who was then in police custody on the same charge, and who was later indicted for the murder along with Danny, told the police that Danny had fired the fatal shots, and that he, Danny, and Danny's sister were all in on the crime. Later that evening, Danny and his sister, now the widow of the deceased, were arrested and taken to police headquarters.

Danny was handcuffed in the back of the police car on the way to the police station when one of the arresting officers told him that DiGerlando had named him as the one who shot the deceased. According to Escobedo's later testimony, the detective also said, "They had us pretty well, up pretty tight, and we might as well admit to this crime," and that Escobedo replied, "I am sorry, but I would like to have advice from my lawyer." A police officer testified that, although Escobedo was not formally charged, "he was in custody" and "couldn't walk out the door."

Shortly after Escobedo and the police reached the police station, his lawyer arrived. The lawyer testified about the ensuing events in the following terms:

> On that day, I received a phone call from the mother of the defendant and, pursuant to that phone call, I went to the Detective Bureau at 11th and State.
>
> The first person I talked to was the Sergeant on duty at the Bureau Desk, Sergeant Pidgeon. I asked Sergeant Pidgeon for permission to speak to my client, Danny Escobedo. . . . Sergeant Pidgeon made a call to the Bureau lockup and informed me that the boy had been taken from the lockup to the Homicide Bureau. This was between 9:30 and 10:00 in the evening. Before I went

anywhere, he called the Homicide Bureau and told them there was an attorney waiting to see Escobedo. He told me I could not see him. Then I went upstairs to the Homicide Bureau. There were several Homicide Detectives around, and I talked to them. I identified myself as Escobedo's attorney and asked permission to see him. They said I could not. . . . The police officer told me to see Chief Flynn, who was on duty. I identified myself to Chief Flynn and asked permission to see my client. He said I could not. . . . I think it was approximately 11 o'clock. He said I couldn't see him because they hadn't completed questioning. . . .

For a second or two, I spotted him in an office in the Homicide Bureau. The door was open, and I could see through the office. . . . I waved to him and he waved back, and then the door was closed by one of the officers at Homicide. . . . I waited around for another hour or two and went back again and renewed my request to see my client. He again told me I could not. . . .

Danny Escobedo knew that his attorney was at the police station and he asked to speak with him but was told by police that he could see the attorney after the interrogation was over. Eventually, after a lengthy interrogation, Escobedo confessed. Actually, he had been told that if he confessed and named Benedict DiGerlando as the shooter, he would be given immunity from prosecution and could go home. However, after he confessed, he was detained and charged with the murder.

At the trial, Escobedo's attorney made a motion to suppress the confession on the grounds that it had been obtained in violation of Escobedo's Sixth Amendment right to counsel. The trial judge denied the motion, and Escobedo was convicted.

The case was appealed to the U.S. Supreme Court, a Court that now had a different composition than the earlier *McNabb* or *Mallory* Courts. This was the **Warren Court**, and it had a decidedly due process orientation. In its decision (*Escobedo v. Illinois*, 1964), the Court held that:

Under the circumstances of this case, where a police investigation is no longer a general inquiry into an unsolved crime but has begun to focus on a particular suspect in police custody who has been refused an opportunity to consult with his counsel and who has not been warned of his constitutional right to keep silent, the accused has been denied the assistance of counsel in violation of the Sixth and Fourteenth Amendments, and no statement extracted by the police during the interrogation may be used against him at a trial.

The Court thought that its decision provided suspects with the constitutional guarantees in the Sixth Amendment. When a person became the focus of an investigation and was a suspect and requested to speak with an attorney, the questioning had to stop. However, the decision lacked any provision for determining when the police investigation made the shift from a ". . . general inquiry into an unsolved crime but has begun to focus on a particular suspect in police custody. . . ." Also, the police were not required to tell the person he or she was the suspect nor advise him or her of the right to speak with an attorney. Consequently, the decision regarding the **right to on-the-spot counsel** after police made that "shift" had little, if any, effect on police procedures.

It was business as usual in many law enforcement agencies, and police continued to offer confessions into evidence if they were given freely and voluntarily.

THE *MIRANDA* CASE

The ***Miranda* warning** was named after the 1966 U.S. Supreme Court decision in which the 1963 conviction of Ernesto Miranda was reversed because the Court believed that he was deprived of his constitutional right to remain silent when questioned by police. The decision was one of the most important cases ever to come out of the Supreme Court. It is one that often has frustrated law enforcement, and one that often has been misunderstood. What follows is an explanation that, it is hoped, will clarify exactly what *Miranda* is and when it is and is not necessary for police to give the admonition to a suspect in a criminal case.

Miranda v. Arizona, 1966

Ernesto Miranda, a 23-year-old man of Mexican descent, was arrested at his home on March 13, 1963, and taken to the Phoenix Police Station, where he was placed in a lineup. He was immediately identified by a woman as the man who had kidnapped and raped her. He was taken into an interrogation room and questioned for two hours, after which he signed a confession to both crimes. His confession was admitted into evidence at his trial, over objections by his attorney, and he was found guilty of both charges. Miranda was sentenced to two concurrent terms of 20 to 30 years. On appeal, the U.S. Supreme Court held that

> . . . the prosecution may not use statements, whether exculpatory or inculpatory, stemming from **custodial interrogation** of the defendant unless it demonstrates the use of procedural safeguards effective to secure the privilege against self-incrimination. By **custodial interrogation, we mean questioning initiated by law enforcement officers after a person has been taken into custody or otherwise deprived of his freedom of action in any significant way**. As for the procedural safeguards to be employed, unless other fully effective means are devised to

inform accused persons of their right of silence and to assure a continuous opportunity to exercise it, the following measures are required.

Prior to any questioning, the person must be warned that he has a right to remain silent, that any statement he does make may be used as evidence against him, and that he has a right to the presence of an attorney, either retained or appointed.

The defendant may waive effectuation of these rights, provided the waiver is made voluntarily, knowingly, and intelligently. If, however, he indictates in any manner and at any stage of the process that he wishes to consult with an attorney before speaking, there can be no questioning. Likewise, **if the individual is alone and indicates in any manner that he does not wish to be interrogated, the police may not question him**. The mere fact that he may have answered some questions or volunteered some statements on his own does not deprive him of the right to refrain from answering any further inquiries until he has consulted with an attorney and thereafter consents to be questioned.

In any case in which a defendant appeals his or her conviction because of some procedural error and wins the appeal, the person may be retried, as long as no evidence that was ruled out because of the appeal is used. That is not double jeopardy. Miranda was retried, without using his confession, and was convicted of the same charges on the testimony of the victim. He was resentenced to two concurrent terms of 20 to 30 years.

That sentence did not mean that he would actually serve 40 to 60 years. It just meant that he would not be paroled right away. Actually, he was paroled in 1972 and returned to his same haunts around Phoenix and Tempe, Arizona. One evening in July 1974, two Tempe police officers observed him driving around town. They stopped him, searched his car, and found a loaded handgun and drugs under the front seat. He was arrested and booked into jail, but no charges were filed because the prosecuting attorney found that the stop, search, and seizure were illegal. However, Miranda's parole agent was not held to the same legal standard as the police. He had Miranda's parole revoked for possession of the gun, and Miranda was returned to prison to resume serving his sentence.

Miranda was paroled again in April 1975 and again returned to his same haunts. One evening in February 1976, while drinking beer in a barrio bar, he got into an argument with a young illegal Mexican who had just entered the country. He stabbed Miranda to death. The bar patrons held the illegal while the bartender called the police.

When the police arrived, the officers recognized Miranda. They searched his pockets and found several cards with the *Miranda* warning printed on them; cards that he was known to sell near the Maricopa

County court buildings. In a touch of irony, one officer stood the suspect against the bar, straddled the dead body of Ernesto Miranda, and read the suspect his rights off of one of the cards taken from Miranda's pocket.

The Meaning of *Miranda*

Our system of justice is called an adversary system because two sides (prosecution and defense) contest against each other in open court, similar to the knights' practice of trial by battle in medieval England. In theory, the legal truth will emerge from their contest. According to the Supreme Court justices, the privilege against self-incrimination that is guaranteed in the Fifth Amendment shares a similar historical development from England and is

> . . . the essential mainstay of our adversary system, and guarantees to the individual the right to remain silent unless he chooses to speak in the unfettered exercise of his own will, during a period of custodial interrogation, as well as in the courts or during the course of other relevant investigations.

In its reasoning for the *Miranda* decision, the Court explained that when a person is held in custody by law enforcement officers:

> . . . the atmosphere and environment of incommunicado interrogation as it exists today is inherently intimidating and works to undermine the privilege against self-incrimination. Unless adequate preventive measures are taken to dispel the compulsion inherent in custodial surroundings, no statement obtained from the defendant can truly be the product of his free choice.

The purpose of the Supreme Court in requiring police to advise an arrested person of his or her rights before questioning was to "police the police." It is similar to the *Mapp* decision in that the Warren Court did not trust the police or what they would do to obtain a confession and conviction. Warren had been a strong law-and-order district attorney in Alameda County, California, and later state attorney general, where he had firsthand experience with what he could expect of overzealous police officers. Those experiences influenced his thinking and the decisions of the Court.

The so-called *Miranda* warning was suggested by the Court as a guideline to follow in providing the acceptable "**preventive measures**" required. Its specific wording is not required, nor is the *Miranda* warning, itself, a constitutional right (see *Michigan v. Tucker*, 1974; *Edwards v. Arizona*, 1981; *New York v. Quarles*, 1984; *Duckworth v. Eagan*, 1989; *Davis v. United States*, 1994; and *Moran v. Burbine*, 1986).

The only requirement is that police provide sufficient procedural safeguards to satisfy the Court that a citizen's knowledge of his or her rights and protection against self-incrimination are assured. In the absence of any other procedural safeguards an agency might have, a law enforcement officer may follow the *Miranda* wording as one way to insure that a citizen in custody and interrogated by police (hereinafter called **custodial interrogation**) knows of his or her Fifth Amendment protection against self-incrimination, and his or her Sixth Amendment right to an attorney, either hired or appointed, to represent him or her at every stage of a criminal prosecution, once prosecution has been initiated. One form of the *Miranda* wording is given below.

The *Miranda* Warning

You have a right to remain silent. Do you understand? (Fifth Amendment right)

Anything you say may be used against you in court. Do you understand? (Fifth Amendment right)

You have the right to the presence of an attorney before and during any questioning. Do you understand? (Sixth Amendment right)

If you cannot afford an attorney, one will be appointed for you free of charge, before any questioning, if you want. Do you understand? (Sixth Amendment right)

A suspect's statements or confession cannot be admitted as evidence against him or her in trial unless it has been given freely and voluntarily. A confession may not be coerced or given after a threat or a promise of leniency made by police, and not until he or she knows and understands his or her Fifth Amendment protection against self-incrimination and Sixth Amendment right to have an attorney appointed and/or present during any questioning. Any evidence obtained in violation of this Sixth Amendment right to an attorney is inadmissible in trial (*Massiah v. United States*, 1964).

Not *Mirandizing* a person in custodial interrogation does not violate his or her constitutional rights. The only time a person's rights are violated is if a person's statements (confession) made without being advised, or otherwise given involuntarily, are admitted as evidence in what is called the prosecutor's case-in-chief, the prosecution's side of the case during the trial (see *United States v. Verdugo-Urquidez*, 1990).

If an officer obtains information about a person's role in a crime during custodial interrogation without first *Mirandizing* the suspect, the evidence cannot be used against the person at trial during the prosecution's presentation of his or her side of the case. However, it may be used for impeachment purposes at trial if the person testifies in his or her own behalf with information contrary to what was stated to police.

Also, evidence derived from the tainted information (confession) obtained by police, such as a gun or other contraband, may be admitted because it does not fit the so-called fruit of the poison tree doctrine (*Oregon v. Elsted*, 1985; *People v. Torres*, 1989; and *United States v. Gonzalez*, 1990), although many state trial judges may not agree. In addition, a peace officer knows that under Chapter 42 United States Code §1983, he or she can incur civil liability for depriving a person of his or her rights.

Until recently, the actual *Miranda* warning was not considered to be a constitutional right, and no civil liability would attach to an officer for interrogation of a suspect without giving the *Miranda* warning (see *Brock v. Logan County*, 1993), or interrogating a suspect in the hope of obtaining incriminating statements to use against a defendant who testifies in court after he or she invoked his or her right to remain silent or to have an attorney . In a recent case, however, a majority of the U.S. Supreme Court held that *Miranda*, itself, is a "constitutional rule" (*Dickerson v. United States*, 2000). In addition, the Ninth Circuit Court of Appeals (*California Attorneys v. Butts*, 1999) ruled that there were possible civil rights violations when two officers continued to interrogate two murder suspects after they had invoked their right to counsel and/or to silence. The officers also made false statements by telling the suspects that nothing they said could be used in court.

As it now stands, an officer may incur a civil rights violation if not adhering to a strict application of the *Miranda* standards. An officer should not question suspects in custody without advising them of their rights and should not question suspects after they invoke either their Fifth or Sixth Amendment rights.

The requirement to admonish an adult suspect of the *Miranda* warning has been so distorted by its use in cop shows on television and in the movies that it is misunderstood by the general public and by some criminal justice personnel as well. Suspects usually are not *Mirandized* immediately upon arrest.

Miranda must be given only when two specific conditions are present at the same time:

- when a suspect is taken into custody or otherwise deprived of freedom in a significant way
- if and when the person is subject to questioning about a crime as a suspect by a police officer

These two conditions are the **elements of custodial interrogation**. Also, the suspect must know that the person questioning him or her is a law enforcement officer. If the person is not in custody and knows that he or she is free to leave, *Miranda* need not be given before questioning by police. And if the suspect is in custody but police do not question him or her, *Miranda* need not be given (see the Sixth Circuit Court of Appeals decision, *United States v. Salvo*, 1998, and the Ninth Circuit Court of Appeals decision, *Bains v. Cambra*, 2000).

The phrase "deprived of freedom in a significant way" means that the person is not free to leave and is restrained in freedom of movement, such as being cuffed and caged in a car or locked in a room at the station (see, *California v. Beheler*, 1983).

Consider the recent case of *Thompson v. Keohane*, 1995, as a clear example of a confession given during noncustodial interrogation.

On September 10, 1986, two moose hunters discovered the body of a dead woman floating in a gravel pit lake on the outskirts of Fairbanks, Alaska. The woman had been stabbed 29 times. Notified by the hunters, the Alaska state troopers issued a press release seeking assistance in identifying the body. Thompson called the troopers on September 11 to inform them that his former wife, Dixie Thompson, fit the description in the press release and that she had been missing for about a month. Through a dental examination, the troopers conclusively established that the corpse was Dixie Thompson. On September 15, a trooper called Thompson and asked him to come to headquarters, purportedly to identify personal items the troopers thought belonged to Dixie Thompson. It is now undisputed, however, that the trooper's primary reason for contacting Thompson was to question him about the murder.

Thompson drove to the troopers' headquarters in his pickup truck, and upon arriving, immediately identified the items as belonging to Dixie. He remained at headquarters, however, for two more hours while two unarmed troopers continuously questioned him in a small interview room and tape-recorded the exchange. The troopers did not inform Thompson of his *Miranda* rights. Although they constantly assured Thompson he was free to leave, they also told him repeatedly that they knew he had killed his former wife. Informing Thompson that execution of a search warrant was under way at his home, and that his truck was about to be searched pursuant to another warrant, the troopers asked questions that invited a confession. Eventually, Thompson told the troopers he killed Dixie.

As promised, the troopers permitted Thompson to leave but impounded his truck. Left without transportation, Thompson accepted the trooper's offer of a ride to his friend's house. Some two hours later, the troopers arrested Thompson and charged him with first-degree murder.

The Alaska trial court, without holding an evidentiary hearing, denied Thompson's motion to suppress his September 15 statements. Deciding the motion on the papers submitted, the trial court ruled that Thompson was not "in custody" for *Miranda* purposes; therefore, the troopers had no obligation to inform him of his *Miranda* rights. Applying an objective test to resolve the "in custody" question, the trial court held that, under the *totality of the circumstances*, a reasonable person would have felt free to leave, it also observed that the troopers' subsequent actions—releasing and shortly thereafter arresting Thompson—rendered the question "very close."

After a trial at which the prosecution played the tape-recorded confession, the jury found Thompson guilty of first-degree murder and tampering with evidence. The Court of Appeals of Alaska affirmed Thompson's conviction, concluding, among other things, that the troopers had not placed Thompson "in custody" and, therefore, had no obligation to give him *Miranda* warnings. The Alaska Supreme Court denied discretionary review.

Thompson filed to the United States District Court for the District of Alaska. The District Court denied his appeal, giving a presumption of correctness under 28 U.S.C. §2254(d) to the state court's conclusion that, when Thompson confessed, he was not yet "in custody" for *Miranda* purposes. The U.S. Court of Appeals agreed (1994).

Thompson's appeal eventually reached the U.S. Supreme Court, and his case was argued on October 11, 1995. On November 29, 1995, by a vote of 7 to 2, the Court held that Thompson was not in custody at the Alaska troopers' police station for purposes of *Miranda*. Consequently, *Miranda* did not apply, and his conviction was upheld. Actually, the Alaska troopers and Thompson were engaged in a deliberate consensual encounter (also see, *Oregon v. Mathiason*, 1977) to question Thompson in the manner they wanted without having to advise him of any rights. This is a common practice now in many states under *Beheler*.

The *Beheler* Admonition

Many law enforcement agencies have a policy that the arresting officer is not to question the suspect about the crime. The officer merely effects that arrest and transports the person to jail. Consequently, no *Miranda* warning is required. If the person voluntarily offers incriminating information as to his or her role in the crime, it is admissible in court. Any *Mirandizing* will be done by the detectives investigating the case, and they usually will videotape, or at least auditorally tape, the officers giving the warning.

When a suspect has not been arrested, it is a common practice for investigative officers to ask a suspect if he or she would mind coming to police headquarters to discuss a matter. When the suspect arrives, he or she is given what is termed the **Beheler** **Admonition** or warning (*California v. Beheler*, 1983), which goes something like the following:

> Thank you for coming down to the station. We want you to know that you are not under arrest and that you are free to leave at any time. We just want to talk to you about a matter. Do you mind answering a few questions?

This creates the situation discussed in the Thompson case, a consensual encounter. It does not constitute custodial interrogation because the suspect is not under any restraint and is free to leave. It is, in a sense, a **consent interrogation**. Then, if a confession or incriminating statements are obtained, they are legally admissible. If the suspect does confess, he or she is still free to leave the station at any time. However, after he or she leaves, the officers will obtain an arrest warrant, using the confession as probable cause, and will arrest the suspect.

More on *Miranda*

In the original *Miranda* decision, the Court also stated that if the suspect indicates, prior to or during questioning, that he or she wishes to remain silent, the interrogation must cease. If he or she indicates that he or she wants an attorney, the interrogation must cease, and may not resume again unless and until the attorney gives permission and is present during any questioning. However, if the suspect does not make a clear invocation of his or her right to remain silent and to have an attorney, and merely asks the interrogating officers about the rights and/or if he or she should have an attorney, the officers must ". . . stop the interview and make a good-faith effort to give a simple and straightforward answer" (see, *Almeida v. Florida*, 1999 and *Florida v. Glatzmayer*, 2001).

If questioning does continue, any incriminating statements made by the suspect will not be admitted as evidence to prove guilt at a trial. However, in some states, it is admissible to counter a defendant's testimony if a defendant does testify at trial. Rarely will this occur because it is uncommon for a defendant to take the stand and testify. When an interrogation is conducted without the presence of an attorney and statements are made by the suspect, a heavy burden rests on the government to demonstrate that the defendant knowingly and intelligently waived his right to counsel.

When a suspect makes some statements without waiving his or her rights, the suspect may stop answering questions and invoke his or her privilege against self-incrimination or right to an attorney at any time during the interrogation. However, if the suspect does waive his or her rights, the waiver may be stated or implied in the responses to the *Miranda* admonition made by the suspect. That is, the suspect need not actually state that he or she waives his or her rights. He or she may imply a legal waiver by merely responding to a police officer's questions after being advised of the *Miranda* admonition (see, *North Carolina v. Butler*, 1979; *United States v. Astello*, 2000).

A **person's right to counsel**, as guaranteed in the Sixth Amendment, attaches to the person only after he or she has been formally charged in court and becomes the defendant in a criminal action. That is when an attorney will be appointed. Therefore, the police do not provide an attorney if a person requests one after being *Mirandized*. The police must stop any efforts to interrogate the suspect. However, after an attorney has been hired or appointed by the court, after formally charging the defendant, the attorney's representation **is case-specific**

(*Texas v. Cobb*, 2001). This means that while police may not question the suspect on the immediate offense without the presence of an attorney, they may question him or her on other unrelated offenses after *Mirandizing* the person and obtaining a waiver.

When *Miranda* Is Not Required

During detention situations, as was indicated, the person is not free to leave and often is asked incriminating questions. However, detention does not constitute an arrest. There are several specific detention situations to take note of, as follows:

- when asking questions of a motorist detained in a routine traffic stop
- when asking routine questions of a DUI suspect
- when there is an immediate threat to public safety, officer safety, victim safety, or suspect safety (refer to The Public Safety Exception section in Chapter 3)
- when no questions (or the functional equivalent) are asked
- when asking general on-the-scene questions
- during lineups, field showups, or photo IDs
- when questioning witnesses
- when statements are made to a private person, or one believed to be a private person by the suspect
- when questioning is in a suspect's office or place of business, as long as the person is free to leave
- in simple detention/stop-and-frisk situations
- even in an interrogation room of the police station if the suspect knows he or she is free to leave, is not locked in, and is not under arrest, but instead remains there freely and voluntarily to talk or answer questions

The Reaffirmation of *Miranda*

As was mentioned previously, when it was announced, the Warren Court's *Miranda* decision was resented both by law enforcement and by staunch law-and-order politicians. As a reaction, Congress enacted a law (Section 3501) in 1968 as an attempt to override *Miranda*. This law allowed a suspect's incriminating statements to be admitted as evidence in federal courts if they were given freely and voluntarily, the old standard. A list of factors was included for determining whether a confession was acceptable in court.

The law was never used because the U.S. Justice Department thought it was unconstitutional. However, a federal prosecutor attempted to apply the law and introduce such non-*Mirandized* statements by Charles Dickerson, then accused of robbing seven banks in Maryland and Virginia. He admitted driving the getaway car on January 24, 1997, when he and an accomplice robbed the First Virginia Bank in Old Town Alexandria. He also admitted that he and the accomplice had robbed 18 other banks in three states. The fourth U.S. Circuit Court ruled in February that they were admissible under Section 3501. Dickerson's attorney appealed the decision. In a 2-to-1 opinion, the U.S. Court of Appeals in Richmond, Virginia, upheld the prosecutor's position and the 1968 law, allowing Dickerson's admission to be admitted as evidence against him. This decision was then binding on all federal courts within the district where it was made, which included the federal courts in Virginia, West Virginia, Maryland, North Carolina, and South Carolina. Dickerson's attorney appealed the case to the U.S. Supreme Court.

The case (*Dickerson v. United States*, 2000) went to the Supreme Court, but in a very unusual move, the Justice Department refused to defend §3501 and Attorney General Janet Reno asked the Supreme Court to uphold *Miranda* and to declare §3501 unconstitutional. Since the Department of Justice would not defend against Dickerson's appeal, justices of the Supreme Court appointed Paul Cassell, a conservative University of Utah law professor who had argued the legality of §3501 before the fourth U.S. Circuit Court, to argue the merits of §3501 and oppose Dickerson's appeal.

If the justices had agreed with Cassell and the Fourth Circuit Court ruling, that failure to give a *Miranda* warning would not necessarily bar the admission of incriminating statements in federal court, it follows that state legislatures would have been free to enact their own versions of §3501, meaning that local law enforcement officers might be able to interrogate a suspect and obtain incriminating statements and/or a confession without ever having to advise the suspect of any rights under the Fourth and Fifth Amendments.

Arguments in the case were heard in April 2000, and a decision was handed down on June 26, 2000. The Supreme Court found that §3501 was insufficient to provide the procedural safeguards required under *Miranda*, **upheld the mandatory use of the *Miranda*** warning by a **vote of 7 to 2**, and stated that ". . . *Miranda* announced a **constitutional rule** that Congress may not supersede legislatively."

In a scathing dissent, Justices Scalia and Thomas stated that the Court's majority had created in *Miranda* a new entity that had constitutional clout but that was not a part of the Constitution. They complained that rules are either required by the Constitution itself or they are not, and the Court had no authority to create it as a rule.

One final word on *Miranda* in adult cases: The private beliefs, thoughts, intentions, or suspicions of a law enforcement officer about a person as a suspect are totally irrelevant to any issue of *Miranda*, just as they are irrelevant in a detention situation. For example, in the

Thompson case, Alaska troopers suspected him of killing his wife and invited him to come down to the station to pick up her effects because they really wanted to talk to him about his role in her death. However, it does not matter what is on the officer's mind. It only matters what the officer does.

Miranda in Juvenile Cases

All the above information on *Miranda* applies only when the suspect is an adult at the time of arrest. Juvenile procedures have more rigorous requirements, in some states, depending on the particular state's law because of a concept known as **independent state grounds**. This means that a state's legislature may enact laws providing greater protection for juveniles than the minimum required by the Constitution and the Supreme Court's interpretation of it. According to Cavin:

> . . . the scope of the additional protection afforded the juvenile ranges from an absolute requirement that an interested adult consent to the waiver to a mere procedural requirement that parents be notified prior to questioning of the juvenile.

These requirements are called **interested adult laws** because they require the advisement and/or consent of any waiver of Fifth and Sixth Amendment rights by some adult having a concern in the minor's welfare. Ohio, for example, requires consultation with an interested adult by the minor before questioning. In Indiana, legislation requires the consent of either the custodial parent, guardian, or attorney before a juvenile's rights may be waived. In California a minor must be advised of his or her rights regardless of whether he or she will be questioned and regardless of what the officer might do with the minor after arrest.

In Connecticut, the Court of Appeals suppressed a juvenile's confession that was first made out of the presence of the father then repeated with the father present after both the father and minor had signed a waiver. Both minor and parent must be advised before any questioning may begin.

In Massachusetts, minors under the age of 14 years must consult with an interested adult before waiving any rights, whereas minors 14 years and older must be advised and given the opportunity to consult with an interested adult. Georgia law requires merely that a minor's parents be advised upon taking a minor into custody and allowed to consult if a request is made by the parent.

Procedures in New Hampshire follow the *totality of the circumstances*. However, it has a list of 15 factors that must be considered in determining the legality of any waiver. Georgia has a nine-factor list. North Dakota statutes and appellate decisions require that an attorney be appointed for any minor not represented by a parent or guardian and hold that a minor absolutely cannot waive his or her rights. Only an attorney, parent, or guardian can initiate a waiver.

In Oregon, police must *Mirandize* a juvenile exactly as they would an adult. Police must also advise the parents before questioning the minor, and the parents or the minor may invoke the minor's Fifth and Sixth Amendment protections. However, if the minor is on probation as a ward of the court, the court may waive the minor's rights (as the substitute and legal parent), and police are not required to advise the natural parents.

Nevada seems to provide juveniles with the most protection. There police must advise the juvenile and the parent of the minor's *Miranda* rights, and both must waive the rights before questioning. In addition, if the minor is of an age, and has committed the type of offense that may allow for his or her waiver of jurisdiction to adult court to stand trial, police must advise him or her that anything the minor says may be used against him or her in criminal proceedings as an adult.

This does not represent the complete list of states that provide greater protection for juveniles than is required under *Miranda*. It is merely a sample of selected laws included to give a better legal context for considering the procedures required in the reader's own state.

This extra protection for juveniles is not constitutionally necessary. Actually, the U.S. Supreme Court has held that the *Miranda* requirement is the same for juveniles (*In re Gault*, 1967, and *Fare v. Michael C.*, 1979).

Note that in the case, *Yarborough v. Alvarado*, 2004, described in Chapter 4, Alvarado was a 17-year-old called down to the police station for questioning. After two hours of questioning, he admitted his involvement. He was allowed to leave and go home with his parents and the situation was termed a *consensual encounter*. He was never advised of his rights, yet he was later arrested, tried, and convicted, and his conviction was upheld by the U.S. Supreme Court. The court ruled that age and inexperience with the justice system are not factors to be considered with *Miranda* (*Yarborough v. Alvarado*, 2004).

Miranda in Federal Juvenile Cases

Section 5033 of Title 18 of the United States Code (USC) prescribe the procedures that federal law enforcement officers must follow when taking a juvenile into custody.

> Whenever a juvenile is taken into custody for an alleged act of juvenile delinquency, the arresting officer **shall immediately advise** such **juvenile** of his legal rights, in language comprehensible to a juvenile, and shall immediately notify the Attorney General **and** the juvenile's **parents**, guardian, or custodian of such custody. The arresting officer **shall also notify the parents**, guardian, or custodian of the rights of the juvenile and of the nature of the alleged offense.

Federal law, then, provides far greater protection for juveniles than is required under *Miranda*. This federal requirement was reaffirmed by the U.S. Ninth Circuit Court of Appeals in their decision *United States v. Rudolfo R.*, 2000.

SUMMARY

The purpose of this chapter was to explain what the requirements are for law enforcement officers under *Miranda*. The defining concept is known as **custodial interrogation**, the questioning of a suspect who is in custody or under similar restraints about his or her role in a crime. Several case situations that were forerunners of the *Miranda* decision also were discussed: the *McNabb* and *Mallory* requirement of prompt arraignment, and the *Escobedo* requirement of on-the-spot counsel. The use of what is known as the *Beheler* Admonition was described, as a contemporary approach to questioning suspects without arresting them. The additional situations in which *Miranda* is not required were explained as well.

The chapter concluded with a summary of how *Miranda* applies in juvenile arrest situations, both within the various states under the concept known as independent state grounds and in federal law enforcement procedures.

ISSUES FOR DISCUSSION

1. Define *custodial interrogation* and discuss the elements that must be present to fit the definition.
2. Discuss the need for a warning such as *Miranda*. Why should people be informed of their rights before interrogation? Does this warning requirement interfere with police in their efforts to solve crimes and arrest suspects?
3. Discuss the methods by which police attempt to gain information from a suspect without having to meet the requirements of *Miranda*. How does the *Miranda* requirement relate to the Social Contract discussed in Chapter 2?

REFERENCES

Cavin, Jeffrey D. "Waiver of a Juvenile's Fifth and Sixth Amendment Rights," *Journal of Juvenile Law*, 1992, v. 13.

Nickelsberg, Jessica E. "Illinois v. Lidster: Continuing to Carve Out Constitutional Vehicle Checkpoints," *The Journal of Criminal Law and Criminology*, Spring 2005, v. 95, No. 3.

Robin, Gerald D. *Introduction to the Criminal Justice System* (3rd edition) New York: Harper & Row, 1987.

Scheb, John M., and John M. Scheb, II. *Criminal Procedures*. Belmont, CA: Wadsworth, 1999.

Zalman, Marvin, and Larry Siegel. *Key Cases and Comments on Criminal Procedure* (1994 edition) New York: West, 1994.

INTERNET REFERENCES

http://www.usconstitution.net/miranda.html
http://publicdefender.cjis20.org/miranda.htm
http://www.emergency.com/miranda.htm
http://www.landmarkcases.org/miranda/home.html

CASE DECISIONS

Almeida v. Florida, 737 So, 2nd 520 (1999)

Bains v. Cambra, 204 F.3d 964, 977 (2000)

Brock v. Logan County, 3 F3d 1215, 1217 (1993)

California Attorneys v. Butts, 195 F.3d 1039 (1999)

California v. Beheler, 463 U.S. 1121 (1983)

Davis v. United States, 512 U.S. 452, 464 (1994)

Dickerson v. United States, 530 U.S. 428, 444 (2000)

Duckworth v. Eagan, 492 U.S. 195 (1989)

Edwards v. Arizona, 451 U.S. 477 (1981)

Escobedo v. Illinois, 378 U.S. 478 (1964)

Fare v. Michael C., 442 U.S. 707 (1979)

Florida v. Glatzmayer, No. SC 00-602 (2001)

In re Gault, 387 U.S. 1 (1967)

Massiah v. United States, 377 U.S. 201 (1964)

McNabb v. United States, 318 U.S. 332 (1943)

Mallory v. United States, 354 U.S. 449 (1957)

Michigan v. Tucker, 417 U.S. 433 (1974)

Miranda v. Arizona, 384 U.S. 444 (1966)

Moran v. Burbine, 475 U.S. 412 (1986)

New York v. Quarles, 467 U.S. 649 (1984)

North Carolina v. Butler, 441 U.S. 369 (1979)

Oregon v. Elsted, 470 U.S. 298 (1985)

Oregon v. Mathiason, 429 U.S. 492 (1977)

People v. Torres, 213 CA3d 1284, 1255 (1989)

Thompson v. Keohane, 516 U.S. 99 (1995)

Texas v. Cobb, 121 S.Ct. 1335 (2001)

Yarborough v. Alvarado, 000 U.S. 02-1684 (2004)

United States v. Astello, 241 F.3d 965 (8th Cir) cert denied 533 U.S. 962 (2001)

United States v. Gonzalez, 894 F2d 1043, 1048 (CA 1990)

United States v. Verdugo-Urquidez, 494 U.S. 259 (1990)

United States v. Rudolfo R., No. 99-5025 (2000)

United States v. Salvo, 133 F 3rd 943 (1998)

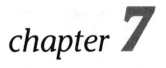

BOOKING AND JAIL CUSTODY PROCEDURES

KEY TERMS AND CONCEPTS

Assault by public officers

Body cavity search

Booking

Cite-and-release program

Classification

Cruel and unusual punishment

Custody

Detention facility

Detention searches

Direct supervision

Failure to appear (FTA)

Gang affiliation

Inhumanity to prisoners

Inmate safety

Medical prescreening

Metal detector searches

Modular housing

Patsearches

Prisoner's rights to phone calls

Required visits

Separation by class and gender

Soliciting for attorneys

Soliciting for bail bond people

Strip search

Treatment of prisoners

Validating the legality of arrest

Weapons control in jails

INTRODUCTION

Many people, and especially those of the media, often use the words *jail* and *prison* interchangeably. Nothing could be further than the truth (Kerle, 2005). Jails are locally operated detention/correctional facilities that temporarily confine individuals either before court or after a court proceeding and decision to hold them. At midyear 2004, 713,990 inmates were detained in jails nationwide (BJS, 2005). However, the majority of adults arrested are not taken to jail. Most of those charged with infractions and most misdemeanors are cited by police to appear in court. Each county maintains a jail, usually under the control of the sheriff, which receives adults for one or more of the following purposes:

- for the detention and presentation in court to answer to the charges after a lawful arrest by a peace officer
- for the detention of persons ordered to jail by the magistrate or judge pending trial
- for the confinement of individuals sentenced to jail following misdemeanor convictions
- for the confinement of individuals committed for contempt, or some civil process, or by other authority of law
- for the detention of individuals committed in order to secure their attendance as witnesses for trial
- for the confinement of persons granted probation but ordered to serve some time in jail as a condition of probation
- for the detention of individuals arrested by county probation officers, county parole officers, or state parole agents and ordered held for probation or parole violation proceedings
- for the temporary detention of individuals in transit from and/or to other county, state, or federal facilities
- for the detention of certain juveniles, as specified in the various state codes

It should be obvious from reading the list of sources of those received in jail that they will be detained for varying lengths of time—some for a few days and some for a year or longer. Regardless of the length of time, all those detained or confined must be treated as prisoners under legal custody, subject to all the rights and treatment required by law.

THE JAIL POPULATION

There are more than 3,300 county jails operating in the United States today, and approximately 20 million individuals are booked into jail each year. The states of California and Texas seem to be competing to be the largest in the nation, with California housing approximately

75,000 a day and Texas nearly 60,000. Overcrowding is a major problem, and many jails are increasing in size and staff at every opportunity. However, jail construction seems to follow the theme expressed in Kevin Costner's movie *Field of Dreams*: build it, and they will come. This could also be expressed in a version of Murphy's Law: the jail inmate population will increase to fill the size of the facilities built to hold it.

For years most jail populations were fairly well balanced between felony and misdemeanor offenders. This balance has shifted to the point where the vast majority have either been charged with or convicted of felonies. This increase has a decided impact on the type of jail construction needed, with an increased emphasis on security that requires more expensive housing. It also affects jail classification procedures. Ironically, one current philosophy of jail construction and management stresses the open, **modular housing**, with its direct supervision of inmates, rather than the traditional linear-style cell blocks.

In many instances, one correctional officer is placed in charge of 50 inmates in open pods, where the inmates are free to wander about the housing unit, and the correctional officer often wanders among them. This requires a strong and amenable interpersonal style to approaching inmate supervision, as opposed to the authoritarian personality type. It also places a special importance on classification and housing procedures.

CUSTODY

A dictionary defines **custody** as ". . . immediate charge and control exercised by a person or an authority over a ward, suspect, or inmate." Another dictionary used the phrase ". . . immediate care or charge." Two aspects of custody are either stated or implied in these definitions:

- control over a person
- safekeeping of the person

Within the limits necessary to maintain proper control, one does not lose his or her rights and protections just because one is in jail. In fact, it is both the legal and moral responsibility of a person having custody of prisoners to insure their safety and humane treatment, as well as to maintain the control and security of the facility.

BOOKING

When a person is first brought into a jail after an arrest, he or she is booked. This term is derived from the early practice of entering all the relevant information about the person and offense in a large book. Today computers have replaced the book, but the practice remains relatively the same.

Booking is simply a procedure in which the suspect is photographed, fingerprinted, and relieved of all his or her personal property, for which a receipt must be given. The property should be accurately described but in generic terms so as not to imply some worth or value. If the person is to be detained, he or she is provided with jail clothing, and his or her personal clothing is stored for return on release.

Validating the Legality of the Arrest

The receiving or booking officer should verify that the documents that request or command detention or confinement are legal. These will include an abstract of a warrant, a valid probable cause arrest by a peace officer, a valid adult court commitment document, and valid probation or parole arrest and detainer documents. Valid court commitment documents include an arrest warrant, a sentencing order, or a remanding order. They must contain the court case and docket numbers, the violation, the amount of bail or information as to sentencing time, and the signature of the proper legal authority—the judge or clerk.

For a warrant to be valid, it either must be in the possession of the arresting officer or its validity must have been confirmed by that officer or a person from his or her agency, and the arresting officer must be in possession of the warrant or abstract at the time of booking. As stated in the previous chapter, by the time an arresting officer reaches the jail, dispatch will have arranged for the abstract or warrant to be there as well. County probation officers will provide their valid arrest and detention orders, as will county parole officers and state parole agents.

When accepting custody from a peace officer after a probable cause arrest, the booking officer will require the arresting officer, or officer doing the transporting after arrest, to provide a copy of the police arrest report or to complete a proper booking sheet, containing the arrested person's name, age, and offense. Persons booked and detained while en route to other facilities will be accompanied by a booking or commitment order signed by some authority. The booking officer should note the legality of that order before accepting custody.

Before accepting anyone for booking, the booking officer should be certain that the person to be booked is not in need of immediate medical care or treatment. If immediate treatment is required, the officer should refuse to accept custody and should request that the arresting peace officer take the prisoner to a hospital or medical facility where treatment can be provided before that person is delivered to jail for booking. This procedure should be followed for three reasons:

- to ensure that treatment is provided to the arrested person as soon as possible

- to prevent the custodial agency from assuming any liability because of the injury or illness for which the treatment is needed
- to be sure the arrested person's insurance company is responsible for the cost of such treatment

Failure of a booking officer to follow this procedure could be very costly to the facility, the county government, and even to the custodial officer if an injury does not receive treatment because of negligence.

MEDICAL PRESCREENING OF ARRESTED PERSONS

Every peace officer is responsible for the care, protection, and safety of each person arrested or otherwise in custody. The initial responsibility of **medical prescreening** lies with the arresting officer to be certain that the person arrested is not suffering from any injury, mental illness, drug overdose or intoxication, or other conditions that might require medication or treatment. If the officer believes that the arrested person is in urgent need of treatment, he or she should immediately take the person to the approved local medical facility, usually the county hospital.

The nature of the injury or other condition, and the treatment it is given, should be noted in the officer's report or notebook. When the prisoner has received the required treatment, the officer will obtain a medical release from the medical practitioner in charge, and can then transport the person to jail.

The jail intake or custodial person receiving the arrested person should complete a medical questionnaire on each person received. And if urgent treatment is required, the person should not be accepted by custody staff. Once custody is accepted, the arresting and/or transporting officer and his or her agency are relieved of any further responsibilities.

PRISONERS' RIGHTS TO PHONE CALLS

Almost immediately after booking, providing that the detainee is cooperative with staff, the person is granted the right to communicate with certain individuals in an effort to gain release from jail and/or assistance of an attorney in answering the charges. Each state's penal code details the procedures that the jail custody staff must follow. It usually includes a time limit within a few hours of custody to allow the individual these rights. In addition, these phone calls may not be monitored, eavesdropped upon, or recorded.

Any police or corrections officer who deprives an inmate of these rights may be charged with a crime, usually a misdemeanor.

SOLICITING FOR ATTORNEYS OR BAIL BOND PEOPLE

In allowing the phone calls, a peace officer absolutely may not suggest the name of any particular lawyer or bail bond person to call. In addition, the officer may not dial a number for the prisoner. The names of attorneys and bail bond persons usually are posted in the booking area, near the phone from which the prisoner will make his or her other calls.

Not only is it an abuse of an officer's position of authority if he or she recommends anyone, friend, relative, or business associate, but the act of soliciting for business is prohibited by law, as a misdemeanor in most states.

REQUIRED VISITS FOR INMATES

Another legal requirement of custody staff is the obligation to allow jail inmates the rights to have visits on demand by certain types of professionals, including physicians, surgeons, psychiatrists, and often psychologists, along with the attorney of record or one requested by the inmate or his or her family.

CITE-AND-RELEASE PROGRAM PROCEDURES

The jails in many jurisdictions are overcrowded and have room only for offenders who present the most serious risk to the community. In addition, it is not necessary to hold some people under lock and key after arrest and during their court proceedings because they do not pose a public threat and/or concern that they might fail to appear in court. Consequently, a procedure known as cite-and-release is used to minimize the unnecessary detention of persons brought to jail after a probable cause arrest.

The staff that operate the programs to implement cite-and-release vary from one jurisdiction to another. They might be probation officers, jail custody officers, or nonsworn personnel, usually trained in interviewing techniques. They will interview the prisoner after booking to determine whether the need exists for further detention. They consider the likelihood of the person appearing in court when required. In doing this, they look for stability and ties in the area such as family, property, and employment.

They also look at the person's prior record to determine if he or she ever failed to appear on previous release occasions. They also consider the risk to public safety that the person might pose if released. This would include whether the person were armed during the commission of the instant offense (offense for which they were arrested), the severity of the instant offense, whether the person were on probation or parole at the time, and the concerns of any victim, particularly in domestic violence cases.

The cite-and-release staff usually have criteria to use in assessing the worthiness of the person for release and usually have limits on their release authority. However, in many jurisdictions, a judge is on call to authorize the release if it is beyond the authority of the program staff. If the person qualifies for release, he or she is given a citation to appear in court, similar to what the arresting officer could have given. A court appearance date is provided on the citation. After signing it, the person is released without bond or bail.

Those who do not qualify for the **cite-and-release program** may pursue the traditional options: posting bail with cash or, in some jurisdictions, with a credit card, or contracting for the services of a local bail bond person. This person will guarantee the bail for the prisoner. If the person's release is followed by a **failure to appear (FTA)**, the bail bond person probably will contract with a bounty hunter for the person's capture and return.

CLASSIFICATION

As individuals are accepted and booked into jail custody, they may not all be housed together, both for staff and inmate safety and for legal reasons. Each prisoner booked into jail should be evaluated to identify characteristics that can be used in determining where and with whom each may be housed. They should be classified during and/or immediately after booking in order to comply with the law, to ensure everyone's safety, and to maintain a secure **detention facility**. It is the responsibility of custody staff not only to protect each other, but to protect the prisoners from each other as well.

Any **classification** procedure should be based on consideration of criminal sophistication, seriousness of crime charged, presence or absence of assaultive behavior, age, and other criteria that will provide for the safety of the prisoners and staff.

Separation by Class and Gender

Individuals detained in jail pending trial and persons convicted and serving a sentence often may not be mixed together or put in the same room except for the purpose of participating in activities under **direct supervision**. Persons committed or detained on a civil process, such as a witness or a person being punished for contempt of court, may not be mixed with those detained for criminal matters. Diplomats also require special consideration. In addition, male and female prisoners, except husband and wife, should not be allowed to sleep, dress or undress, bathe, or perform eliminatory functions in the same room. Male and female prisoners must be separated at all times unless they are participating in certain recreational or educational activities that are supervised (Brennen & Austin, 1997).

Separation by Gang Affiliation

The growth of gangs and gang violence is alarming, and it is everywhere. Juvenile and adult gangs often form among those of economically and/or socially disadvantaged families living in the poorer areas of a community. They also seem to cluster along the major transportation corridors throughout a state in order to create favorable drug distribution networks. One of the primary activities of some street gangs is drug sales, and much of the violence between gangs is over the control of drug distribution.

Gangs fight each other over territory as well. There also are gangs formed along racial and even sectional-racial lines, such as the rivalries often found between two Hispanic gangs, those from the north and those from the south, or black gangs against white gangs.

Gangs have expanded their repertoire of crimes, as well, to broaden the threat they pose to the general community. Some gangs, particularly certain Asian gangs, specialize in extortion and home invasion robbery. The victims are often Asians themselves, many of whom do not trust the American institutions, such as banks and police. Other gangs specialize in carjacking, and still others in party-crashing robbery. The so-called Russian Mafia is becoming an increasing threat as well.

It is beyond the scope of this text to present all the details and complexities of the gang phenomena. Specific gang recognition characteristics and classification requirements will be provided to detention personnel in their various correctional academies. Suffice it to say here that gangs form primarily around racial lines, with the Hispanics forming two rival factions divided between those from the north and those from the south. The other basic rivalry is between the blacks and/or between blacks and the white supremacist gangs. Many subgroups have developed over the years from these primary gangs, all of which must be identified, classified, and usually separated during detention.

Separation for Inmate Safety

Several categories of prisoners are often separated from the main-line inmates because they might need protection from other prisoners. Besides rival gang members, these would include former peace officers and correctional officers who have been arrested, police informants, homosexuals, youthful and/or vulnerable prisoners, and certain sex offenders, such as child molesters, exploiters, or pornographers. This is particularly true if it is a high-profile case. A good example of this is Richard Allen Davis, who kidnapped, sexually assaulted, and murdered 12-year-old Polly Klass in northern California in October 1993. He required separation and protection in the county jail for nearly three years pending trial and now requires protection in San Quentin Prison, where he was received on death row in August 1996, because of the nature of his crime and the vulnerability of his victim. In addition to loathing his crime, many inmates blame him for provoking that state's legislature into enacting a *three-strikes* law because of the publicity and public attention his crime received. In fact, shortly after arriving at San Quentin, he was attacked by inmates while he was exercising in the small yard off of death row, right under the protection of a gun tower.

Other prisoners might require separation because they pose a threat to their own safety or the safety of others. These would include suicide risks, those with communicable diseases, such as AIDS and hepatitis, along with the injured or sick prisoners, those with mental disorders, and alcoholics or addicts who are detoxing.

Those who are physically or developmentally disabled also will need special classification and treatment.

If an arresting officer has any indication that a person he or she is booking might require special classification, he or she should immediately bring this to the attention of the booking intake staff for their consideration.

DETENTION SEARCHES

Patdown and Metal Detector Searches

These are the least intrusive searches performed by peace officers and are preferred in cases that present limited risk to officer or facility safety. Aside from the field patdown by a police officer, **patsearches** and **metal detector searches** are performed on misdemeanor and infraction offenders who are booked into jail but who will soon be released. They also are used in screening visitors to prisoners and private persons who will be touring a jail facility.

Strip and Body Cavity Searches

Most of the procedures designed to control the behavior of peace officers came into law as the result of isolated cases of serious abuses by a few officers or a pattern of complaints about some particular abuse. However, there were more than a few instances of abuse of prisoners, particularly female prisoners, when it came to requiring **strip** and/or **body cavity searches**. Apparently, some females were searched by males, while other males watched, and in some cases females would be searched then released.

In addition, some procedures violated state and federal constitutional rights to privacy and freedom from unreasonable searches and seizures. Just because a person is in jail, he or she does not lose his or her rights. Consequently, many states enacted laws to protect the rights of prisoners by establishing statewide policies placing strict limits on who can be searched and when.

In spite of all the state and federal procedural controls placed on strip searches, abuses by correctional staff have climbed dramatically during the past 20 years. In the usual case, the staff are male and the person ordered to strip is a female. In the year 2000, the city of New York, alone, paid out up to $50 million to settle lawsuits alleging improper searches in jails. Cities in other states are currently facing similar situations (Layman, McCampbell, and Moss, 2000).

TREATMENT OF PRISONERS BY PEACE OFFICERS

State penal codes provide for criminal penalties for any peace officer who mistreats a prisoner. Mistreatment usually includes the following:

- **inhumanity to prisoners**
- **assault by public officers**
- **cruel and unusual punishment**
- depriving a person of his or her rights under the color of authority

Examples of mistreatment and the legal consequence can be found in every state and at every level of corrections. For example, in January 1998, a criminal investigation was initiated in Los Angeles, California, involving several deputy sheriffs who allegedly arranged for certain jail inmates to beat other selected inmates charged with child molestation. Two deputies were suspended as of this writing and more suspensions are expected, along with criminal prosecution.

On February 26, 1998, eight correctional officers at the Corcoran State Prison in California were indicted by a federal grand jury on nine counts of conspiracy, civil rights violations, and deprivation of rights under color of authority that could result in life sentences for some of the officers, if convicted. It is alleged that they entertained themselves by arranging for rival prison gang members to be together in the exercise yard. Naturally, this resulted in fights between the rival inmates. Then as one officer was quoted as saying to another, "It's going to be duck hunting season." The officers shot and killed at least six inmates during these fights.

It was stated in the beginning of this chapter that custody staff have a moral, or ethical, as well as a legal responsibility to protect prisoners and to care for them because they are in the charge of the prisoners. The legal requirements are detailed in the law; the ethical responsibilities are derived from the professionalism of the job.

It is hoped that the personnel selection processes in all the states will strive to ensure employment of individuals who have the moral capacity to meet their responsibilities. Those who do not have this capacity face state prosecution for violating their state's penal code. In addition, they might well face federal prosecution for a violation of federal civil rights laws. They also will face civil liability for money damages, for both doing what is prohibited and not doing what is required.

WEAPONS CONTROL IN JAILS

Current law places specific limits on anyone bringing weapons into or possessing weapons in a custodial institution, including prisons, jails, road camps, or other facilities described in the law. The word "anyone" includes peace officers. Therefore, peace officers need to know the conditions that prohibit and allow them to bring weapons into a jail, and how to secure their weapons when they are not permitted to bring them in. Each state code will have one or more controlling sections.

Each police agency or detention facility also will have its own policy and procedure for securing weapons outside the custodial setting. Usually a jail will have secure lockers just outside the booking intake area in which police may lock their weapons. This includes their primary and backup guns, knives, and any other type of weapon. These could be locked in the trunk of the patrol car as well. The baton should be left inside the patrol car. Lockers are also provided in most cases inside the jail lobby area in which police detectives, private detectives, and others entering the jail by the front door may secure their weapons.

SUMMARY

The focus of this chapter has been the requirements of peace officers, either custodial staff or patrol officers, when dealing with persons in county detention facilities. It began with a look at jail populations and their increasing demands of bed space and institutional security. The booking process was described, including the responsibility of booking staff to validate the legality of the arrest and/or custody, medical pre-screening, and the rights of prisoners to phone calls and selected visits. The prohibition against police or detention personnel from soliciting for certain attorneys or bail bond people was discussed as well.

The requirements of classification were described and included classification by gender and class, by gang affiliation, and for inmate security. The types of detention searches were defined, and the law controlling body cavity searches was discussed. The treatment of prisoners was described within the specific laws that prohibit certain types of treatment, rather than any criteria that required certain treatment. This included inhumanity to prisoners, assault by a peace officer, and cruel and unusual punishment. The chapter concluded with an examination of the law controlling the possession of weapons within a detention facility.

This chapter stressed the point that prisoners, when in the custody of police and custody staff, are in their care. That carries with it the dual responsibility by staff to ensure the safety and protection of the prisoners, as well as the security of the facility. Compliance with all the legal requirements will keep them free from criminal prosecution and civil liability, and fulfillment of their ethical responsibilities will help to professionalize an important element of the justice system, the group of peace officers who work within local correctional facilities.

ISSUES FOR DISCUSSION

1. What purposes should county jails serve?
2. What rights and privileges should be given to those jail inmates awaiting trial?
3. How can we best balance the need for jail security with that of personal privacy when carrying out the various types of jail searches?
4. What are the important elements of inmate classification?
5. What constitutes inhumane treatment for jail inmates? Should there be a difference in treatment between those inmates awaiting trial and those sentenced?
6. What are the benefits and shortcomings of a cite-and-release program operating in a jail?

REFERENCES

Brennan, Tim, and James Austin. "Women in Jails: Classification Issues," Washington, D.C.: National Institute of Corrections, U. S. Department of Justice, 1997.

Collins, William C. "Jail and Prison Legal Issues: An Administrators' Guide," *Jail & Prison Legal Issues*. American Jail Association, 2005.

Kerle, Ken. "American Jails: There Is a Difference Between Jail and Prison, and It Matters," *American Jails*, 2005.

Layman, Elizabeth P., Susan W. McCampbell, and Andie Moss. "Sexual Misconduct in Corrections," *American Jails*, Nov./Dec. 2000, www.cipp.org/sexual/article2.html.

Nelson, William "Ray." "New Generation Jails," http://www.prop1.org/legal/prisons/97jails.htm.

Moore, Delancey H. "The Complexity of Jail Classification of Gang Members," *American Jails*, Mar./Apr. 1997, pp. 81–84.

Rowan, Joseph R. "Corrections in the 21st Century," *American Jails*, Mar./Apr. 1997, pp. 32–34.

INTERNET REFERENCES

http://www.ojp.usdoj.gov/bjs/jails.htm
http://www.texasescapes.com/Texas_architecture/TexasJails.htm
http://www.ojp.usdoj.gov/bjs/pubalp2.htm
http://www.vadoc.state.va.us/facilities/jails/default.htm
http://ourworld.cs.com/historicjails/index.htm?f=fs
http://www.corrections.com/aja/publications/index.shtml
http://www.corrections.com/index.aspx
http://www.corrections.com/aja/publications/magazine_about.shtml
http://www.therapeuticjustice.com/programPDFs/JAILS%20are%20not%20prisons.pdf

THE ADVERSARY SYSTEM
ROLES OF THE PROSECUTION AND DEFENSE

KEY TERMS AND CONCEPTS

Appointed counsel	Indigent
Complaint desk	Pretrial motions
Conflict attorney	Private counsel
Constitutional rights	Prosecuting attorney
Contract counsel system	Public defender
Count	Scottsboro Boys
Defense counsel	Self-representation
Discovery	Traditional prosecution
District attorney	Vertical prosecution
Enhancement	

INTRODUCTION

At the heart of our court process is the **adversary system** in which the prosecution and defense, having fair and equal access to the same resources and information, compete in open court to arrive at the legal truth in a case. It is a battle in which the prosecution represents the people of the state, and the defense represents the constitutional rights guaranteed to every individual.

This chapter begins by examining the role of a prosecutor and the manner in which cases are prosecuted. It concludes with a description of the various defense attorney systems used in the country. This includes a review of selected appellate cases that eventually insured that every individual, rich or poor, has adequate counsel for his or her defense.

THE PROSECUTION OF CRIMINAL CASES

The Prosecuting Attorney

Each county has a **prosecuting attorney**, known as the **district attorney** (DA), or county prosecutor, who usually is elected by the general public every four years. He or she is the only person with the legal authority to charge someone with a crime. His or her role is not just to prosecute criminal cases, but **to insure that justice is done** for the public he or she serves. Therefore, he or she is obligated not to charge a person unless the evidence is sufficient to warrant a trial. The district attorney has a weighty responsibility and a great deal of power.

The office of the district attorney is staffed by a number of deputy district attorneys (or deputy county attorneys), depending on the size of the office and the prosecution workload. Under the **traditional prosecution model**, each attorney is assigned to a specific duty within the department. For example, one might be assigned to a lower court to represent the State during all initial appearances by accused persons. Another attorney might conduct all preliminary examinations. Another might prosecute offenders in misdemeanor trials or handle all traffic matters, while another, more experienced, deputy might handle only felony trials. And yet another experienced deputy will be assigned to the complaint desk.

The deputy assigned to the **complaint desk** reads the police reports or reviews them with a liaison officer from the police department then makes several crucial decisions about each person arrested and against whom the police are requesting a complaint. First, he or she **decides whether to charge** the suspect with a crime. The deputy DA looks to see if the reporting officer has described the elements of a crime, if there is sufficient evidence to support a charge, and if the conduct of the officer was legal. Next, the DA **decides what to charge**: felony or misdemeanor; multiple counts; or, in some states, a Class A or Class B felony and so forth. Each separate crime charged is called a **count** and each count must be proven beyond a reasonable doubt.

Many crimes are punishable as either a felony or a misdemeanor, at the discretion of the DA. These are called **wobblers** because they wobble on the fence and fall on one side or the other as a result of the punishment given. In some states, a few crimes, such as petty theft, may be charged as either a misdemeanor or an infraction, at the discretion of the DA. Also, the DA needs to review the prior conviction record of the suspect to determine if that person has any priors that can be charged as **strikes**, a prior violent felony conviction, as defined in Chapter 1, or charged under some habitual offender law.

Enhancements

In addition to any crime charged, there might be sufficient aspects of the crime, or incidents in the prior record of the accused, to allow the DA to charge one or more **enhancements**, as defined in Chapter 1. In California, for example, if the crime meets the legal definition of a criminal street gang crime, the DA may charge it as a separate offense and, upon conviction of the crime, an extra term of one, two, or three years will be added as the enhancement.

If the accused carried a firearm on his or her person or in a vehicle during the commission of the gang crime, an additional enhancement can add one, two, or three more years to the sentence. If a person uses a firearm during the commission of any felony, the sentence can be enhanced by three, four, or 10 years.

Factors to Consider in Charging

In deciding whether to charge and what to charge, the DA considers the following factors:

- The sufficiency of the evidence
- The legality of the police officer's behavior
- The seriousness of the crime
- The wishes of the victim
- The risk posed to the public safety
- The sentiments in the community regarding the offense
- The potential punishment upon conviction and whether punishment is mandatory
- The person's role in the crime
- The offender's prior record
- The willingness of the accused to cooperate with the investigation or prosecution
- The motives of the complainant
- The impact of the trial on the victim, particularly if the victim is young

This is not an exhaustive list.

In some instances the DA will charge as many separate counts as he or she can find described in the police report, knowing full well that he or she does not have sufficient evidence to win a conviction, or that if convicted, the defendant could not be sentenced on all the charges. That way, he or she can drop some of the weaker counts as a part of a plea bargain and still end up with convictions on those charges that actually would have held up in court.

In some cases the DA can find several code violations to describe the same act. For example, if a person is arrested for possession of a loaded and concealed handgun in a town, the DA can charge two crimes: possession of a concealed firearm and possession of a loaded firearm within the city limits. However, since they both arise out of the same act, only one can receive punishment, regardless of whether both receive convictions.

A 1997 case in Port Washington, Wisconsin, demonstrates how the DA's disregard of community sentiments about a situation and/or his prosecution by the letter of the law rather than the spirit of the law, can rile and unify the community in opposition to him. Reportedly, an 18-year-old boy and his 15-year-old girlfriend from the community had a consensual sexual relationship and she became pregnant. They intended to marry and raise their child. The DA prosecuted him for the Wisconsin crime of "sexual assault on a child," punishable by up to 40 years in prison. The jury did not want to convict him but were led to believe that they had to if they followed the law, so they did. There was a strong public outcry against the prosecution and a plea for leniency in sentencing. On June 24, 1997, the boyfriend was granted two years probation and ordered to register as a sex offender. Now the defense will seek a pardon. Without a pardon, that sex offender registration order could last for the life of the defendant.

A similar situation faced the DA in Sonoma County, California. In Petaluma, the town still reeling over the abduction and murder of Polly Klass, a 24-year-old man and his fiancée were in an upstairs room of their house at about 8:00 p.m. on May 7, 1997, when they heard the sound of glass shattering downstairs. The man grabbed a baseball bat and went downstairs, where he found a burglar climbing in the broken kitchen window. He struck the man on the head with the bat, and as the man tried to escape, he chased and struck him at least three more times. In the meantime, the fiancée called the police.

When officers arrived, they found the bat-wielding young man standing guard, as it were, over the limp body of the alleged burglar. The burglar was taken to the hospital, where he was treated for a fractured skull and bleeding in his brain. He was unconscious for almost 40 hours. He recovered and was prosecuted on burglary charges, his third strike.

The police arrested the homeowner who hit the burglar on a charge of assault with a deadly weapon because he had become the aggressor when he chased the man trying to escape. The police investigation showed that the burglar had a long criminal record, including burglaries, and he had been paroled from the state prison in Vacaville, California, only four hours before his break-in and beating. He also had a blood-alcohol level of .21.

The homeowner claimed that he was defending his home and used force to detain the burglar for police. The people in the community called the man a hero and were outraged at his arrest and possible prosecution. The DA finally decided not to charge the man. He indicated that the arrest by police was based on probable cause, making it the proper action to take, but that he needed proof beyond a reasonable doubt to convict and that it was lacking in this case.

Traditional Versus Vertical Prosecution

Traditional prosecution, as it is used here, means the assignment of prosecutors to specific jobs throughout the court process, based on a function to fulfill. That is, one deputy DA is assigned to a complaint desk, another DA is assigned to handle the arraignment calendar, another DA handles the prelims, and so on. This is the common method the DA has of allocating resources, and these assignments might be for one to three years. This is the practice followed in most counties. The justification for this is, in part, the need to develop the expertise of a new attorney by having him or her begin with the least complex of cases and procedures and move to the more complex as one gains competence at each level.

Vertical prosecution is a relatively new method in which one deputy DA handles all the cases of a certain type from the point of filing the complaints or grand jury indictments all the way through to trial and sentencing. Jurisdictions are beginning to use this method in sensitive cases, such as child molestation or sexual assault. This also allows the victim to deal with only one prosecutor, with whom he or she can develop a rapport, and allows the prosecutor to develop an expertise in certain cases. County prosecutors are using this approach in other types of cases, such as career criminal prosecution, repeat sexual offender prosecution, street gang prosecution, and auto theft.

COUNSEL FOR THE DEFENSE

Role of a Defense Attorney

A defense attorney does not defend what his or her client did, nor what the client is accused of doing. In fact, the criminal charge against the accused is irrelevant to the responsibility of the defense attorney. He or she defends the **constitutional rights** of an accused person because every person has these same rights. That was one purpose in writing the Constitution in the first place, to protect the citizens against government actions that might illegally deprive them of their freedom.

We all have these rights, and the first thing anyone, even a police officer, will do when charged with a crime, is to obtain an attorney to protect those rights. In protecting the accused, it is the responsibility of the defense attorney to be certain that all the actions of the police, the court, and correctional personnel are legal. That is why they challenge the conduct of the police officer in every arrest and search, to test the legality of official conduct. This is the perspective taken by any good defense attorney. It is the only way he or she can do an effective job.

Every person accused of a crime has always had the right to an attorney, if he or she could afford one. But it is only recently that those who could not afford an attorney actually received the assistance of counsel.

It took more than 30 years, beginning in 1932, and several appellate decisions of the U.S. Supreme Court for those who could not afford an attorney to have one appointed. The discussion below first reviews four appellate cases from which right of **indigents** to appointed counsel was created. Following that, the chapter details four ways by which a person can be represented by an attorney. The chapter concludes with a summary of the most common motions a defense attorney makes in court and two motions made by a prosecutor.

The Right to Counsel Cases

The Scottsboro Boys   On March 25, 1931, nine young black men, ages 13 to 21 years; seven young white men; and two young white women were riding in the same freight car traveling across Alabama when a fight broke out. The white men were thrown off the train.

They immediately notified the sheriff, and, in addition to their assaults, claimed that the two white girls were raped. The train was stopped by a sheriff's posse in the small town of Paint Rock, Alabama, and the young black men were arrested. When mob violence seemed imminent, the National Guard was summoned for protection and sheriff's deputies loaded the nine men on to a flatbed truck and moved them to the Jackson County jail in Scottsboro, Alabama.

There the nine uneducated, illiterate, poor men were tried for the capital offense of rape, without the assistance of adequate counsel. On the first day of the trial, the judge did appoint a local lawyer, Milo Moody, to assist in their defense, but he had no preparation for the case. The nine were tried in groups of three, and it took three days to try and convict eight of the nine, even though medical testimony contradicted the girls' claims of rape. The judge declared a mistrial in the case of the 13-year-old. The eight convicted men, known as the **Scottsboro Boys**, were sentenced to death.

Their case immediately made national headlines and motivated several defense attorney organizations to step in on behalf of the convicted men. On appeal, their convictions were reversed (*Powell v. Alabama,* 1932), and the Supreme Court ruled that **an indigent is entitled to the appointment of free counsel in capital cases**. This was the first precedent to be set on the right to counsel.

The case was set for retrial in March 1933, with the assistance of counsel. The trials lasted more than five years because of a number of legal motions and complications. In the meantime, all nine men remained in the Jackson County jail. Finally, charges were dropped against five of the nine. The other four were tried, convicted, and sentenced to life in prison. Eventually, three were paroled and one escaped.

Years later, one of the girls recanted her story and admitted that it was a lie. The second girl went to her grave without changing her story. The Scottsboro Boys eventually were pardoned by Governor Wallace of Alabama, although not all were living at the time.

The Betts Case   In 1941 an out-of-work farm hand on county relief named Betts was indicted for robbery in the Circuit Court of Carroll County, Maryland. He was unable to afford an attorney, so he requested that counsel be appointed for him at arraignment. The judge denied his request and said that it was not the practice in Carroll County to appoint counsel for indigent defendants, except in prosecutions of capital cases.

Without waiving his asserted right to counsel, Betts pleaded not guilty and asked to be tried without a jury. At his request, witnesses were summoned on his behalf. Betts cross-examined the State's witnesses and presented his own. The latter gave testimony tending to establish an alibi. Although afforded the opportunity, Betts did not take the witness stand. The judge found him guilty and imposed a sentence of eight years.

He appealed, alleging that he had been deprived of the right to assistance of counsel guaranteed by the Sixth Amendment by virtue of the Fourteenth Amendment. His appeal was denied all the way through the state's appellate system and up to the U.S. Supreme Court. Justice Roberts issued the Supreme Court's opinion on June 1, 1942 (*Betts v. Brady*, 1942). The court held that:

> The Sixth Amendment of the national Constitution applies only to trials in federal courts. The due process clause of the Fourteenth Amendment does not incorporate, as such, the specific guarantees found in the Sixth Amendment.

Thus, Betts's conviction was upheld and he remained in prison to serve his sentence. Precedent was set by this case. Indigents accused of felonies in state courts did not have a constitutional right to appointed counsel, unless some **special circumstances** about the case, such as illiteracy or mental incompetence, would make **self-representation** unfair.

For the next 20 years, thousands of indigent defendants were convicted without the assistance of counsel and were sent to prison. And every time a conviction was appealed, the Supreme Court referred to *Betts* as precedent, and had to look for special circumstances if a conviction was to be reversed.

The Gideon Case   In 1963 the U.S. Supreme Court did an unusual thing. It completely reversed itself on the *Betts* precedent in the case of ***Gideon v. Wainwright***.

In 1960 Clarence Earl Gideon, a 48-year-old itinerant laborer from Hannibal, Missouri, was arrested and charged with breaking into the Bay Harbor Pool Room in Panama City, Florida, and stealing about $65 out of the coin-operated machines, as well as some beer, wine, and Coca-Cola. The charge was felony burglary. He requested an attorney, but the trial judge, Robert L. McCrary, Jr., refused based on existing practice and precedent. Gideon attempted to defend himself against the skills of prosecutor Bill Harris, but he was convicted and sentenced to a term of five years at the Union Correctional Institution in Raiford. Gideon appealed to the U.S. Supreme Court, in his own handwritten petition, with the help of Joe Peel, a former lawyer and city judge who was in Raiford serving time on a murder conviction.

The Supreme Court heard the case and announced its unanimous opinion on March 18, 1963. Justice Black wrote the opinion, stating that:

> The right of one charged with crime to counsel may not be deemed fundamental and essential to fair trials in some countries, but it is in ours. From the very beginning, our state and national constitutions and laws have laid great emphasis on procedural and substantive safeguards designed to assure fair trials before impartial tribunals in which every defendant stands equal before the law. This noble ideal cannot be realized if the poor man charged with crime has to face his accusers without a lawyer to assist him.

The Gideon decision made it mandatory that judges in state courts **appoint free counsel to indigents accused of felonies**. The Supreme Court stated that it ". . . was a fundamental right, essential to a fair trial."

Gideon's case was set for retrial before the original court in Panama City. The prosecutor, Bill Harris, offered a plea bargain whereby Gideon would plead guilty to the charge in return for a sentence of time served. His defense attorney, a local lawyer appointed to represent him named W. Fred Turner, suggested that he take the deal. Gideon refused and demanded a jury trial. With the assistance of Turner, he was found not guilty and the charges were dismissed. In fact, the testimony at the second trial showed that Gideon might have been framed by the man who testified at the first trial, Henry Cook, who claimed to have seen Gideon in the pool room when it was burglarized (*Daily Journal*, p. 22; Lewis).

The *Gideon* decision was made **retroactive**, which meant that the officials in every state had to review their prison records to determine who had been convicted without the help of an attorney. Anyone so convicted, and there were thousands, had to be either retried or released. Imagine the impact of this decision.

Gideon had one more brush with the law. He was arrested for vagrancy in Kentucky in 1965, claiming he had lost all his money on the Kentucky Derby. He spent one night in jail. He died in poverty, and as a family outcast, on January 18, 1972. He was buried in a pauper's grave, with a wooden marker, in Hannibal, Missouri, and not even the remaining members of his family who lived there attended his funeral. Ten years later, however, members of the American Civil Liberties Union (ACLU) felt that Gideon had made such a contribution to the livelihood of so many lawyers that on the 10th anniversary of his death, they collected funds from attorneys nationwide, erected a marble headstone at his grave site, and held a belated funeral service commemorating his contribution.

Many thought that the *Gideon* decision meant that anyone charged with a crime could have free counsel, but it actually included only accused felons. It took one more decision to fulfill the Sixth Amendment right.

The Argersinger Case   In 1969 another indigent in Florida, named Argersinger, was arrested and charged with possession of a concealable firearm, a misdemeanor punishable by a jail term of up to six months or a $1,000 fine. He was not informed of a right to an attorney at arraignment, and he pled guilty. He was given a 90-day jail sentence. He appealed his conviction, claiming that he had been denied his Sixth Amendment right to an attorney, even though he was released long before the appeal was ever argued. Justice Douglas wrote the Supreme Court's opinion (*Argersinger v. Hamlin*, 1972), which was released on June 12, 1972, and stated that:

> The right of an indigent defendant in a criminal trial to the assistance of counsel, which is guaranteed by the Sixth Amendment as made applicable to the States by the Fourteenth, is not governed by the classification of the offense or by whether or not a jury trial is required. **No accused may be deprived of his liberty as the result of any criminal prosecution, whether felony or misdemeanor, in which he was denied the assistance of counsel**.

The assistance of counsel, a right that people today take for granted, has been in practice for felons in all the states only since 1963, by *Gideon*, and finally in 1972, for all defendants who stand to lose their freedom, by *Argersinger*. That is not very long ago.

Those decisions not only gave indigents a new constitutional protection and released many convicted inmates from prisons and jails, it also created an immediate need for states to establish public defender systems and other appointed counsel methods.

TYPES OF DEFENSE REPRESENTATION

The defendant's first appearance in court, called the *arraignment*, is the point in the legal process where the Sixth Amendment right to an attorney attaches to the accused. That is, this is the point at which he or she is advised of the right to have an attorney to represent him or her. Of course, by that time many individuals have already hired attornies to represent them in court.

There are basically four types of **defense counsel** representations: private counsel, public defender, conflict attorney, and the contract counsel system. Each of these is examined below.

Private Counsel

Private counsel is an attorney chosen and paid for by a defendant who can afford one. Attorneys' fees vary, often with the reputation of the attorney for winning cases. Two or three hundred dollars an hour is not unusual. When one well-known and highly skilled attorney (who shall remain nameless) was asked by a prospective wealthy client what his fee would be to represent him in a murder case, the attorney replied, "Whatever you have."

Many attorneys have set fees relative to the nature of the case and how far through the system the case is likely to go.

Public Defender

The vast majority of defendants arraigned in criminal court cannot afford an attorney. After arraignment, when the judge asks the defendant if he or she wants an attorney, most of the defendants say, "Yes!" When the judge asks if he or she can afford one, the answer usually is, "No!" Therefore, the judge will appoint an attorney to represent the defendant.

A **public defender** is a county-paid attorney who represents defendants who cannot afford their own attorney. He or she is no better and no worse than a private attorney, although some public defenders have accumulated a negative reputation over the years. Frequently, the **appointed counsel** can represent the defendant more effectively because he or she works within the system and knows all the players and the processes, both formal and informal.

The main disadvantage of having a public defender is that he or she has very limited time to spend with the client, seemingly just a few minutes before court. Nevertheless, an experienced public defender has handled most every type of case and has heard most every explanation given by a suspect. Also, he or she knows what the going rate is for the crime charged, and knows best how to work with the judge and opposing DA.

Selecting an attorney is an individual matter. There are both excellent and incompetent attorneys in both private and public defense systems, just as there are good and poor levels of competence in any occupation. As a general rule, the public defender system is used in the following states: California, Colorado, Florida, Illinois, Louisiana, Minnesota, Missouri, Nevada, New Jersey, New York, Pennsylvania, Utah, Wisconsin, and Wyoming.

Contract Counsel System

In some sections of the country, we find the use of what is called the **contract counsel system**. This is a system used primarily in rural counties in which having a full-time public defender's office might be too expensive. In this system all appointed defense attorneys are private attorneys who work at the prevailing hourly rate when appointed, and there is no public defender's office. The indigents still receive free attorneys, and the counties save money by not having to pay employee benefits, retirement, and vacation time. This system is used primarily in Arizona, Idaho, Kentucky, New Mexico, Oregon, and Washington.

Self-Representation

The defendant may waive his or her right to counsel and represent him- or herself, which is called standing in *propria persona* (in one's own proper person), which is usually shortened to *pro per*. Originally, in a 1942 case, *Adams v. United States*, the U.S. Supreme Court held that if a defendant wanted to waive his or her right to counsel, the judge had to be satisfied that the defendant was capable of self-representation before a waiver could be accepted. However, in *Faretta v. California*, 1975, the U.S. Supreme Court ruled that when a defendant "knowingly and intelligently" waives his or her right to an attorney, he or she has a constitutional right to self-representation. The judge, however, may appoint a stand-by counsel to assist the defendant, to act as cocounsel, or to take over if self-representation is terminated (*McKaskle v. Wiggins*, 1984).

When a person is considering self-representation, he or she should heed the advice of Clarence Darrow, one of this country's great lawyers: "Anyone, even a lawyer, who defends himself has a fool for a client."

The Conflict Attorney

If two or more defendants are being prosecuted for the same crime, they cannot have the same attorney or even an attorney from the same office. There will always be a conflict of interest between codefendants.

Their roles and motives in the crime are different, and their backgrounds are different. Even husband and wife codefendants have differing interests in the outcome of their cases. Consequently, if the codefendants are indigent, the judge will appoint the public defender to represent one and a conflict attorney to represent the other. A **conflict attorney** is an attorney in private practice who is willing to be appointed to represent indigents at the prevailing county pay rate.

Many attorneys just starting out in practice accept this type of appointment because it gives them a steady income, experience in court, and visibility within the community as they attempt to develop their own paying clientele.

PRETRIAL MOTIONS

There are a number of **pretrial motions**, which are legal requests that are made before the trial actually begins or before the case reaches a settlement. Two of the most common ones, the motion for a **continuance** and to **suppress the evidence**, are discussed in the next chapter.

Motion for Discovery

An important motion that is almost always made is the motion for **discovery**. This is a request by one attorney to have copies or access to all the evidence in the possession of the opposing attorney.

Some states limit the use of discovery to the defense and do not allow it for the **prosecuting attorney**. The reasoning is that it is a necessary element of preparing a defense because one cannot possibly prepare a defense unless one knows what to defend against. In those states where victim advocate groups have had influence over legislation, the prosecution now has the right to discover what evidence the defense might use as long as it does not include any evidence that might tend to incriminate the defendant.

Present Sanity Motion

A motion to determine the present sanity of the defendant is made when the defense believes his or her client is insane and does not know what is happening to him or her and cannot participate in his or her own defense. It would not be fair to try a defendant in this condition. Psychiatric testimony is used to determine the present sanity, and it has no bearing on the mental state of the defendant at the time of the actual crime. If the defendant is found to be sane, the legal process continues. If found insane, the defendant is sent to a hospital until he or she is sane enough to return for trial.

Motion to Consolidate

If a defendant has several legal matters pending in different courts, the defense can make a **motion to consolidate** them all into one court proceeding. This saves time and money for everyone. And frequently, a defendant can work out a plea bargain with the court by agreeing to plead guilty to some of the charges if others are dismissed.

Motion for Severance

If the defendant is charged with multiple counts but wants a separate trial for each count, the defense can make a **motion to sever the counts**. This might be granted if the counts are unrelated as to type or the time in which they occurred. Similarly, if two or more defendants are to be tried for the same crime, their defense attorneys may make a **motion to sever the defendants**. Each will have a separate trial. That way only a limited amount of evidence, which is relevant to each specific defendant, will be presented at trial.

The Kelly-Frye Motion

If the defense wants to challenge the scientific basis for identifying the evidence, he or she can make what is called a Kelly-Frye motion. This is done when the defense claims that the scientific foundation of identifying some piece of physical evidence is faulty. DNA evidence was challenged in this manner when it was newly introduced into the courts (*People v. Kelly*, 1976).

The Pitchess Motion

This is a request to have access to the personnel file of the arresting officer. In cases that involve a charge of assault or battery against a peace officer or resisting arrest, the defense may make a **Pitchess motion**. This is done when the defense wants to show that the officer's conduct was overly aggressive and/or brutal and wants to substantiate this by showing that the officer has had a series of complaints of brutality against him or her. The judge will review the personnel file, determine the merits of any information it contains, and will allow the defense to have access only to the information relevant to the motion.

Change of Venue Motion

An important motion for the defense in cases that receive extensive pretrial publicity or incur the wrath of the community is a motion for a **change of venue**. This is a motion to change the location of the trial to some other venue (county). If the judge agrees that the defendant cannot receive a fair trial in the original venue, he or she will grant the motion, and the entire trial proceedings will be relocated to the new venue.

This can be an expensive proposition because all the expenses, including room and board for the prosecuting attorney and witnesses, must be paid by the charging county, not the host county.

Motion to Quash Inflammatory Evidence

This is derived from the evidence code in some states. It is a request to disallow the admission of certain inflammatory evidence, such as vivid photographs, that the defense thinks might unreasonably stir the emotions of a jury and result in an unfair trial. The judge will exclude these only if he or she is convinced that the jury would be biased against the defendant by viewing the questioned evidence. After all, the photographs, regardless of how inflammatory, usually convey a picture of what happened. They are not some out-of-context creations of the DA.

Motion to Compel Exemplars

There are a number of other legal motions that a defense attorney may make, but it is beyond the scope of this introductory text to include them all. However, the prosecution does have the opportunity to make one important motion called a **motion to compel exemplars**. This is a request to require the defendant to provide any and all nontestimonial samples of him- or herself, such as samples of voice, hair, semen, prints, blood, or photographs.

Obviously, if these exemplars match something found at the scene of a crime and incriminate the defendant, it will make conviction much easier. DNA matches are considered almost foolproof.

The taking of exemplars does not violate the defendant's Fifth Amendment protection from self-incrimination as long as it does not include any statements made by the defendant.

SUMMARY

As was stated in the beginning of this chapter, the responsibility of a prosecutor is to represent the people of his or her state and to see that justice is done. The prosecutor has a great deal of power in the justice system because he or she has complete say in the charging process. Many of the factors considered by a prosecutor when deciding who to charge and what to charge were listed, and a comparison was made between traditional prosecution and vertical prosecution.

The second portion of this chapter examined the role of a defense attorney. Every person accused of a crime has always had the right to an attorney. However, as mentioned, it took more than 30 years, beginning in 1932, and several appellate decisions of the U.S. Supreme Court for those who could not afford an attorney to have one appointed.

This chapter reviewed four appellate cases from which right of indigents to appointed counsel was created. We then examined three ways by which a person can be represented by an attorney, as well as self-representation. We concluded with a summary of the most common motions for a defense attorney along with the motion to compel exemplars usually made by the prosecutor. The stage is nearly set for the trial, but first we will study the array of pretrial procedures found in the next chapter.

ISSUES FOR DISCUSSION

1. Discuss the initial impact on the justice system of the *Gideon* and *Argersinger* cases. How do these cases impact the system now?
2. Should all defendants receive free appointment and use of a defense attorney at taxpayers' expense?
3. Discuss the types of defense representations. Which type is used predominantly in your area?
4. Compare and contrast the traditional and the vertical prosecution models. What are the advantages and disadvantages of each?

REFERENCES

Adversarial System, Wikipedia, the Free Encyclopedia, http://en.wikipedia.org/wiki/Adversarial_system.

Carter, Dan T. *Scottsboro: A Tragedy of the American South*, 2nd ed. Baton Rouge: Louisiana State University Press, 1984.

Cinetel Productions, (1998) "The Greatest Trials of All Time: Scottsboro Boys," (aired on *Court TV*).

Dixon, Brenda A. *The Adversary System: A Brief Philosophical Analysis*, (1998) http://mywebpages.comcast.net/badixon1/adversary.htm.

Dudley, Mark E. *Gideon v. Wainwright (1963): Right to Counsel*. Twenty-First Century, 1995.

Ingram, Jefferson L. *Criminal Procedures: Theory and Practice*. Prentice Hall, 2004.

Lewis, Anthony. *Gideon's Trumpet*. New York: Random House, 1964.

LIFE, "Scottsboro Boys Once More on Trial," (July 19, 1937).

Motion Practice in Criminal Cases: Pretrial Motions in Criminal Cases (2001) http://www.criminaldefense.homestead.com/MotionPractice.html.

Serious Criminal Defense, (2006) http://www.thebestdefense.com/criminalprocess/thecase/motions.html.

Sherrow, Victoria. *Gideon v. Wainwright: Free Legal Counsel*. Berkeley Heights, NJ: Enslow, 1995.

CASE DECISIONS

Adams v. United States, 317 U.S. 269 (1942)
Argersinger v. Hamlin, 407 U.S. 25 (1972)
Betts v. Brady, U.S. 445 (1945)
Faretta v. California, 422 U.S. 806 (1975)
Gideon v. Wainwright, 372 U.S. 335 (1963)
McKaskle v. Wiggins, 79 L.Ed 2d 122 (1984)
People v. Kelly, 17 Cal.3d 24 (1976)
Powell v. Alabama, 287 U.S. 45 (1932)

THE COURT STRUCTURE AND PRETRIAL PROCEDURES

KEY TERMS AND CONCEPTS

Accusatory pleading	Indictment
Appellate jurisdiction	Information
Arraignment	Justice Court
Arraignment calendar	Justice of the peace
Bail	Limited jurisdiction
Circuit court	Lower courts
Court consolidation model	Municipal court
Court of appeals	*Nolo contendre*
Deferred judgment	Own recognizance (OR)
District court	Preliminary hearing (PX)
Diversion	Preplea investigation and report
Dual plea	Preventive detention law
Enhancement	Probable cause
First-person hearsay	State supreme court
General jurisdiction	Superior court
Grand jury	Supervised OR
Held to answer	Suppression hearing

INTRODUCTION

Within the United States there are two distinct court structures: the federal courts and the state courts. These correspond to the one set of federal laws and federal justice system, and the fifty differing state laws and state justice systems.

This chapter begins with a brief description of the federal court structure then follows with a more detailed presentation of the state courts and pretrial proceedings at the state court level. The scope and jurisdiction of each court is detailed first so the reader will understand which of the procedures described in the balance of the chapter occur in which level of the courts. The remaining portions of the chapter include a summary of various alternatives to formal prosecution, the formal complaint and grand jury processes, the initial appearance of the accused person before the court, the preliminary screening process in felony cases, and the additional procedures followed in the preparation of a case for trial.

This latter portion also includes an examination of the procedure most often used to settle a case, plea bargaining.

THE FEDERAL COURTS

The U.S. Supreme Court

The U.S. Supreme Court is composed of nine members: eight associate justices and one chief justice. Vacancies on the Court are filled by an appointment by the president, with confirmation (approval) by the Senate. Once confirmed, a justice sits for life, or until he or she retires. They are beyond political control and they are not accountable to anyone for their work or their decisions.

The annual term of the Supreme Court begins on the first Monday of October and runs through sometime in July. Their primary responsibility is to exercise **judicial review** of state court decisions and state laws that are questioned by someone's appeal to them. They do not seek out cases to hear but wait for an appeal from some lower court that the justices believe presents some **significant constitutional issue**. They are selective and might agree to hear approximately 100 cases out of the several thousand that are appealed to them each year.

When someone wants to appeal a conviction, he or she prepares a Writ of *Certiorari*, a legal document requesting an appellate review of the case. The justices meet behind closed doors and vote on what cases they want to hear. It takes a vote of four to hear a case. The one who appealed and the opposing attorney, usually from some state attorney general's office, are notified. Each submits a written argument of their positions, which are supported by any prior cases they can find in which precedent was set. Then the case is scheduled for oral arguments before the Court in which each attorney has 30 minutes to present his or her position.

After the oral arguments, the justices meet, again behind closed doors, to discuss and vote for or against the appeal. Many of their decisions are not unanimous. A vote of 5 to 4 is sufficient for a binding decision. After the vote one justice is assigned to write the majority opinion, which is circulated and signed. When the decision is made public, it becomes law, or legal precedent.

The U.S. Courts of Appeals

The nation is divided into 12 judicial appellate districts, which include Guam, the Virgin Islands, the Northern Mariana Islands, and Puerto Rico. Cases from the federal trial courts within those regions are appealed directly to the respective court of appeal. In addition, these courts hear appeals from the various state courts within their regions that pose some constitutional issue.

There are approximately 165 appellate judges, who are appointed by the president with confirmation from the Senate and sit for life. They hear appeals in panels of three judges. Their decision is binding within the appellate district they serve, unless it is overturned by the U.S. Supreme Court. The decision by one appellate district in not binding outside of its own district, but it may be cited as precedent in some other appellate case.

The Federal Trial Courts

For purposes of federal trials, the nation and its territories are divided into 94 judicial districts. There are 650 judgeship positions within this court structure, but many are unfilled at this time because of political (philosophical) differences between the president, who appoints the judges, and the controlling party of the Senate, who confirms the appointments. A somewhat similar situation exists in the courts of appeals. Consequently, there is a heavy workload for each court.

This is the felony trial court for violations of all federal crimes. In addition to the judges, each district court has an assistant U.S. attorney and staff to prosecute the cases and a U.S. probation officer and staff to assist the court with investigations and the supervision of any offenders who are granted probation after conviction. These attorneys serve at the pleasure of the president, whereas the probation staff serve at the pleasure of the presiding federal judge in the court to which they are assigned.

There also is a lower trial court, called a U.S. magistrates court, within each district to serve as the trial court for any federal misdemeanors and to hear the preliminary matters in felony cases, such as arraignment, bail, and supervised release pending trial.

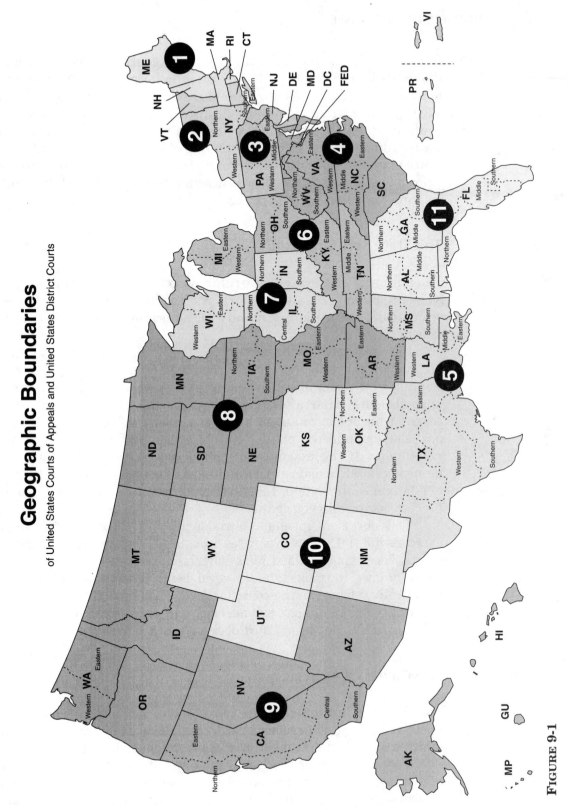

Geographic Boundaries

of United States Courts of Appeals and United States District Courts

FIGURE 9-1

137

THE STRUCTURE OF THE STATE COURTS

In most states the judicial authority of the courts is distributed among the courts in a four-tier court structure, similar to that of the federal system described above: a state supreme court, a first-level court of appeal, a felony trial court, and lower trial court for hearing misdemeanor and/or traffic cases and the preliminary matters in felony cases. This has been the traditional model since the founding of our country, although several states have devised more complex organizations. This traditional structure is examined below, followed by a description of an alternative structure emerging in several states, the consolidation model.

The State Supreme Court

The authority of a **state's supreme court** is the highest and its decisions are binding on all the courts within the state. The court consists of one chief justice and a number of associate justices, ranging from four to eight.

In most states judges are appointed by the governor as positions become vacant, and those appointments are confirmed by the state's senate or by a commission established to review and approve judicial appointments. Thereafter, depending on the state, appointees may serve for life or their names may be placed on the ballot at the next general election, and the public votes to either confirm or deny their appointments. If the appointment of a justice is confirmed, his or her name is placed periodically on the ballot for reconfirmation. If the voters deny a confirmation, the governor appoints someone else, and the process begins all over again.

The court is an appellate court, having **appellate jurisdiction**, that exercises judicial review over cases brought to it by appeals from the lower courts. These appeals must raise some issue relative to the state's constitution or laws. In some states, however, death penalty convictions are automatically referred to the court for review. This court does not have the authority to alter, amend, extend, or change any procedure or law established by a U.S. Supreme Court decision (*Fare v. Michael C.*, 1979).

The Courts of Appeals

The **court of appeals** (DCA) consists of a network of appellate districts and is located to serve a state's population centers and areas from which a substantial number of appeals are raised.

The appointment process to the court of appeals is similar to that of a state's supreme court, and the qualifications are the same as well. These courts primarily have appellate jurisdiction and hear the majority of cases on appeal from the felony trial courts within their districts.

GEORGIA COURT STRUCTURE

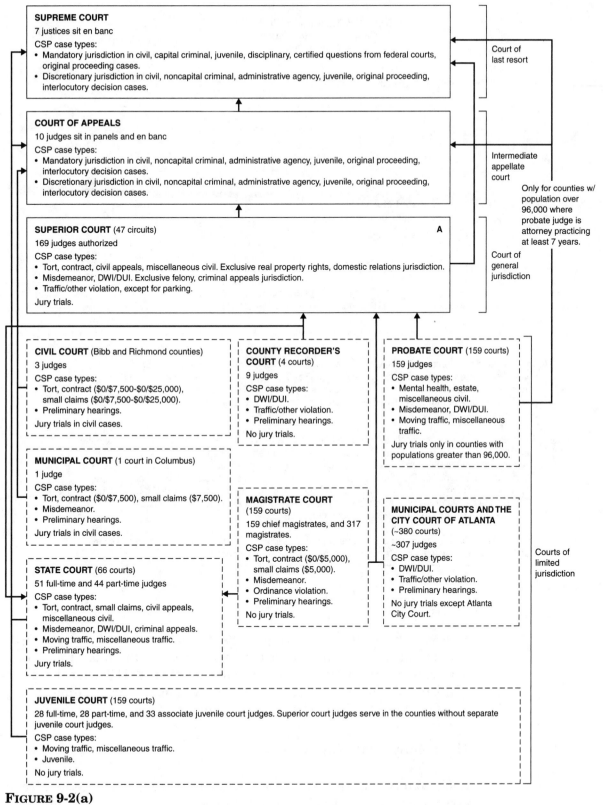

SUPREME COURT

7 justices sit en banc

CSP case types:
- Mandatory jurisdiction in civil, capital criminal, juvenile, disciplinary, certified questions from federal courts, original proceeding cases.
- Discretionary jurisdiction in civil, noncapital criminal, administrative agency, juvenile, original proceeding, interlocutory decision cases.

Court of last resort

COURT OF APPEALS

10 judges sit in panels and en banc

CSP case types:
- Mandatory jurisdiction in civil, noncapital criminal, administrative agency, juvenile, original proceeding, interlocutory decision cases.
- Discretionary jurisdiction in civil, noncapital criminal, administrative agency, juvenile, original proceeding, interlocutory decision cases.

Intermediate appellate court

Only for counties w/ population over 96,000 where probate judge is attorney practicing at least 7 years.

SUPERIOR COURT (47 circuits)   A

169 judges authorized

CSP case types:
- Tort, contract, civil appeals, miscellaneous civil. Exclusive real property rights, domestic relations jurisdiction.
- Misdemeanor, DWI/DUI. Exclusive felony, criminal appeals jurisdiction.
- Traffic/other violation, except for parking.

Jury trials.

Court of general jurisdiction

CIVIL COURT (Bibb and Richmond counties)

3 judges

CSP case types:
- Tort, contract ($0/$7,500-$0/$25,000), small claims ($0/$7,500-$0/$25,000).
- Preliminary hearings.

Jury trials in civil cases.

COUNTY RECORDER'S COURT (4 courts)

9 judges

CSP case types:
- DWI/DUI.
- Traffic/other violation.
- Preliminary hearings.

No jury trials.

PROBATE COURT (159 courts)

159 judges

CSP case types:
- Mental health, estate, miscellaneous civil.
- Misdemeanor, DWI/DUI.
- Moving traffic, miscellaneous traffic.

Jury trials only in counties with populations greater than 96,000.

MUNICIPAL COURT (1 court in Columbus)

1 judge

CSP case types:
- Tort, contract ($0/$7,500), small claims ($7,500).
- Misdemeanor.
- Preliminary hearings.

Jury trials in civil cases.

MAGISTRATE COURT (159 courts)

159 chief magistrates, and 317 magistrates.

CSP case types:
- Tort, contract ($0/$5,000), small claims ($5,000).
- Misdemeanor.
- Ordinance violation.
- Preliminary hearings.

No jury trials.

MUNICIPAL COURTS AND THE CITY COURT OF ATLANTA (~380 courts)

~307 judges

CSP case types:
- DWI/DUI.
- Traffic/other violation.
- Preliminary hearings.

No jury trials except Atlanta City Court.

Courts of limited jurisdiction

STATE COURT (66 courts)

51 full-time and 44 part-time judges

CSP case types:
- Tort, contract, small claims, civil appeals, miscellaneous civil.
- Misdemeanor, DWI/DUI, criminal appeals.
- Moving traffic, miscellaneous traffic.
- Preliminary hearings.

Jury trials.

JUVENILE COURT (159 courts)

28 full-time, 28 part-time, and 33 associate juvenile court judges. Superior court judges serve in the counties without separate juvenile court judges.

CSP case types:
- Moving traffic, miscellaneous traffic.
- Juvenile.

No jury trials.

FIGURE 9-2(a)

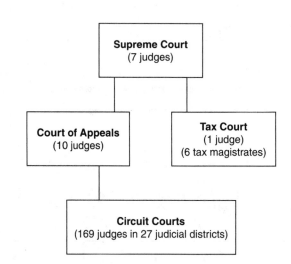

OREGON JUDICIAL DEPARTMENT
Court Jurisdiction Structure
(July 1, 2003)

The judges of the Supreme Court, Court of Appeals, and Tax Court are elected by voters in nonpartisan statewide elections for six-year terms. The judges of the circuit court are elected by voters in nonpartisan judicial district elections for six-year terms. There are 27 judicial districts, composed of one or more counties. The governor has authority to appoint judges to fill vacancies between general elections.

The 1981 Legislative Assembly consolidated Oregon's district courts, circuit courts, tax court, and the appellate courts into a unified, state-funded court system, effective January 1, 1983, known as the **Oregon Judicial Department**. Effective September 1, 1997, the legislature created a Tax Magistrate Division in the Oregon Tax Court to replace the administrative tax appeals structure formerly in the Department of Revenue. The tax magistrates are appointed by the Tax Court Judge. Effective January 15, 1998, the legislature abolished the district courts and merged their judges and jurisdiction with that of the circuit courts to form a single, unified trial-court level.

NOTE: Municipal, county, and justice courts continue as limited jurisdiction tribunals outside of the state-funded court system and are not subject to its administrative control.

FIGURE 9-2(b)

Cases are heard by a panel of justices. The panel's decision (the court's opinion) affects the specific case on appeal, and can be used as precedent within that district if the decision is published. However, decisions of the panels do not set statewide precedent and are not binding on any court outside of the district in which they are made.

The Felony Trial Courts

Each county within a state has a felony trial court, often called a **circuit court** or **superior court**. It is known as the court of **general jurisdiction** because it has the authority to hear any type of case, in-

NEW YORK COURT STRUCTURE

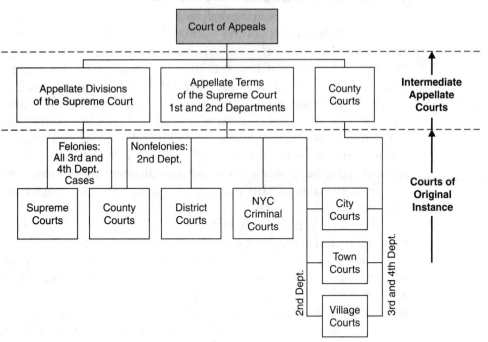

FIGURE 9-2(C)

cluding criminal, civil, juvenile, probate, or family matters. Each court may have a number of divisions and judges, depending on the case workload. This could vary from a single judge in some rural county to more than 300 judges in metropolitan areas.

Newly created judgeships and vacancies on any existing bench are filled in one of three ways:

1. By appointment of the governor or an appointment followed by a nonpartisan election
2. A partisan election process in which candidates are associated with a political party ticket and campaign
3. What is known as the *Missouri Plan*, in which a commission reviews the qualifications of selected individuals and refers the most qualified three to the governor for the final appointment

This last option tends to minimize the political nature of the judicial selection process.

In this text we are primarily concerned with the courts' jurisdiction in felony cases. However, these represent the least work done by these courts of general jurisdiction. For example, of the 1,000,000 cases filed in various superior courts within a state, approximately 150,000 will be criminal matters. This example might also serve to indicate why most attorneys practice some sort of civil law.

The Lower Trial Courts

In many states, each county (a parish in Louisiana) is divided into judicial districts according to population, and each district is authorized to have some form of lower trial court, having **limited jurisdiction**. These courts are known as **district courts**, **municipal courts**, or courts of common pleas, and hear both designated civil and criminal matters. They are often referred to as the people's court because they serve as small claims courts in which individuals can bring civil suits without the need for an attorney and without having to wade through a lot of legal paperwork. In some jurisdictions these **lower courts** are run by a **justice of the peace**, who often sits as a part-time judge in one district while working as an attorney in other districts.

The municipal, or district, court has original jurisdiction in all misdemeanor and infraction cases, both criminal and traffic. It also has jurisdiction in small civil suits and/or in small claims actions. The judge of this court also sits in the capacity of a judicial officer called a **magistrate** with the authority to preside over preliminary hearings in felony cases (discussed later in this chapter). Also in noncapital felony cases, when the defendant pleads guilty or no contest, the municipal court judge in some jurisdictions may preside at the sentencing hearing and may sentence the defendant.

As indicated above, the municipal, district, or **justice court** has limited jurisdiction in felony cases. Under the traditional two-tier model, the initial appearance and preliminary matters are conducted in the lower court; then the case is forwarded to superior court for trial.

The details of this process are presented later in this chapter. However, this two-tier trial model is gradually being replaced by a more efficient structure in which all courts are consolidated into one general court.

The Court Consolidation Model

The primary reason that counties have a two-tier court structure, with the jurisdiction of the lower court limited to hearing misdemeanors and felony prelims, is because that is the way it started. If one will refer back to the history of the court development under Henry I and Henry II, discussed in Chapter 1, it will become readily evident that very little has changed since that structure was developed in that time. In the past five years or so, the courts have been going through a reorganization at the administrative level to improve efficiency. Also, in many states, superior and municipal court judges are being cross-assigned. That is, judges at each level are being assigned to hear cases in the other level: lower court judges can hear superior court cases, and vice versa.

This **cross-assignment approach** has helped in reorganizing the work assignments, but it still leaves the two-tier structure, which many think is inefficient. Consequently, states are beginning to move toward an alternative model in which the lower court is abolished and all judicial jurisdiction is vested in a single circuit or superior court, with all judges having identical powers. This distributes the workload more evenly and allows each case to be heard and completed in the same court. Oregon is the latest to join this reform effort, as its **court consolidation model** became effective January 15, 1998. On that date district courts ceased to exist, leaving only the circuit court. District court judges became circuit court judges. Thus, Oregon became one of a dozen states to consolidate its court structure. Other states probably will soon follow.

For example, on June 2, 1998, the voters in California approved a senate constitution amendment that allowed each county to abolish the municipal courts, leaving only the superior courts to hear all the civil and criminal matters, provided that the judges in each county also approved it. The judges in most of the counties approved the consolidation within the first year. The last county, the County of Kings, unified its court system in January 2001.

THE ACCUSATORY PLEADINGS

The Complaint Process

An **accusatory pleading** is the generic name of any legal document used to charge a person with a crime. There are three basic types of pleadings that are used, depending on what state one is in and where the case is in the court process:

1. Complaint
2. Information
3. Indictment

Some states use the document called a **complaint**, in which a DA names the person being charged and describes the crime charged, along with any **enhancements**, and the date the alleged crime was committed. Both felony and misdemeanor complaints are filed in the lower court within 48 hours after the person is booked into jail. If the defendant is still in jail, he or she is brought into the lower court for the initial court appearance. If the defendant is out on **bail** or was cited and released, either by law enforcement at the crime scene or by the jail cite-and-release staff, he or she will appear in court on the date stated in the citation.

Some states do not follow the complaint process. Rather, the initial charging document is the indictment, which is filed with the grand jury (discussed below), a body of peers who will determine if sufficient evidence exists to have a trial.

Arraignment

The initial appearance of the defendant before the court is the **arraignment**. *To arraign* is a verb that can be conjugated like any other verb. Consequently, one can say that he will be arraigned, or has been arraigned, and the process of actually doing it is called *arraignment*.

Typically, one judge hears the **arraignment calendar**, which includes all the cases of defendants who will be arraigned that day. The judge calls each case in turn and arraigns the person called. *To arraign* means to call a defendant before the court and provide him or her a copy of the complaint, advise him or her of the charge(s) and maximum possible penalty allowed by law, and advise him or her of the right to have an attorney represent him or her at every stage of the proceedings. The defendant also is advised of his or her right to have an attorney appointed free, or at a nominal cost, if the defendant is indigent and cannot afford an attorney.

In misdemeanor cases the defendant need not personally appear and can have an attorney appear instead. However, in that case, the court will require the defendant to sign and file with the court a form titled "Waiver of Defendant's Personal Presence."

The Defendant's Response to the Charges

After arraignment, the defendant needs to respond to the charge(s). The defendant must enter a plea or refuse to plea and stand mute. In the latter event, the judge will enter a not-guilty plea and the matter will proceed.

A defendant may plead **guilty**, acknowledging full responsibility for the act and the outcome of what occurred. He or she may plead **not guilty**, which is denying responsibility for the act. Another plea, common in misdemeanor cases, is known by the Latin phrase ***nolo contendre***. This translates into a plea of **no contest**, in which the defendant neither admits nor denies responsibility but will not contest the charge and is willing to be sentenced as if he or she were guilty. This plea is used in cases in which a possible civil suit for money damages might arise. It separates the criminal from the civil matter, in that the judge may proceed to sentence the defendant, but any civil damages must be proven in a separate court on their own merits.

If a defendant claims insanity, he or she enters what is called a **dual plea**. In effect, the defendant enters a plea of not guilty and not guilty by reason of insanity. When one considers what is meant by these two pleas, it is like saying, "I didn't do it, but if I did, I'm not responsible." In this event there will be two trials. The first will determine if the defendant is guilty or not. If the verdict is not guilty, the charges are dismissed and no one cares about the issue of insanity. If the verdict is guilty, there will be a second trial, usually before the same jury, in which the defendant has the burden of proving he or she was insane at the moment the act was committed.

Other pleas available but rarely used are **once in jeopardy** and former judgment of conviction or acquittal of the offense charged. In making this plea, the defendant is claiming to have already been tried and acquitted of the same charges or charges arising out of the same act.

If the case is for a misdemeanor, every effort is made to settle it quickly. Even though we operate by the legal principle of innocent until proven guilty, one gets the feeling sitting in court that the judge and both attorneys sometimes work on the assumption that the defendant is guilty of something and will plead guilty if an attractive bargain can be found. It is rare to have a misdemeanor go to trial. They usually are continued for some further proceeding, diverted, or bargained down and settled quickly so the prosecutor's resources can be devoted to the more serious felony cases.

In these misdemeanor cases, the defendant might or might not have an attorney. However, a judge will not accept a plea of guilty unless he or she is satisfied that the defendant knows of all his or her rights, voluntarily waives them, and acknowledges that there is a factual basis for the plea.

An attorney usually is appointed or retained in a felony case because the consequences of a conviction might be serious. Typically, an attorney is appointed immediately after arraignment, and he or she assumes command of the case. He or she will **stipulate** to (agree to) proper arraignment, **waive time** for a speedy trial, and ask that the matter be set for the next stage, the preliminary hearing.

Bail and OR Investigations

When individuals are arrested by police and booked into jail, the first thing they want to do is get out. Some post bail and others use the bail bond system. Also, many jurisdictions operate some form of a **cite-and-release program** on a 24-hour basis, as described in Chapter 7, in order to reduce the jail population as much as possible. Consequently, many individuals come to their arraignment from their homes. However, there are a substantial number of defendants who cannot make bail and who do not qualify for cite and release.

Immediately after arraignment and the appointment of counsel in these cases, the attorney will make a motion to have his or her client released on what is termed **own recognizance (OR)**, or at least to have him or her released on a lower bail. Usually, the judge knows nothing about the defendant at this point and wants additional information about him or her in order to rule appropriately on the motion.

The proceedings will be continued for a day or two, and the matter will be referred to the county probation officer, who serves as the investigative arm of the court, for an **OR investigation** and report. A deputy probation officer working in the investigation unit will investigate the defendant's background and make a recommendation to the court as to how to rule on the defense's motion, based on the defendant's ties in the area, potential for harm to the victim or others, and the likelihood that he or she will return to court when required.

Based on the probation officer's recommendation, the judge may grant the motion for OR release, deny the motion but lower the bail, raise the bail, or order that the defendant be denied bail. This latter decision is derived from what is termed a **preventive detention law** in many states, by which the judge may deny bail if he or she has a reasonable belief that the defendant poses a threat to the community or will flee the jurisdiction of the court.

In recent years, the county jail populations in most states have increased to the point where there just is not any bed space left. And many counties simply cannot afford to build a new jail, given today's high construction costs. The populations inside the jails, which once represented the full range of offenders, from the hard core to the light weight, now are primarily the serious and violent offenders. Minor offenders are cited either by the police or by the jail's cite-and-release staff. In fact, in many cases some of the less violent serious offenders must be cited out to make room for the more violent. Consequently, there is a category of defendants, whose number is increasing, who cannot be fully trusted in the community but whose behavior is not serious or threatening enough to warrant complete detention.

In response to this, many jurisdictions have established a creative method of releasing these defendants from jail, pending trial, called **supervised OR**. These are offenders who are released without having to post bond, but they must agree to abide by certain conditions and supervision by the enforcement arm of the court, the probation officer, until their case has been settled. Conditions might include antinarcotic/drug testing, nonassociation with certain other individuals, restriction from certain locations, curfew, requirement to submit to search at any time, and any other condition that the judge or probation officer thinks is appropriate. A violation of any condition could result in the judge revoking the supervised OR status and ordering jail confinement.

This supervised OR will continue until the case is settled by trial or other means, which often will take months or more than a year. It is far cheaper to have one probation officer supervise 75 to 100 OR'ed defendants than it is to keep them housed in a jail. Whether the community is as safe is another question. It is a program that usually is money driven.

The officer supervising the OR'ed defendant often has a great deal of discretion in overlooking or holding accountable the defendant for violations of the court-imposed conditions. For example, one officer might overlook a dirty narcotic test now and again, whereas another officer might rearrest after the first dirty test. Or one officer might conduct searches of the offender and his or her residence or automobile on a regular basis, whereas another officer might not have the time or make the effort to search at all. In most jurisdictions there are no standards for supervision compliance, and officer discretion is the rule.

The Preliminary Hearing

In those states that use the complaint process rather than the grand jury, the law requires that a felony complaint be set for a **preliminary hearing (PX)** within two to 10 days after the initial arraignment. It is often referred to as a **prelim** or in it's abbreviated form, a **PX**. It is held in a lower, municipal, county, or justice court before a judge who serves in the capacity of, or uses the title of, magistrate during this proceeding. The use of this term is archaic now and will probably fade away through disuse.

The prelim is a **probable cause hearing** in which the DA must present just enough evidence to the judge to convince him or her that the evidence shows that a crime occurred and the accused probably did it.

Until recently, the victim of the crime usually had to testify in person in order to establish the elements of probable cause. Now, however, in many states a peace officer with several years of experience and who is directly involved in the investigation of the case may testify in place of the victim and state what the victim said to him or her. This is called **first-person hearsay** testimony because it is only once removed from the victim's own story.

This type of testimony has provided tremendous relief to young or otherwise vulnerable victims because they do not have to testify in court at this point. However, if the case goes to trial, the victim will have to testify because the Sixth Amendment guarantees that a defendant has the right to face his or her accuser. As we shall see, however, very few cases ever actually go to trial. In addition, if the victim does testify at the prelim and is under the age of 16 years, the judge may close the hearing to the press and public to protect the minor's reputation.

In establishing probable cause, the DA will present whatever physical and/or testimonial evidence is necessary but not all the evidence that is available. The defense attorney may cross-examine any of the state's witnesses and present witnesses on behalf of the defendant. Also, the defendant may waive the right to have a preliminary hearing and have the matter immediately certified to superior court for trial. This is seldom done, however, because the defense gains an opportunity to size up the DA's case and evaluate the witnesses and other evidence at the prelim. The prelim is the heart of any felony case, and this is where the defense will attack the conduct of the police in order to have the evidence suppressed.

The officer will be examined by the defense attorney at length as to the validity of any search warrant, the search and seizure of any evidence, the detention and/or arrest, and any interrogation in which the defendant might have given incriminating statements. As soon as the defense finds a piece of evidence that he or she thinks was obtained illegally, he or she will make a motion to suppress the evidence.

Sometimes the judge can rule on the motion immediately. Other times he or she will want the opposing attorneys to write and submit briefs (their argued positions on the motion, supported by any precedent-setting cases). If it appears that it will take time to decide on the motion, the judge can schedule the matter for a **suppression hearing**, which is a separate hearing just on the issue of the legality of the evidence.

Once the judge rules on the defense's motion to suppress, the prelim is resumed. If the evidence is suppressed, the DA might not be able to establish **probable cause**, and the case will be dismissed. If the evidence is admitted, the prelim will continue until both attorneys have presented their evidence and the judge rules whether there is probable cause.

If the judge finds that there is not sufficient evidence to establish probable cause, the case is dismissed. This is not the end of the case, necessarily, because if the DA obtains additional evidence, he or she often may initiate the process again by filing a new complaint. This is not double jeopardy because jeopardy attaches (begins) when the trial starts. If the judge does find probable cause, he or she holds the defendant to answer. The phrase ***held to answer*** means that the defendant's case will be certified to superior court and he or she will be bound over to that for trial.

The Information

As stated earlier in this chapter, an accusatory pleading was defined as the generic term for a legal document used to charge a person with a crime or crimes. The most common example of it is the complaint filed in municipal court that initiates the prosecution process. Once a felony case reaches superior court, however, a new charging document is used, the **information**. It looks like a complaint but has a different title and lists the crimes that the defendant was held to answer for at the preliminary hearing. These counts might be more, less, or different than the original counts in the complaint because the judge at the prelim might dismiss one or more counts or make other changes in the charges.

There is a time limit within which the information must be filed in superior court after the preliminary hearing. When a defendant is held to answer at a prelim, he or she will be advised of the date to appear in superior court. If he or she is still in jail, the detention staff will have a record of the court date and will bring him or her to the court. When the defendant appears in superior court for the first time, he or she is given a copy of the information and is arraigned on the new charging document. This means that he or she is advised of the charges again and of his or her rights at trial.

After arraignment, the defendant may enter a plea or may have the matter continued for further proceedings. Typically, at this point, the defendant is represented by an attorney, who will **waive time** for a speedy trial, enter a plea of not guilty, and make a motion for (ask for) a continuance, to continue the proceedings until some later date.

The word *continuance* is the most frequently uttered word in the court process. Many cases will be continued and continued for months or a year or two. Usually it is the defense who requests a continuance. It is to the defendant's advantage. Witnesses might forget what they saw or move or die. Any passions that might be aroused within the community over the crime will have had time to cool. And the attorney will have sufficient time to investigate the case and prepare a defense. Eventually, the case will be set for trial, but it probably will be settled without a trial.

The Grand Jury Process

By law in most states, every county must have a **grand jury**. The number of grand jurors that a county must have also is determined by law and can vary from nine in very small rural counties to as high as 23 jurors in counties having a large population. Some counties also may have a second grand jury at the discretion of the presiding superior court judge.

To be eligible to serve on a grand jury, a person usually must be a citizen, be over the age of 18 years, be a resident of the county for at least one year, possess a command of the English language, be of sound mind, be of ordinary intelligence, and be of an honest and fair character.

Grand jurors usually serve for a one-year term. In most states, the grand jury has two functions: a watchdog over county government and to hear evidence in criminal matters. However, some counties might have a separate grand jury for each function.

In the first function listed, its role is to investigate the actions of government agencies and officials to insure honesty in local government. In this capacity, the grand jury serves in an investigatory and advisory capacity and reports its findings, along with any recommendations, annually to the presiding judge and/or county board of supervisors for review and action, if warranted.

The second function of a grand jury is to serve as a panel that screens cases to determine if a trial is warranted. In some states, notably the eastern states, the law requires the prosecutor to use the grand jury process in every felony criminal matter. In these situations, they would bypass the complaint process, and the case would go directly to court for trial. This can be a costly and time-consuming requirement to fulfill. Some state laws provide for two grand juries: one to perform civil investigations and one to hear criminal matters.

In those states in which the use of the grand jury is not mandatory, the prosecutor has the discretion to use it. That is, if the DA does not want to prosecute a felony case by the traditional complaint–municipal court arraignment–preliminary hearing route, he or she may convene the grand jury for a **secret probable cause hearing**.

The only persons allowed to be present at a grand jury hearing are the prosecutor, the members of the grand jury, and those witnesses the DA wants to present. The defendant and his or her attorney are not present and might not even know that a criminal investigation is under way. If the DA convinces the grand jury that probable cause does exist to show that a crime occurred and that the suspected felon probably did it, the grand jury foreperson signs an accusatory pleading called an **indictment**.

The indictment is filed in superior court by the prosecutor and lists the charges and the name of the accused person. If the person is not yet in custody, a warrant will be issued for his or her arrest. When arrested or summoned by the DA to appear in superior court, the defendant is arraigned on the indictment, enters a plea, and the matter is set for trial or other proceedings. There is no prelim and no chance for the defense to view the prosecution's case, except through a motion for discovery.

The grand jury is a **secret process** conducted at the direction of the district attorney. And even though the Fifth Amendment to the Constitution guarantees that no person will be tried for an infamous crime without having the case screened first by a grand jury, an accused person has no control in how the prosecution will be initiated, by the traditional procedure or the grand jury in those states where the use of the grand jury is not mandatory. Actually, no defendant would ever want the grand jury process because it works entirely to the advantage of the prosecution. However, at the federal level, all felony crimes are charged through the indictment process. The defendant has no choice.

Nationwide there are about 1,100 federal grand juries, having 23 members. They meet twice a week unless cases require meeting more often, they meet in secret, and they are sworn to secrecy about their proceedings.

A person summoned to appear before the grand jury must testify and is not allowed to have an attorney or other advisor within the hearing room. As Nancy Panzke said when she was called to testify regarding her boss, former Representative Dan Rostenkowski, "You're trapped like a rat. . . . I kept having nightmares about it. (*Chicago Tribune*, February 19, 1998)."

The Preplea Referral

In some states at the request of the defense and after arraignment the judge may refer the matter to the probation department in either a felony or misdemeanor case for what is called a **preplea investigation and report**. Read the following definition carefully. It is a tentative and "iffy" procedure. The preplea referral is a temporary suspension of criminal proceedings and the referral to the probation department for an investigation into the background of the defendant to determine if he or she might make a good candidate for probation if convicted.

The probation officer assigned to the investigation reads over the police report, talks to the victim and any witnesses to determine what happened in the offense, then researches the defendant's background, including any prior record, to determine what type of character and potential the defendant has. He or she will interview the defendant in this process, but because it is "preplea" and the defendant retains his or her Fifth Amendment protection against self-incrimination, the probation officer may not ask the defendant what or why he or she did what is alleged in the complaint. They may not discuss the offense.

Based primarily on this character study, the probation officer recommends to the judge that if the defendant is convicted, the probation department will probably recommend that he or she either be granted probation, sentenced to jail or prison, fined, or any other appropriate sentence. In this manner, the defendant has a reasonably good idea what the likely sentence will be. If he or she is willing to accept the recommended sentence, he or she will then enter a plea of guilty. The case will then be rereferred to the probation department to complete the investigation and report, which includes a full discussion of the defendant's role in the crime. Thereafter, the probation officer makes a final recommendation to the judge as to the appropriate sentence.

This procedure works to the definite advantage of the defendant because he or she can learn what the probable sentence will be before having to plea to the charge. If the final recommendation or the judge's decision is different than the initial tentative one, and the defendant does not like it, he or she may withdraw his or her guilty plea, enter the new and different plea of not guilty, and ask that the matter proceed to trial. The State does gain a little time and money by this procedure if the defendant likes and accepts the final sentence without having a trial. Otherwise, the defendant is the benefactor, and it consumes a great deal of probation resources.

Plea Bargaining

The vast majority of criminal cases, from 90 to 96 percent, are settled without ever going to trial by the process known as **plea bargaining**. It is a negotiation process between the prosecution and defense (and sometimes, but not always, the judge) to settle the case without a trial, and to the best advantage of both sides, by a plea to some charge in return for some consideration. The types of possible bargains include, but are not limited to, the following:

- A plea to one count or more of a multiple count complaint, with the other counts dismissed
- A plea to some lesser but included offense (e.g., from grand theft to petty theft, from murder first to murder second or manslaughter, from driving under the influence of alcohol to a wet or dry reckless driving charge, from burglary first to burglary second, etc.)
- A plea to a charge with the enhancement(s) dismissed
- A plea to a misdemeanor, reduced from a felony charge
- A plea to some charge in return for a guaranteed sentence or immunity from prosecution

In whatever form the bargaining takes, the State (DA) obtains a conviction to something and the defendant usually receives less of a penalty than he or she otherwise would if convicted of all the original counts. The defendant must give up most of his or her Fifth and Sixth Amendment rights in the plea bargaining process because in pleading guilty or no contest, he or she agrees to waive the right to a trial and all its attending requirements, and to the protection against self-incrimination.

In fact, before the guilty plea is accepted in court, the parties will go through a litany in which the judge or DA advises the defendant of each and every right he or she is giving up, and the defendant acknowledges he or she understands these rights and freely and voluntarily waives them. Thereafter, the matter is set for a sentencing hearing.

ALTERNATIVES TO PROSECUTION

Diversion

It is expensive to process a defendant all the way through the system, especially if he or she wants a jury trial. Also, as the result of a criminal conviction, the defendant often ends up with this conviction on his or her record. To avoid spending the time, effort, and money to prosecute a case to its fullest, and to avoid a conviction record for certain types of offenders who deserve a second chance, the legislature created two alternatives to formal prosecution: **diversion** and **deferred judgment**. Diversion is defined as the temporary suspension of criminal proceedings and the referral of the defendant to some type of education, training, or treatment program.

The most common diversion program is **traffic school**, in which a person cited for a minor traffic offense attends several classes to learn about safe and defensive driving. Often this education type of program is conducted by either private vendors or local colleges, and the traffic violator pays a fee for the privilege of not going through the formal traffic (criminal) process. After completing the traffic school, the charge is dismissed and the person's record remains clear, providing the additional benefit of not having increased car insurance rates.

A second type of diversion is **drug diversion**. A defendant might qualify for diversion to a drug program approved by the district attorney if the drug or narcotic were for personal use, and if the following criteria are met:

- defendant has no prior drug charges
- the present crime did not involve violence or the threat of violence
- the present circumstances indicate that there is no related drug charge other than the one being considered for diversion
- defendant has not had any prior grant of probation or parole revoked
- defendant has not received drug diversion in the past five years
- defendant has no prior felony drug convictions in the past five years

Also, the defendant must waive time for a speedy trial when accepting diversion.

If a defendant is eligible for drug diversion, the matter usually is referred to the county probation department for screening and to coordinate the diversion. The diversion is for up to two years, and if the defendant successfully completes it, the court dismisses the charges and deems that the arrest never occurred.

However, if the defendant later applies for any peace officer job within five years, he or she must acknowledge the arrest and diversion. If the defendant does not successfully complete the program, the diversion is terminated, after a hearing, and criminal proceedings resume. However, any statements made to any justice system personnel or diversion staff that might tend to incriminate the defendant cannot be used against him or her if prosecution is resumed.

A third type of diversion is called **misdemeanor diversion**. This usually includes theft- or vice-related crimes wherein the defendant meets the same criteria mentioned above. Programs such as Project Intercept, for theft crimes, or prostitution diversion with AIDS counseling are the most common. Often these are six-month programs based on a fee determined by the defendant's ability to pay. Completion of the program results in the charges being dismissed.

Additional types of diversion include programs for mentally challenged defendants, for bad-check writers, and for parental diversion in cases in which the charge is contributing to the delinquency of a minor.

The purpose of these diversion programs is to settle as many cases as possible without having to go to the expense of a trial if they are the types of cases that would result in lenient treatment and/or probation anyway. The state saves time and money, and the defendant saves having a criminal conviction. The courts are so impacted today with cases that almost any creative way to expedite a case out of the system will be considered if justice can still be served.

Deferred Judgment Cases

This is a procedure similar to diversion; however, it occurs after conviction, and it includes those cases in which the defendant is charged with some type of abuse or molesting of a minor child. At the discretion of the district attorney, he or she may enter into an agreement with the defense in which the defendant admits to all the charges and enhancements in return for having the judgment (sentence) delayed and instead is referred to an approved counseling program.

On successful completion, the guilty plea is withdrawn and the charges are dismissed. The defendant would have to demonstrate a strong potential to change his or her behavior to persuade most DAs to consider this option, and long-term counseling usually would be made a condition of deferring the judgment. If the crime is within the family, both the defendant and victim may receive treatment of some type in an effort to reunify the family. Programs such as Parents United and Children United have demonstrated remarkable results in this regard.

A similar procedure is used in cases of domestic violence, which used to qualify for diversion. However, in many states the laws have changed and these cases can no longer be diverted. Now in most cases, they must follow the procedures in the deferred judgment process. This was done as another effort to intervene more effectively in domestic violence situations.

The primary justification for using these alternatives to formal prosecution is that they save the county time and money, allowing scarce resources to be used in more serious cases.

SUMMARY

This chapter began with a brief description of the federal court structure, followed by an overview of how most states structure their courts along the four-tier model. In many counties the two-tier structure is the traditional method of processing cases, but it is all but disappearing because the courts are being reorganized along more efficient lines by consolidating the jurisdictions of the courts into one court of general jurisdiction.

The prosecution of a defendant using the traditional complaint-arraignment-prelim process was presented in detail and was contrasted with that of using the grand jury. Alternatives to a formal prosecution were described, including various diversion programs and the deferred judgment law, as was the manner of settling most criminal matters without a trial by plea-bargaining. Procedures to reduce bail or have the defendant released on OR or supervised OR were discussed, as were the pleas that a defendant may enter and the alternatives to prosecution.

ISSUES FOR DISCUSSION

1. Discuss the differences and similarities of the accusatory pleadings: complaint, information, and indictment.
2. What are the advantages and disadvantages of using the grand jury process?
3. What are the advantages of the court consolidation model over the traditional two-tier structure?
4. Discuss the extent and process of plea bargaining. Is it an efficient way to expedite cases through the system or does it undermine the very nature of justice?

REFERENCES

del Carmen, Rolando V. *Criminal Procedure: Law and Practice*, 6th ed. Belmont, CA: Wadsworth, 2003.

Ferdico, John N. *Criminal Procedure for the Criminal Justice Professional*. Belmont, CA: Wadsworth, 2004.

Ingram, Jefferson L. *Criminal Procedures: Theory and Practice*. Prentice Hall, 2004.

Jacobs, Susan. *Case Studies in Criminal Procedure*. Prentice Hall, 2005.

Scheb, John M., and John M. Scheb, II. *Criminal Law and Procedure*, 4th ed. New York: Wadsworth, 2001.

INTERNET REFERENCES

http://www.ncsconline.org/D_KIS/info_court_web_sites.html (Provides access to various state court sites)

http://en.wikipedia.org/wiki/Image:Circuitmap.png

http://www.ncjrs.gov/app/topics/topic.aspx?topicid=22

http://www.law.cornell.edu/donors/solicit.php?http_referer=/supct/

CASE DECISION

Fare v. Michael C., 442 U.S. 707 (1979)

chapter *10*

TRIAL PROCEDURES

KEY TERMS AND CONCEPTS

Case-in-chief	Opening statement
Chain of evidence	Peremptory challenge
Change of venue	Physical evidence
Circumstantial evidence	Privileged communication
Confessional evidence	Scientific evidence
Cross-examination	Scientific jury selection
Direct evidence	Subpoena
Direct examination	*Subpoena duces tecum*
Gag order	Testimonial evidence
Hung jury	Transferred evidence
Indirect evidence	Venire list
Instrument of a crime	Venue
Jeopardy	*Voir dire*
Oath	

INTRODUCTION

A public myth has been created over the years by the media and entertainment industries about the nature of criminal proceedings and the extent to which cases are resolved by trial. As indicated in the previous chapter, relatively few cases ever go to trial. They are settled by a plea bargain. Nevertheless, many of the serious cases do go to trial, cases in which the defense has too much to lose from a conviction and the prosecution has too much to lose by bargaining.

The adversary system is still alive and well, particularly in serious cases. It is here that the two sides clash in battle, each using all the legal skills they possess, and from their contest the legal truth shall emerge.

This chapter presents the trial procedures, most of which are derived from a portion of the Sixth Amendment. We begin with a discussion of just what is a speedy and public trial, then examine the State's burden of proof in a criminal case, followed by a comparison of the relative advantages of a court trial and a jury trial. Next, the selection of jurors, by both the traditional method and a scientific selection process, is presented, as is the selection and preparation of witnesses. We also examine the issues surrounding the number of jurors used in a trial. People who have lived all their lives in a state where a jury is composed of 12 members tend to think that the same requirement applies elsewhere. It does not.

Once the jury is sworn and seated, jeopardy attaches to the defendant and the actual trial begins. We will examine the trial in two parts. This chapter presents the prosecution's side of the case. The defense's version of the case is discussed in the chapter that follows.

Because the State is charging an individual with a crime, the State (DA), must prove the individual guilty **beyond a reasonable doubt**. That means that the DA must present his or her side of the case first. This is called the prosecutor's **case-in-chief**.

TRIAL PREPARATION

A Speedy and Public Trial

A defendant who has entered a plea of not guilty to a misdemeanor charge has the right to have a trial within 30 days if he or she is confined in jail pending trial or 45 days if he or she is not confined. In a felony case, the defendant has the right to a trial within 5 to 60 days after arraignment in superior court on the information or indictment. However, in most cases, the defense attorney will **waive time**, meaning that he or she gives up that right for the defendant, and will ask that the trial date be continued until some future time.

This time waiver usually works to the advantage of the defense to delay the trial in a serious case until the emotions of the community have quieted, witnesses' memories have faded, and there has been ample opportunity to investigate the case and prepare an adequate defense. When the attorney waives time, the judge usually will explain to the defendant what that means and ask if the defendant joins in that waiver.

It is unfortunate that in many cases a long delay in bringing a case to trial works a hardship on the victim and on witnesses. This is particularly true in a homicide case. The family of the victim needs closure on the tragedy, which includes having the suspected killer of their loved one tried and, if convicted, punished. Delays work against this and keep the emotional wounds of the victim's family open for months or even years. Of course, the justice system was not established, nor is it maintained, to provide solace and satisfaction to the victim.

A **public trial** means just that, a trial where the State must prove its case against the accused in an open public forum, free from any government coercion, tricks, and schemes. In addition, members of the public are free to attend to be certain that justice is done in their community. A judge can order any pretrial proceeding closed to the public and even the press, if all parties to the case agree, to ensure a fair trial for the accused (*Gannett v. DePasquale*, 1979). However, the judge may not close an actual trial to either the press or the public.

The U.S. Supreme Court ruled in a 7-to-1 decision (*Richmond Newspapers v. Virginia*, 1980) that both the public and the press have an absolute constitutional (First Amendment) right to have access to a trial, and the openness of a trial is an indispensable part of American justice. Space may limit access by all the public who might want to attend, but a representative public will attend in any event. And, of course, the press will always be there.

Challenging the Judge

If a judge has personal knowledge about a case that might bias him or her, or has a personal, financial, or other interest in a case, he or she should disqualify him- or herself. Either attorney also may move to disqualify a judge for cause if he or she can convince the judge, or an appellate court, that the judge is biased. In addition, each attorney can exercise what is called a **peremptory challenge** of the judge's qualifications. This disqualifies a judge without having to provide a reason, and each attorney may exercise one peremptory challenge in each trial. This is a rare occurrence because most judges are fair minded and have the respect of the attorneys within their community.

The Selection of Jurors

Trial by a jury of one's peers is an integral part of our adversary system. However, the term *peers* can mean different things to each person. Does it mean a group of one's own age, gender, race, or status?

Legally, a jury of one's **peers** is a randomly selected group of qualified individuals from within the venue where the trial will be held. If one's own age or ethnic group or gender is not represented on the jury, yet the jury was randomly selected, it is a legal jury. However, it is not legal to deliberately exclude any one particular group.

The Venire List

The **venire list** is the list of individuals within a county who are eligible to be considered as **potential jurors**. In each county, a court administrator or jury commissioner mails out questionnaires to county residents whose names are taken from the list of registered voters and DMV records. The individuals complete the questionnaire, giving a few facts about themselves including their age, county of legal residence, any felony convictions, and claiming any hardships that they might incur by serving on a jury.

When a jury is needed, the jury commissioner or administrator randomly selects the number that might be needed to arrive at a panel of qualified individuals, plus several alternates, in the event that problems arise with one of the regular jurors during the trial. These potential jurors are sent a **summons**, commanding them to appear at the jury waiting room on a given date and time. Often a phone number is listed on the summons that may be called the night before the juror is to appear just to confirm that their appearance the next day is necessary. If not, it saves the juror from having to take a day off of work or other activities when his or her presence is not needed. Perhaps they will be asked to appear in another day or two.

The number actually summoned depends on the number a state requires on a jury, the nature of the case to be tried, and the length of time it will take. The summoned pool might range from 30 individuals for a simple burglary case to 500 or more for a serious homicide. Those summoned will arrive at the jury waiting room of the courthouse, all primed and ready to serve or else anxious to be excused for any reason. They soon will come to understand why it is called a waiting room.

The Jury Size

In many states, 12 jurors are required on a felony jury and any number from 6 to 12 on a misdemeanor jury, if all parties can agree to a number (*Patton v. United States*, 1930). However, it is rare that a defendant would agree to less than 12. Also, the U.S. Supreme Court has ruled (*Duncan v. Louisiana*, 1968) that the Sixth Amendment right to a trial by jury applies only to crimes in which the possible penalty is more than six months' incarceration. States are free, however, to provide juries in all criminal cases. This is an example of independent state grounds, where a defendant receives greater protection under the law in many states than is required by the Constitution.

Some states require 12 on a felony jury, but that number is not constitutionally required. They use 12 just because that is the way juries started in King Henry's time. States such as Florida, New York, Virginia, and Georgia have long used juries composed of less than 12. The first case to test the constitutionality of this was *Williams v. Florida*, 1970, when a bank robber named Williams was convicted by a jury of six and was sentenced to prison. The U.S. Supreme Court found through research that the practice of using 12 on a jury was the result of a historical accident. Consequently, the Court held that 12 jurors were not needed.

Although the Supreme Court ruled that 12 jurors were not needed, it did not say how many were required. By the mid-1970s, more than 30 states had reduced the size of their juries, many to as low as six. Georgia even went lower. Finally, the Supreme Court realized that a minimum limit was necessary and, in 1978, ruled that **six is the minimum** that a jury must have (*Ballew v. Georgia*, 1978). Today, the following states use a six-person jury in felony trials: Florida, Louisiana, Oregon, and Rhode Island. Utah and Arizona use 8, and the other states use 12. In misdemeanor trials the number varies among 6, 7, 8, or 12.

A strong argument can be made for the use of six on a jury. According to management theory, six is an ideal number for consensus decision making. Twelve can hardly agree on where to go for lunch. Those states that have reduced the size of their juries have found that the conviction rates have increased, there are fewer hung juries, it saves time and money, and there is less likelihood that the jury will have a dissenter or holdout. On the other hand, with smaller juries there is less likelihood of minority representation, fewer opinions to consider, and a smaller representation of the community at large, whereas the collective opinion of 12 is better informed and more thorough in its thinking and deliberation.

Those who favor 12 on a jury seem to have a defense orientation, whereas those who favor a six-person jury seem to have a prosecution orientation.

Qualifying the Jurors: The *Voir Dire* Process

Once the prospective jurors are called into a courtroom to be considered for the jury panel, the judge begins a process of qualifying who can serve as a fair and unbiased juror. First, the judge might explain to the potential jurors what the case is about, the names of all the parties involved in the presentation of the case, and approximately how long the trial will last. If anyone knows any of the parties or will suffer hardship by sitting on a jury for the time mentioned, he or she will be dismissed.

After this initial screening is completed, the court clerk will randomly draw numbers, perhaps out of a box, that match the numbers on the jurors' summons stubs. When the number called matches, the person walks up from the audience to sit in the jury box. Anywhere from six to 12 will be called to fill the jury box, and several alternates will be called as stand-by jurors.

When the jury box and alternate juror seats are filled, the real qualifying process begins, the questioning process called ***voir dire***. This term, formed by two French verbs meaning *to see* and *to tell*, which when loosely translated means *to understand and tell the truth*.

This is a process in which the judge asks each prospective juror a series of questions, depending on the nature of the case, in order to determine whether the individuals can be fair and unbiased in considering the evidence and can abide by his or her instructions on how to judge the evidence and the law in reaching a verdict. The two opposing attorneys either may submit questions for the judge to ask or they might be able to ask some questions directly of the prospective jurors, depending on the court and the policy of the judge.

Challenging the Prospective Juror

When the *voir dire* is over, each attorney in turn may **challenge** and excuse any of the potential jurors in two ways, similar to how they can challenge a judge. Each attorney may challenge and have the judge excuse any number of prospective jurors **for cause**. That is, any number can be challenged for demonstrating that they cannot be fair and unbiased, and cannot accept the adversary system of justice, with its attending protections against the accused, especially the defendant's right to remain silent. However, the attorney will have to convince the judge that his or her reasons for claiming bias, etc., are sound. In addition, each attorney may exercise a limited number of **peremptory challenges**, challenges without giving a reason. When a juror is challenged and excused, a new prospective juror is randomly chosen and subjected to *voir dire*.

The defense attorney also may challenge the entire jury and claim that the entire venire list has a bias against the defendant, usually because of some pretrial publicity. In this case, the defense would make a motion for a **change of venue**. The judge is well aware of the delicate balance between freedom of the press and a fair trial for the accused.

Attorneys frequently rely on hunches, experience, and old wives' tales about what makes a good jury in deciding who to challenge. In some cases an attorney will hire a jury watcher or jury consultant to assist is assessing the types of responses jurors make during the *voir dire*. In the past this left a great deal to chance and to gut feelings. Today a more sophisticated method is available.

The Gag Order

The judge cannot control the press because the First Amendment gives the press the right to freely investigate and publish the news.

However, the judge may control the information available to the press by issuing what is called a **gag order**, limiting the release of information by all the parties that have a legal role in the case (*Estes v. Texas*, 1965; *Sheppard v. Maxwell*, 1966; and *Rideau v. Louisiana*, 1963).

Scientific Jury Selection

The traditional method of selecting jurors is giving way to science. What is termed **scientific jury selection** is the use of some type of social science research method(s) to assess the attitudes of individuals within the venire list or within the community at large. Such methods include field interviews and/or questionnaires within the population at large, random surveys, or questionnaires given to a large portion of individuals from the venire list who are summoned as potential jurors.

The scientific selection method got its start in the mid-1970s in a small county in North Carolina. On January 15, 1974, a 20-year-old black woman named Joan Little and her younger brother were arrested for stealing $850 from two mobile homes, and were booked into the Beaufort County Jail in North Carolina. Both were charged with burglary. The brother worked out a plea bargain and was granted probation. She demanded a jury trial, was convicted, and was sentenced to prison for 7 to 10 years. She appealed and had to remain in jail pending her appeal. On her 81st night in jail, a 62-year-old white night jailer entered her cell, and she stabbed him 11 times with an ice pick, took his jail keys, and escaped. She turned herself in to the state police about a week later and was returned to Beaufort County to face trial on a charge of first-degree murder (Robin, p. 285).

The prosecutor claimed that she had the ice pick hidden in her cell, lured the jailer in on a pretext, then killed him. She claimed that he entered her cell, threatening her with the ice pick (which had come from the jail kitchen), and demanded sexual favors. She acted as though she were giving in; then at the right moment, in his heat of passion, the jailer dropped the ice pick. She picked it up and stabbed him in self-defense (Robin, p. 285).

The Joan Little case was an early *cause celebre* in the women's rights movement, and sympathetic individuals from around the nation responded with both moral and financial support. In fact, this writer can recall having students in the administration of justice classes, while teaching at California State University, San Jose, who collected and contributed to the Joan Little Defense Fund. These funds probably went to the Southern Poverty Law Center, the organization who helped fund her eight-member defense team, social science experts, and field interviewers. They raised substantial funds and hired several social science researchers from local universities and 70 interviewers to conduct public opinion surveys among the Beaufort County residents.

The survey results showed that most people had heard of the case because of extensive pretrial publicity and that they had already made up their minds. The survey also showed a strong racial bias against blacks in the community (Robin, p. 285). Armed with this information, the defense requested and was granted a change of **venue** to Wake County. There the team of social science researchers conducted another survey to assess the community attitudes and to attempt to develop a profile of a favorable juror. They hired 20 interviewers, who interviewed 954 potential jurors, collecting demographic information on them and asking questions to learn of their attitudes and activities.

These surveys did not show the racial bias that had existed in Beaufort County, so the venue was acceptable. However, their questions did reveal characteristics of favorable jurors for the defense and favorable jurors for the prosecution. Therefore, during the *voir dire*, which was conducted primarily by the attorneys, the defense team asked questions similar to those asked in the survey. When the responses matched those of a favorable juror, they did not use a challenge, but if the responses were unfavorable, they would exercise one of their peremptory challenges. Eventually, the jury was acceptable to both parties, and the trial continued.

Joan Little was found not guilty of any crime because the jury was not convinced by the circumstantial evidence that she was guilty beyond a reasonable doubt. Her defense team credited the scientific survey and jury selection process for the verdict. The cost of her defense was approximately $325,000 (Robin, p. 286).

From that humble but expensive beginning, the use of jury questionnaires has grown until today it is the common method in serious cases in which a large jury pool is needed to be certain that a fair and unbiased jury is selected. Instead of using private funds or allowing one side to have the advantage of the information gathered, a **standard questionnaire** is administered at county expense and completed by all those individuals summoned in a case, and both sides share in the results. However, each side can still use the information as a basis for further questioning in the *voir dire* process.

A recent example of this is the O. J. Simpson case in Los Angeles in which the jury questionnaire had 94 pages of questions and required about four hours to complete. Similar examples can be found in courts throughout the country. The uses of these questionnaires are still the same: to eliminate the obviously biased or unqualified individuals, to move for a change of venue if it is appropriate, and to attempt to select the most favorable jurors and challenge the unfavorable ones by asking questions from the information given in the answers.

A COURT TRIAL

The Sixth Amendment guarantees an accused person the right to a jury trial. However, there are times when it is in the best interests of the defendant not to have a jury trial, but to have the trial by a judge sitting alone. This is called a ***court trial***; the terms judge and court are used interchangeably within this context.

In situations where the accused faces heinous charges that might stir the emotions of individuals on a jury, or where they might find the defendant or his or her appearance offensive, the jury might find it difficult to render a fair verdict. Theoretically, a judge can rise above the emotions of a case and rule on the factual evidence and the law.

The defendant may waive his or her right to a jury (*Patton v. United States*, 1930) and proceed with a court trial if the prosecutor agrees to the waiver. Ironically, the U.S. Supreme Court has ruled that although the Constitution guarantees the accused the right to a trial by jury, it does not give him or her the right not to have a jury. Consequently, the DA must concur with the defendant's waiver (*Singer v. United States*, 1965). And the waiver must be made personally by the defendant in open court.

The importance of this personal waiver was pointed out in the results of an appeal in a northern California case in 1994. A defendant appeared in superior court for arraignment on an information charging two counts of second-degree (vehicular) homicide. The attorney waived his client's right to a jury, with the client standing alongside of him, and requested a court trial. The attorney affirmed this request at a later hearing, with the defendant again standing beside him. However, the defendant did not say a word in court, and the judge did not ask him if he personally agreed to the waiver.

The defendant was convicted and sentenced to prison for two terms of 15 years to life. Approximately five years later, on appeal, the state supreme court reversed the conviction because the waiver was not personally made in court by the defendant (*People v. Ernst*, 1994). Eventually he was recharged, but a plea bargain was arranged where the defendant pled guilty in exchange for a suspended sentence and four years' probation.

LET THE TRIAL BEGIN

It is not uncommon to have all the parties assembled and ready for trial only to have the attorneys agree to a last-minute plea bargain. The jurors are stunned, but they are thanked for their time and willingness to serve. If the trial does take place, it is the responsibility of the judge to control and orchestrate the events to ensure a fair trial, to rule on the admissibility of evidence or on the questioning practices of the attorneys, and to serve as arbitrator in disputes between the attorneys.

The prosecutor has the responsibility to prove the State's case **beyond a reasonable doubt**. It is the responsibility of the defense to challenge the presentation by the DA on his or her case every time there are questions of fairness or the rights of the client.

The Attachment of Jeopardy

In a court trial, **jeopardy** attaches when the first witness is sworn in and seated. In a jury trial, jeopardy attaches when the jury is sworn and seated. The phrase *jeopardy attaches* means that the defendant has been placed in a position of jeopardy at that moment, and the trial must continue to a conclusion. From that moment on, the defendant cannot be retried if the conclusion is a not guilty verdict. However, if proceedings are stopped at any time before jeopardy attaches to the defendant, proceedings against the accused usually may be resumed or renewed by a new complaint.

If the trial is stopped at the end because of what is termed a **hung jury**, a jury which cannot decide on a verdict, it is not considered to be a conclusion of the trial. A trial concludes only when there is a verdict. Consequently, the DA may refile the charges and the judge may start the trial over again with a new jury and not place the defendant in double jeopardy, as defined under the Fifth Amendment. Legally, it is single jeopardy over again.

The Prosecutor's Case-in-Chief

The prosecutor begins the presentation of the trial because it is the State that charged the defendant and it is the responsibility of the DA to prove that charge without the help of the defendant. If the DA fails to prove the State's side of the case, the matter may be dismissed without the defense ever having to present their side. The entire case presented by the prosecutor, including all the witnesses and other evidence, is called the **case-in-chief**.

A trial is similar to a college term paper. It is composed of three parts: the introduction, body, and conclusion. A term paper without a good introduction becomes a maze of meandering verbiage. Thus, a good introduction sets the jury's focus and thinking as to what will be shown in the body of the trial. The prosecutor begins his or her introduction, called an **opening statement**, or opening remarks, to the jury. This outlines the State's case and tells the jury what the DA thinks the evidence will show and how he or she intends to show it. The defense attorney may follow with his or her own opening statement, or he or she may wait until the DA has finished with the State's case.

The prosecutor attempts to prove the truth of the charges by the presentation of three types of evidence: physical, confessional, and testimonial.

Physical Evidence   **Physical evidence** refers to evidence that is physical in nature, such as solids or liquids, and includes bodies, blood, semen, bullets, empty shell casings, fingerprints, hair, writings, documents and records, photographs, and other tangible items such as weapons or stolen property. Some of these are known as **fruits of a crime**, such as the stolen property. Others are called the **instrument of a crime**, such as the item used to force open a door or window or the weapon used in an assault or homicide.

Another category of evidence is called **transferred evidence**. This includes any physical item left at the scene by the suspect, such as hair, blood, or semen, or any items removed from the scene, such as the stolen property, particles of material from a rug, or blood from the victim.

The careful collection, analysis, and preservation of any physical evidence is crucial in obtaining a conviction. Care must be taken to not break the **chain of evidence**, which means to break the continuity of its possession so as to cast doubt that the evidence in court, before the jury, is the same evidence taken at the scene or from the suspect and that it has not been tainted in any way. This also includes the care that must be given in lab analysis and the testimony used about it.

The DA usually will introduce the physical evidence into trial by the person who first obtained it, followed by the one who controlled it pending trial, and ending with the one who performed any analysis or testing of it to maintain the integrity of the evidence presented.

The prosecution would be barred from admitting any physical evidence that had been seized illegally, obtained in violation of the Exclusionary Rule and the Fourth Amendment, discussed at length in Chapter 3.

Confessional Evidence   **Confessional evidence** refers to any confessions or incriminating statements made by the defendant to peace officers during their investigation. Obviously, the Exclusionary Rule is an overlay used by the court in determining the legality of any confessions or admissions by the defendant. If statements were made while the defendant was in custody, the defendant must have been *Mirandized* before questioning.

If a confession is used as evidence when it should have been suppressed, it does not necessarily mean that the conviction is not valid or that the conviction will be reversed. On any appeal it will be up to the appellate court to determine whether the defendant would have been convicted anyway, regardless of the admissibility of the confession (*Arizona v. Fulminante*, 1991). If the appellate court is convinced that the defendant would have been convicted anyway, the use of the illegally obtained confession is called a harmless error, and the conviction need not be reversed. However, in light of the *Dickerson* decision, discussed in Chapter 6, the police interrogation without *Miranda* might constitute a violation of the defendant's constitutional rights and might also be a civil rights violation, making the officers libel in civil court. We will have to look to future appellate decisions to clarify the situation.

Testimonial Evidence   **Testimonial evidence** refers to the testimony given in court by witnesses. The term *witnesses* does not mean just those who witnessed the crime; there are two types of witnesses: expert witnesses and lay witnesses.

An **expert witness** is a person who has some special understanding or knowledge about a particular subject and/or aspect of the crime because of some special training or education in that subject. This includes such individuals as doctors, DNA experts, crime lab analysts, accident reconstruction specialists, and fingerprint and other forensic experts. These individuals may offer opinions and conclusions based on the facts of the evidence, and their opinions are considered to be evidence. However, the jury is advised that they are the ones who determine how much weight to give the opinions of any expert.

The judge will determine if the witness is to be considered an expert. One consideration will be whether the witness has ever testified as an expert in any other court. In addition, the opposing attorney may subject the witness to *voir dire*. That is, the attorney may question him or her as to the expertise he or she has by asking about education and/or training. Or the opposing attorney also may **stipulate** (agree to) that the witness is an expert.

A **lay witness** is a person who might have some knowledge about the events of the crime but has no special training or education in any aspect about which he or she will testify. Most witnesses are lay witnesses, including a majority of the police officers involved in the case. These witnesses may testify about what they have personal knowledge of by virtue of the five senses: what they heard, saw, tasted, touched, or smelled. They cannot offer opinions that would be beyond the common knowledge of a lay person.

Direct and Indirect Evidence   Evidence of any type may be placed into one of two additional categories: direct and indirect evidence. **Direct evidence** is evidence that directly proves a specific fact. **Indirect evidence** does not stand on its own as a relevant fact or truth. It requires the jury to make the connection between sets of facts or to logically infer that something probably is true. For example, if a man testifies that he saw the defendant coming out of his neighbor's house at 8:00 p.m. of the evening that the house was burglarized, it is direct evidence. It stands alone as a fact and directly puts the defendant at the scene of a burglary, leaving the house at a specific time.

When the fingerprint expert testifies that the prints he found on the outside rear door handle and on a glass in the kitchen sink match those of the defendant, it is indirect evidence in that the jury must infer or conclude that the defendant's prints must have been left at the scene that same evening, during the burglary.

Indirect evidence is also called **circumstantial evidence** because whether it is relevant to consider as evidence depends on the total circumstances in which it is included and considered. It requires the jury to infer the connection between it and some more tangible direct evidence.

Scientific Evidence   Science and technology have advanced at a rapid pace during the 20th and 21st centuries, particularly during the past 25 years. Today physical evidence can be collected and tested by methods that would have been impossible only a few years ago, resulting in **scientific evidence**. The newest scientific method for testing evidence, and the one about which there is still argument, concerns the reliability of DNA testing.

The analysis of a person's DNA can either place him or her at a crime scene or conclusively prove that he or she was not the offender by a method that only the analysts seem to understand. As of this writing, DNA analysis has helped free 82 inmates from prisons, many of whom had proclaimed their innocence for years.

The traditional standard for determining the reliability of any scientific method, known as the *Frye test* or *Kelly-Frye test* (*People v. Kelly*, 1976), was described initially more than 75 years ago in the decision *Frye v. United States*, 1923. The court stated that:

> Just when a scientific principle or discovery crosses the line between the experimental and demonstrable stages is difficult to define. Somewhere in this twilight zone the evidential force of the principle must be recognized, and while courts will go a long way in admitting expert testimony deduced from a well-recognized scientific principle or discovery, the thing from which the deduction is made must be sufficiently established to have gained general acceptance in the particular field in which it belongs.

The use of fingerprint analysis met that test many years ago. The use of a lie detector test has not, and probably never will, because it is the polygraph operator who interprets the results. The use of DNA print testing, though still questioned by some, apparently has crossed ". . . the line between the experimental and demonstrable stages . . ." and is fairly well accepted in most states.

Hypnotically Enhanced Memory as Evidence   The reliability of hypnotically enhanced memory is another area where even the so-called experts disagree. The issue seems to center around whether testimony given after hypnosis is really enhanced memory or memory created by the hypnotist or by the subject just to please the hypnotist. Some state courts have ruled that induced memory might be tainted; therefore, it is not reliable because the truth of it cannot be validated. If the defendant wants to testify at trial and has had his or her memory enhanced through hypnosis, he or she must be allowed to testify. Otherwise, it would deny him or her the right to testify on his or her own behalf (*Rock v. Arkansas*, 1987).

Enhanced memories can be very useful in situations where a witness saw a license plate or a person but just cannot recall. The vision is still there and can be recalled by hypnosis.

Viewing the Crime Scene

Viewing the Crime Scene   The members of the jury are instructed by the judge not to visit or view the crime scene on their own. In fact, they are not to receive any evidence on their own outside of the courtroom unless the judge directs them. If the judge thinks that the jury needs to view the actual crime scene in order to better understand the testimony of witnesses, the judge will arrange for all the jurors to view it together in the presence of the two attorneys, the defendant, and the judge.

Direct and Cross-Examination

Direct and Cross-Examination   The word *examination*, when used in this context, means questioning of a witness in court by an attorney. **Direct examination** is the questioning of a witness by the attorney who called the witness to help prove his or her side of the case. For example, when the prosecutor is attempting to prove the guilt of the defendant, he or she will call and question by direct examination such witnesses as the arresting police officer, the victim, and any eyewitnesses to the crime. When the opposing attorney questions the witnesses, it is called **cross-examination**. Therefore, when the defense attorney questions the victim or the police officer who arrested his or her client in order to show that his or her client is not guilty, it is cross-examination.

After one attorney completes his or her cross-examination of a witness, the other attorney may requestion his or her own witness. This is called *redirect*. Following that, the other attorney may requestion the witness by **recross**, and so it can go until the witness's testimony has been exhausted.

During direct examination an attorney may not ask what are called **leading questions**, questions in which the desired answer is stated or implied. It is assumed that this witness is friendly to the attorney and will cooperate because he or she was called to testify by that attorney. If that witness becomes uncooperative in answering the attorney's questions, the attorney may ask the judge to declare the person to be a hostile witness. Then the attorney may ask leading questions because that may be the only way to get that witness to testify. In addition, attorneys may ask leading questions during their cross-examinations.

Before any witness is allowed to take the stand, he or she will be sworn in as a witness. A witness may swear an **oath** before God that he or she will tell the truth or, if a witness prefers not to include God in the process, he or she may simply affirm that the testimony will be the truth. Some courts have even allowed witnesses to make up their own affirmation.

Witnesses are directed to come to court to testify by the use of a legal document that commands their appearance called a **subpoena**. Failure to respond to a subpoena is contempt of court. When an attorney wants to have the court command a witness to bring certain documents with him or her to court, the attorney has the court issue a ***subpoena duces tecum***, meaning *bring the documents*.

Objections to the Question   During the questioning of a witness by one attorney, the opposing attorney might challenge the admissibility of a particular question of the witness or the answer by the witness. The attorney does this by filing an objection with the court: "I object to that question, Your Honor."

The basis for making an objection might be that the question calls for a conclusion or opinion from a lay witness, is a leading question, has been ruled as inadmissible, or would call for hearsay information. **Hearsay information** is what a witness might have learned from another source but does not know firsthand. There are a few exceptions to this hearsay rule, such as a dying declaration by one person to another, certain business records, or a spontaneous statement made by the victim or some witness.

Each attorney might argue his or her positions on whether to allow the question or to admit the answer. Finally, the judge will rule on the objection. If the judge says, "I **sustain** the objection," it means that he or she agrees with the attorney who made the objection and the question may not be asked or answered. If it already had been answered, the judge will order that the answer be **stricken** from the record and will tell the jury to disregard it. Of course, the jury cannot disregard it because they heard it. However, they may not refer to it or use it in their deliberation over the guilt of the defendant.

If the judge does not agree with the attorney who made the objection and will allow the question and answer, the judge says, "I **overrule** the objection."

Privileged Communication   Not all testimony can be admitted at trial. Some individuals are protected by law against having to testify, even though they might know what happened. For example, the defendant is protected against having to testify by the Fifth Amendment to the Constitution. If the State accuses a person of a crime, the State must prove it without that person's help.

There are others who know the defendant and might have communicated with the defendant about the crime, but they do not have to testify because of what is termed **privileged communication**, a vestige from common law. They have a privileged relationship with the defendant and may not reveal anything they know about the matter. These privileged communication relationships include those between husband and wife, attorney and client, doctor and patient, therapist and patient, clergy and penitent, sexual assault victim and counselor, and domestic violence victim and counselor.

Conduct of the Jury As stated above, the jury may not receive any evidence or information outside of the courtroom. For example, in one case a petite female of 98 pounds was on trial for killing her husband by shooting him with his own Ruger .44-caliber magnum revolver, a large gun. The defense claimed that she did not have the strength to pull the trigger alone and that her husband was pulling the trigger during a struggle in which she was trying to defend herself, and the gun went off.

The jury was deadlocked in its deliberation, with some of them believing the defense's theory. However, one of the jurors, also a small and light-weight female, fired her husband's Ruger .44-caliber revolver and told the other jurors how easy it was. The verdict was a quick guilty, until the defense learned about her telling the jurors of her experience. The error was grounds for a new trial.

In addition, the jury must be attentive during the trial, must not hear or read about the case, must not discuss the case among themselves or with anyone else during the trial, and must not form any opinions as to the defendant's guilt until the jury begins its deliberation.

In some instances a judge will **sequester** a jury either during the entire trial or just during the jury's deliberation. To *sequester* a jury means to isolate them from outside influences, such as requiring them to return to a hotel room at the end of each day.

The Prosecution Rests This means that the prosecution has presented all his or her evidence and that the State's case is over. At this point the jury has heard only one side of the matter, the prosecution's case-in-chief. Also by this time, the defense has determined what would be the best defense strategy to counter what the prosecutor's evidence has shown.

SUMMARY

This chapter presented the trial procedures up to the point where the prosecution completed the presentation of his or her side of the case, the case-in-chief. We began with a discussion of just what is a speedy and public trial then examined the State's burden of proof in a criminal case followed by a comparison of the relative advantages of a court trial and a jury trial. Next, the selection of jurors, by both the traditional method and a scientific selection process, was presented, along with the selection and preparation of witnesses.

We also examined the issues surrounding the number of jurors used in a trial. People who have lived all their lives in a state where a jury is composed of 12 members tend to think that the same requirement applies elsewhere. It does not.

Once the jury is sworn and seated and the actual trial begins, the prosecution's version of the case is presented, along with all the evidence available to the DA. Following that, it is the defense's turn to represent the interests and rights of his or her client, as discussed in the chapter to follow.

ISSUES FOR DISCUSSION

1. What situations would justify a change of venue?
2. Discuss the differences between an expert witness and a lay witness.
3. Discuss what the ideal size of a jury would be to ensure a fair trial yet expedite the deliberation and decision on a verdict.
4. After the *voir dire*, what would justify dismissing a prospective juror for cause?
5. For what reasons might the prosecution and defense dismiss a prospective juror via a peremptory challenge?

REFERENCES

del Carmen, Rolando V. *Criminal Procedure: Law and Practice*, 6th ed. Belmont, CA: Wadsworth, 2003.

Ferdico, John N. *Criminal Procedure for the Criminal Justice Professional*. Belmont, CA: Wadsworth, 2004.

Ingram, Jefferson L. *Criminal Procedures: Theory & Practice*. Prentice Hall, 2004.

Jacobs, Susan. *Case Studies in Criminal Procedure*. Prentice Hall, 2005.

Robin, Gerald D. *Introduction to the Criminal Justice System*, 3rd ed. New York: Harper & Row, 1987.

Scheb, John M., and John M. Scheb II. *Criminal Law and Procedure*, 4th ed. New York: Wadsworth, 2001.

INTERNET REFERENCES

http://www.ncjrs.gov/

http://www.statelocalgov.net/index.cfm

http://www.hierosgamos.org/juryselect-serv.asp

http://www.juryduty.org/JuryDuty.htm

http://www.lawmall.com/criminal/

http://www.michiganprosecutor.org/Process.htm

http://www.in.gov/judiciary/rules/jury/index.html

CASE DECISIONS

Arizona v. Fulminante, 499 U.S. 279 (1991)

Ballew v. Georgia, 435 U.S. 223 (1978)

Duncan v. Louisiana, 391 U.S. 145 (1968)

Estes v. Texas, 381 U.S. 532 (1965)

Frye v. United States, 293 F. 1013 (D.C.Cir. 1923)

Patton v. United States, 281 U.S. 276 (1930)

People v. Ernst, 8 Cal 4th 441 (1994)

People v. Kelly, 17 Cal 3d 24 (1976)

Richmond Newspapers v. Virginia, 448 U.S. 555 (1980)

Rideau v. Louisiana, 373 U.S. 723 (1963)

Rock v. Arkansas, 483 U.S. 44 (1987)

Sheppard v. Maxwell, 384 U.S. 333 (1966)

Singer v. United States, 380 U.S. 24 (1965)

Williams v. Florida, 399 U.S. 78 (1970)

chapter 11

DEFENSE STRATEGIES AND TRIAL OUTCOMES

KEY TERMS AND CONCEPTS

Closing argument	Nonunanimous verdict
Defense strategies	Poll the jury
Deliberation	Prejudicial error
Direct verdict	Rebuttal
Hung jury	Unanimous verdict
Instructions to the jury	Verdict
Mistrial	

INTRODUCTION

The basic role of the defense attorney is to defend the constitutional rights of the accused, as described in Chapter 8. This is done by challenging the prosecution at every turn and forcing him or her to actually present enough legal evidence to prove the client guilty beyond a reasonable doubt. Every piece of evidence is challenged and each witness is cross-examined in an effort to test the strength of the State's case and the legality of the arrest and evidence-gathering processes.

Once the prosecution has rested his or her case, the defense attorney will counter the State's case by presenting some form of defense.

This chapter examines the various defense strategies used by the defense in that effort. It concludes with discussion of the verdict, including the issues of an unanimous versus a nonunanimous verdict.

DEFENSE STRATEGIES

There are three general categories of **defense strategies** discussed below, with several specific defenses under each category. However, before the defense attorney needs to present an active defense, it may make a motion to the court to dismiss the case, as follows.

A Motion for a Direct Verdict

The defense might believe that the evidence presented was not sufficient to prove his or her client guilty, or he or she might just want to test what the judge's thinking is about the sufficiency of the evidence. The defense may make a motion for a **direct verdict** (or **direct verdict of acquittal**, as it is also known), a motion for a **judgment of acquittal** by the judge. Before making such a motion, the attorney will either ask that the jury be excused or indicate to the judge what the motion will be; then the judge will excuse the jury.

The defense does not want the jury to hear what will occur during this process. In making this motion, the defense attorney is claiming that the prosecution did not present enough evidence to legally prove his or her client guilty, that the State did not make its case. Therefore, there is nothing to defend. The judge can respond with one of three rulings:

1. The judge can grant the motion, find the defendant not guilty, and dismiss the case. Obviously, this means that the judge agrees that the State did not prove its case.
2. The judge may reduce the crime to some lesser but included crime. This means that the state did not prove all the elements of the crime charged but did prove the elements of the lesser crime.
3. The judge may deny the motion and order the trial to continue.

In this last decision, the judge is in effect saying that the State did prove its case and that the defense attorney should prepare a defense. Obviously, the defense would not want the jury to know if this is the judge's thinking.

Not Guilty by the Evidence

This might be a strategy used by the defense when the State's case is based primarily on circumstantial evidence; there is no direct evidence or eyewitnesses to conclusively prove the matter or to connect the defendant with the crime. The defense might attempt to cast doubt on the State's argument and create **another reasonable explanation** for what occurred through the presentation of his or her own witnesses or through the cross-examination of the State's witnesses.

This strategy could also include the specific arguments that follow:

- The victim consented
- The defendant was framed
- Mistake in the identification of the suspect
- The defendant did not have guilty knowledge of a crime
- The defendant is of such good character

Guilty but to Some Lesser Charge

This is a strategy the defense might use when the direct evidence is strong and there is no doubt that a crime occurred and the defendant committed it. However, what did he or she really do? He or she did the act, but what he or she did does not fit the degree of the crime charged. It fits some **lesser crime**. As an example, a defendant charged with first-degree murder might admit to the killing but try to prove that it was in the heat of passion and lacked the specific intent of first degree.

If the defense is successful, it might substantially reduce the penalty the defendant will receive. And maybe that is the best that the defense can hope for.

Not Guilty Because of Legal Justification

In the two defense strategies discussed above, the defense often can succeed just by weakening the argument of the prosecution. However, under this third category, the defense must offer what is termed an *affirmative defense*; it must actually present a real defense and prove the justification.

This would be a situation in which the prosecution's evidence proved beyond the doubt of anyone that an act occurred and the defendant did it. However, the defense will attempt to prove that the defendant had a **legal right** to do what he or she did.

This would include the following:

- Self-defense
- Insanity
- Accident or misfortune
- Entrapment

- The defendant was acting under a threat or duress
- The defendant was unconscious of the act (through intoxication or a drug overdose induced by someone else) so as to not understand his or her own actions
- The defendant had a legal duty, privilege, or immunity

In this last example, a police officer or state correctional officer facing a homicide charge could argue that he or she had a legal right to shoot a person, or in the case of carrying a concealed weapon, a person could argue that he or she had a permit, had a fear of immediate harm, or other legal excuse.

It is beyond the scope of this text to discuss the juvenile justice system in any detail. Nevertheless, one aspect of it should be noted here. In theory, juveniles do not commit crimes; they commit delinquent acts.

In any juvenile case in which the minor is under the age of legal adulthood, as defined by a state's juvenile code, the minor will remain within the juvenile court's jurisdiction regardless of what type of offense he or she did. In these cases, however, the defense might be that the minor did not have the capacity to appreciate the nature and consequences of his or her act. The burden of proof is on the State to prove by clear and convincing evidence that the minor did have this capacity (*In re Manuel L.*, 1993).

In whatever defense the attorney uses, the process of presenting the witnesses and other evidence will be the same as it was during the case-in-chief.

Testimony by the Defendant

One of the most important decisions that the defense attorney must make is whether to put the defendant on the witness stand to testify in his or her own behalf. The defendant does not have to testify, and the prosecution is prohibited from making any comment to the jury if the defendant does not take the stand (*Griffin v. California*, 1965).

If the defense plans to put the defendant on the stand, the attorney must consider how the defendant's testimony will impact the jury. The defendant also will be available for cross-examination by the prosecutor, which will really test the facts given by the defendant.

If the defendant made any incriminating statements to police during their investigation that were ruled inadmissible because they were obtained in violation of *Miranda*, they may be used to impeach the defendant's story if what he or she says on the stand is different than what he or she told the police (*Harris v. New York*, 1971; *People v. May*, 1988). Consequently, a defense attorney must be certain that he or she is on solid ground before exposing the client to cross-examination.

CONCLUSIONS OF THE TRIAL

The Rebuttal

Once the defense has presented its side of the case and has rested, the prosecution may have another turn to convince the jury of its argument. The DA may present witnesses to rebut (counter) the version of the truth created by the defense. These witnesses may be cross-examined by the defense as well. Following that, the defense also may present **rebuttal** witnesses, which in turn may be cross-examined by the prosecution. Finally, when all the witnesses have been exhausted, literally, the trial is over.

The Closing Arguments

The **closing argument** is similar to the summary and conclusion of a term paper. It is the opportunity for each attorney to address the jury and to summarize what the evidence has shown. They will stress the strong points of their cases and draw attention to the weaknesses of their opponent's case. The prosecutor must be careful not to make what is termed a **prejudicial error** by stating something inadmissible that might prejudice the jury against the defendant.

For example, the prosecutor cannot mention the defendant's prior record, refer to him or her in repugnant terms, or say that he or she has personal knowledge of the defendant's guilt. If the prosecutor makes a prejudicial error and the defendant is found guilty, the defense has grounds for an appeal. On the other hand, if the defendant is found not guilty, nothing said by the defense attorney is appealable. Consequently, the defense has far greater latitude in wording his or her summary of what occurred.

Instructions to the Jury

The judge must explain to the jury what its responsibilities are. This includes giving them an explanation of the laws in the case, the elements of each possible crime that might be considered (the *corpus delicti*), and any other instructions requested by the attorneys. Specifically, the judge must give **instructions to the jury** on the laws that apply in any situation related to the defense theory offered during the trial. When there have been expert witnesses, the judge might clarify for the jury that just because someone is called an expert does not mean that what that person says is true.

The jury must decide how much weight to give to the testimony by any expert. In addition, the judge must instruct them on which side has the burden of proof and on what is meant by the phrase *beyond a reasonable doubt*.

The legal language of what constitutes reasonable doubt might not be clear to a lay person. Consequently, the judge should describe it in lay terms for the jurors because it does little to explain the concept. The clarity of the instructions of the judge are crucial to the jury's proper interpretation of the laws and the evidence. And improper or incomplete instructions could be the basis of a later appeal after conviction. Some states have realized how complex the legal language is for the average juror to understand and have revised their jury instruction to use plain, straightforward language. In some cases several hundred commonly used terms replaced the legaleze.

Jury Deliberation

In the discussion on jury selection, it was noted that several alternate jurors were selected in addition to the regular panel, in case a regular juror becomes ill or is disqualified from the jury for some reason. At the point in the proceedings where the jury sits alone in that closed room to deliberate on a verdict, the alternates cannot participate. Only the seated panel members deliberate. And they must deliberate until they reach a verdict or until they are sure that they cannot reach a verdict.

The jurors first select a foreperson by an informal election process. Then it is the responsibility of the jurors to review and weigh the evidence objectively, decide on the credibility of any testimonial evidence, and judge the facts within the limits of the law as explained to them by the judge.

There will be two possible results from the jury's **deliberation**. If a jury finds that it cannot reach a **verdict** because the jurors disagree on what the verdict should be, they will inform the judge. The judge probably will explain to the jury that they are a panel of reasonable people and that there is no reason to believe that any other chosen panel could make any better judgments. He or she will encourage the jury to continue its deliberation. If the jury absolutely cannot decide on a verdict, the judge will declare a **hung jury**, dismiss the jurors, and allow the DA to decide on whether to prosecute the case again with a new jury.

If the jury has reached a verdict, the judge is informed, and all the participants gather in the courtroom. When everyone is there and the judge is seated, the jury is brought into the room by the bailiff. The judge asks if the jury has reached a verdict, and the foreperson says, "Yes." Then the judge instructs the foreperson to hand the signed verdict to the bailiff, who hands it to the clerk, who hands it to the judge, who either reads it or hands it back to the clerk to read. In many courts the judge asks the defendant to rise and face the jury while he or she reads the verdict.

Once the verdict is read, the jurors think that their services are over. They deliberated in secret and let someone else tell the defendant what the verdict was. Now they are ready to go home. However, in many cases the attorneys have a surprise for them, one more procedure for them to complete.

Polling the Jury

Each attorney may **poll the jury**. This is a process in which an attorney faces each individual juror and asks the juror how he or she voted. The jurors must respond. The defense attorney is looking for some hesitation, some expression of doubt from a juror, something to indicate that the deliberation was not done legally or that duress was used to force a change of vote by some juror. Then the attorney will pursue that line of questioning.

If the attorney is able to find some irregularity in the deliberation or it is disclosed that the jury received information or evidence outside of the courtroom, it might be grounds for a **motion for a new trial**. If some irregularity is discovered during the trial, before the verdict is in, it would have been grounds for what is called a **mistrial**.

The prosecution probably will poll the jury in the case of a hung jury. The DA will want to know what the actual vote was in order to determine whether it is worth trying the case again. If a verdict is 11 to 1 for conviction, it might indicate that some holdout hung the jury. In that case the DA probably would recharge the defendant. However, if the verdict is 8 to 4 for acquittal, the DA knows that either the evidence was weak or his or her presentation was not adequate.

After the jury is polled and both attorneys are satisfied that the jury's services are no longer needed, the judge will dismiss the jury, commending them on how well they fulfilled their civic responsibility. In a guilty verdict case, the defense might follow the jurors out of the courtroom, hoping to speak with one or more of them, again seeking to find some irregularity in the deliberation process.

Unanimous Versus Nonunanimous Verdicts

Many people think that a **unanimous verdict** always is required in a criminal trial. It is required by the law in some states, but it is not required under any constitutional guidelines. In fact, the U.S. Supreme Court ruled in two cases (*Johnson v. Louisiana*, 1972, and *Apadoca v. Oregon*, 1972) that a unanimous verdict is not required to insure a fair trial for the accused. A verdict may be delivered by a three-fourths majority.

However, in a follow-up case (*Burch v. Louisiana*, 1979), the Supreme Court did rule that a unanimous verdict is required in nonpetty cases with a jury composed of only six persons. Nonpetty cases are those in which the possible penalty is longer than six months' incarceration.

The use of a **nonunanimous verdict** is still controversial because its use can discount the opinions of some jurors, and it also means that there is doubt in the minds of some jurors. Several states, such as Louisiana and Oregon, used nonunanimous verdicts before 1972, and others have adopted them since that date. Its use has shortened deliberations and resulted in an increased conviction rate. It also has saved counties money in jury and trial expenses. In addition, one could argue that since we live in a democracy where majority rules in the political arena, why not apply this to the legal arena? As an example of majority rule, the Supreme Court justices decided the *Johnson* case by a vote of 5 to 4. It would have been ironic if they had ruled to require a unanimous verdict by the same vote.

Another Motion for a Direct Verdict

After the verdict is in and if the verdict is guilty, the defense may make another motion for a direct verdict. As before, the defense is claiming that the State did not prove its case. In addition, the defense is claiming that the jury made an error of law in reaching its verdict. The judge, being the expert on how the law should be applied in the case, may make the same three rulings as were cited above in the discussion of a direct verdict.

The defense might make this motion just for the record, realizing full well that the trial judge will deny his or her motion. In this case the defense is thinking ahead toward an appeal, and the federal appellate courts will not hear a case on the issue of the sufficiency of the evidence to prove guilt unless the defense has made this motion during trial.

SUMMARY

This chapter focused initially on the strategies used by the defense in countering the prosecution's case-in-chief. Then the concluding aspects of a trial were discussed, including the deliberation by a jury; the verdict, both unanimous and nonunanimous; and polling of the jury by the attorneys.

The verdict in a criminal case is either guilty or not guilty. No one is ever found innocent because that means that he or she did not commit the crime. The jury has no way to determine that. The term *not guilty* means that the State did not prove that the person did it, a far cry from actual innocence. If the person is found not guilty, the matter is dismissed and everyone goes home. If the verdict is guilty, the case is set for the next stage in the proceedings, sentencing. That is the subject of the next chapter.

ISSUES FOR DISCUSSION

1. Discuss the three basic types of defense strategies and the various arguments that might be put forth under each. How do these fit within the context of the adversary system and the search for truth and justice?

2. Why do we have a jury system for a trial when a judge may independently grant a motion for a direct verdict, even after a jury has given its verdict?

3. What are the advantages and disadvantages of having a unanimous versus a nonunanimous verdict? Which would result in the most fair verdicts?

REFERENCES

del Carmen, Rolando V. *Criminal Procedure: Law and Practice*, 6th ed. Belmont, CA: Wadsworth, 2003.

Ferdico, John N. *Criminal Procedure for the Criminal Justice Professional*. Belmont, CA: Wadsworth, 2004.

Ingram, Jefferson L. *Criminal Procedures: Theory & Practice*. Prentice Hall, 2004.

Jacobs, Susan. *Case Studies in Criminal Procedure*. Prentice Hall, 2005.

Robin, Gerald D. *Introduction to the Criminal Justice System*, 3rd ed. New York: Harper & Row, 1987.

Scheb, John M., and John M. Scheb II. *Criminal Law and Procedure*, 4th ed. New York: Wadsworth, 2001.

INTERNET REFERENCES

http://www.crfc.org/americanjury/jury_deliberation.html

http://www.courts.state.wi.us/services/juror/docs/deliberate.pdf

http://www.nolo.com/article.cfm/objectID/07BA0993-2B75-48E6-8AD65D205B6A39CE/104/143/153/ART/

http://www.annals.org/cgi/content/full/126/5/389

http://www.in.gov/judiciary/rules/jury/index.html

http://en.wikipedia.org/wiki/Jury

CASE DECISIONS

Apadoca v. Oregon, 406 U.S. 404 (1972)

Burch v. Louisiana, 441 U.S. 130 (1979)

Griffin v. California, 380 U.S. 609 (1965)

Harris v. New York, 401 U.S. 222 (1971)

In re Manuel L., 11 CA 4th 529 (1993)

Johnson v. Louisiana, 406 U.S. 356 (1972)

People v. May, 44 CA 3d 309 (1988)

chapter 12

SENTENCING PROCEDURES AND ALTERNATIVES

KEY TERMS AND CONCEPTS

Aggravated term	Probation
Determinate Sentence Law	Punishment
Deterrence	Recidivism
Expungement	Recidivist
General deterrence	Rehabilitation
Incapacitation	Retribution
Indeterminate Sentence Law	Shock probation
Mandatory Sentence Law	Specific deterrence
Mitigated term	Straight probation
Presentence report	Victim impact statement
Presumptive term	Vindication

INTRODUCTION

This chapter deals exclusively with sentencing and the alternative procedures most commonly used. It includes the types of sentencing laws, sentencing options in both misdemeanor and felony cases, and the primary alternative to sentencing—probation. The roles of probation in the sentencing process, as well as in the procedural aspects of supervision, revocation, and honorable termination are detailed, as are the legal aspects of probation that affect police procedures. A brief summary of federal sentencing procedures is included as well.

THE SENTENCING PROCESS

The Goals of Sentencing

Sentencing is one of the most important functions of the justice system because it affects not only the punishment for the offender, but also the feelings of the victim and the safety of the community. There are three basic types of felony sentencing laws: mandatory, indeterminate, and determinate. Each is often related to a particular goal that the Legislature had in mind when it enacted a particular type of sentencing law. Sentencing in misdemeanor cases usually is limited to a fine and/or jail sentence. It might also include some sort of community service work.

The goals of sentencing include the following:

- **Incapacitation.** This means to neutralize the defendant's capacity to commit further crimes by imposing strict custody requirements and has the public safety as its primary concern.
- **Retribution.**   This is similar to revenge or the belief of an eye for an eye. The offender is made to pay harshly for the crime committed, and the victim often feels better, thinking that justice has been done.
- **Deterrence.**   This means to stop criminal behavior. This is further divided into **general deterrence**, which is the deterrent effect the punishment of an offender has on the general public at large, and **specific deterrence**, which is the deterrent effect that the punishment has on the specific defendant who is punished.
- **Rehabilitation.**   This means to effect a change on a person's attitude and/or conduct so that he or she changes from criminal to noncriminal behavior in some lasting way.
- **Vindication.** This means to make the law right, or to uphold or support the value of the law broken, by giving a sanction to one who violates the law.
- **Punishment.**   This is a just-desserts approach that seeks to punish each offender fairly and equally for the crime committed. Punishment usually is equated with years of prison time. It does not take into account any consequences that might result from the punishment time given.

SENTENCING LAWS

The Mandatory Sentence Law

The **Mandatory Sentence Law** is a type of law enacted by a state legislature or Congress in which specific sentences are mandated for certain crimes and no judge has any discretion. Or it could be a situation in which the legislature designates mandatory prison sentences for certain types of crimes and prohibits the judge from granting **probation** as an alternative.

The Indeterminate Sentence Law

Various states enacted the **Indeterminate Sentence Law** (ISL), which initiated parole into the community as an extension of the offender's sentence after serving some portion of it in prison. Both parole and the ISL were products of the reform model that entered American corrections in 1870, when it was first established by Zubalon Brockway, Warden at New York's Elmira Reformatory. This is not to say that parole originated in America. It had been in use in Australia, England, Ireland, and France long before it came to this country. Historically, parole has always been associated with some type of ISL, and the goal of both was **rehabilitation**.

This is a sentencing law in which the legislature sets a minimum and a maximum for the offender to serve, and a parole board conducts an annual review of the inmate's progress toward rehabilitation to determine when the optimum time is for his or her release. For example, a sentence might be from 5 years to life or 1 to 10 years. Somewhere within those limits, the offender knew he or she could get parole when he or she was rehabilitated. If an offender was kept too long, he or she might become bitter and angry. If released too soon, he or she might not yet be rehabilitated.

The use of this law created a great deal of disparity (wide differences in the time individuals served for the same crime), and did not prove effective in the rehabilitative process. Approximately 70 percent of those released returned to crime within a two-year period. **Recidivism** is the return to crime by a person released from prison, and the person who fails and returns to prison is a **recidivist**.

During the 1970s there were many individuals and groups criticizing the ISL and attempting to enact a replacement law. They represented a wide spectrum of interests: conservative law makers, law-and-order lobbyists, and members of humanist organizations, such as the American Friends Society (Quakers), all calling for the abolition of the ISL. The conservatives wanted longer prison terms, while the Quakers wanted fair and equal punishment.

By the mid-1970s their influence, combined with the strong punitive feelings within state governments and an increasingly punitive public, to abolish the ISL and enact its replacement, the Determinate Sentence Law. Maine was first state to act, followed by California and a majority of other states. Maine also abolished parole, but no other state did. However, the ISL is still used in the states of Alabama, Alaska, Connecticut, Georgia, Missouri, Nevada, Massachusetts, Ohio, Oklahoma, South Carolina, South Dakota, and Vermont. And its use is returning in some states, such as California, for certain serious crimes.

The Determinate Sentence Law

The **two primary goals** of the **Determinate Sentence Law** (DSL) were a punishment for each crime in proportion to the seriousness of it and the elimination of the **disparity** in sentencing.

These laws were enacted because the legislatures and the governors had given up on the ideal of rehabilitation. They concluded that the only thing one can accomplish for certain is to take away some years from a person's life. That we can do well.

The DSL applies to felony sentencing and equates punishment with time, time out of a person's life, without any regard for the results of what occurs to the person during that time. However, 98 percent of all those sent to prison return some day to the community, and the public would be safer if they came back better instead of worse.

The laws vary to some extent between the states, but basically, the legislatures have provided three specific times that a convicted felon may serve, and the sentencing judge chooses the most appropriate time after conducting a hearing and considering all the relevant factors.

The middle time (or term) is called the **presumptive term** because it is presumed that the judge will impose the middle term if everything else is equal. The upper time is called the **aggravated term** because the judge may impose it if there are factors about the crime or the role of the defendant that make it aggravated. The lower time is called the **mitigated term** because the judge may impose it if there are factors about the crime or role of the criminal that make it less serious than the average.

It would be interesting for the reader to refer to the penal codes within his or her own state to compare what any given felony sentence is today with what is was 20 years ago.

Needless to say, the prison times have changed dramatically, especially the maximum number of years; they have increased in most states. In addition, under the DSL, parole eligibility is no longer connected to the sentence. Now all one needs to do is to serve the time, and release is automatic and in many states cannot be denied, regardless of attitude or intentions. In addition, there are work-time laws that allows an inmate to earn one day or more off his or her sentence for each day worked, and everyone is given the opportunity to work. Participation in educational or vocational programs usually is equated with working for purposes of earning half-time off of a sentence.

THE PRE-SENTENCING PROCESS

After a felony conviction, either by verdict or plea, the matter is set for sentencing at some later date, often four to six weeks from the date of the verdict. During the time between the verdict and sentencing, the case is referred by the court to the probation department for an investigation and report as to the proper sentence. Often this is termed a PSI, for **presentence investigation**, or an RPO, for a report of the probation officer.

The Presentence Report

The probation officer and his or her deputies serve as both the investigative and enforcement arms of the court. When a felon has been referred for the sentencing investigation, the case is assigned to one of the deputy probation officers who works in the investigation unit. This assignment usually is given to the deputy who has investigated the fewest cases so far during the month. This keeps the workload even.

The probation officer will conduct a thorough investigation into the nature of the crime; the role of the defendant and codefendants, if any; and the social and personal life of the defendant. Any and all the significant information collected by the probation officer is summarized in what is called a **presentence report**. The report contains the details about the offense; the defendant's statement as to his or her role in it and motives for it; **victim impact statement**; an assessment of the prior record, if any; and the potential of the defendant to reform.

This is one of the most important documents filed with the court. Since the judge knows nothing about those 90 percent (plus) of the cases that are convicted by plea bargain, he or she must rely on the RPO to provide all the relevant information on which to base a sentence. The information also will be used later, either in developing a plan for probation supervision or for prison classification. It will be considered later in determining parole conditions and perhaps much later in preparing any subsequent presentence reports if the defendant reoffends.

In many states the law requires an RPO in felony cases and makes it discretionary in misdemeanor cases. However, most probation departments are too busy and overworked with felony matters to have the time to deal with misdemeanor investigations.

The probation officer evaluates the case to determine if the defendant is eligible for probation and, if so, whether he or she will make a good candidate for probation. If so and if the probation officer recommends probation, he or she will include a list of the terms and conditions that he or she thinks should be made a part of the probation order. If the defendant is not eligible for or deserving of probation, the probation officer will recommend whatever sentence is legally required and/or appropriate in the case.

The probation officer also might include in the RPO an assessment of the defendant's ability to repay any of the cost of any appointed counsel services, any restitution to the victim or the state's restitution fund, and/or in some states a victim penalty assessment fund and the cost of his or her own presentence investigation. The probation officer also must advise the victims of the hearing date, and usually the victims will be allowed to personally address the court as to the impact the crime had on them or their families.

The Sentencing Hearing

The presentence report is filed with the court, and the judge must sign it, stating that he or she has read and considered the report. Copies also are given to the prosecution and the defense so that they can prepare any arguments about sentencing at the sentencing hearing. At the hearing, both sides may present additional evidence that they want the judge to consider, and they may argue for or against the recommendation of the probation officer. They also may put the probation officer on the stand and question him or her about the information contained in the report.

Following the arguments or comments on the RPO, the judge will pronounce the sentence. Or if he or she does not want to sentence the defendant, or if he or she does not want the defendant to serve a sentence that has been given, the judge may instead grant probation. The details of probation as the alternate to sentencing are presented below, in a later section of the chapter.

Sentencing Options

The law is very clear about what sentences crimes may receive. Misdemeanors are punishable by a jail term of up to one year (or in some cases, up to six months), by fine, or by both jail and fine. Felonies are punishable by one of the prison times provided by the law. Often felonies can be punishable by a term in county jail, which makes the crime a misdemeanor.

If a judge desires more information about a felon than that provided in the RPO, he or she may suspend criminal proceedings and refer the defendant to the state's department of corrections for a diagnostic study. Similar referrals may be made to youth facilities for juveniles. The report from either facility will provide a diagnostic evaluation of the defendant and a recommendation about the appropriate sentence.

THE GRANT OF PROBATION

Probation is not a sentence. No one is ever sentenced to probation. It is an alternative to, in lieu of, and instead of a sentence. Loosely translated from the Latin, it means *I prove*. It is used as an opportunity for the defendant to prove him- or herself worthy to remain in the community and not have to be sentenced or to serve a sentence. It may be defined as the suspension of the imposition or execution of a sentence and the order of conditional and revocable release in the community under the supervision of a probation officer.

The legal definition means that, one way or another, there is a suspension of a sentence. The words *imposition* and *execution,* as they are used here, require further explanation.

To impose a sentence means to give one. Therefore, to suspend the imposition means that no sentence is given, pending successful completion of probation. If all goes well during the period of probation, it will terminate without the person ever being sentenced. If all does not go well and the defendant's probation is revoked, then the judge will choose what the sentence is to be.

To execute means to carry out. Therefore, when a judge wants to give a sentence but not have it carried out, pending successful completion of probation, he or she imposes a sentence but suspends the execution of it. If all goes well, the defendant will never have to serve the sentence imposed. However, if probation is revoked, the judge will order that the sentence previously given be carried out. The defendant knows the entire time he or she is on probation how much time he or she must serve if probation is revoked.

Two other words in the definition given above need an explanation: *conditional* and *revocable*. The word *conditional* means that the judge will grant probation, but there will be conditions attached. If the defendant breaks one of the conditions, the judge can find that the defendant is in violation of probation and may revoke probation. If the defendant does not like the conditions required by the judge, the defendant may refuse probation, leaving the judge no alternative but to sentence the person. Consequently, when a defendant accepts probation, he or she freely and voluntarily agrees to abide by the conditions imposed and to not object when the probation officer enforces them (*People v. Bravo*, 1987).

The meaning of the word *revocable* is self-evident. It means that if probation is revoked, it is taken away, and a sentence will be imposed, or if one was previously imposed but its execution suspended, the execution of that sentence will be carried out.

The Terms of Probation

Misdemeanor probation may be granted for a term usually up to three years. If a condition is imposed, a defendant must be reasonably able to complete that condition during that period, or it is unfair and illegal to impose it.

Probation in a felony case may be granted for terms of varying lengths, depending on the state and the type of crime. Usually, however, felony probation is granted for terms of three to five years. That is a long time for a person to abide by the conditions imposed, and it is sufficient time for a person to prove him- or herself worthy to remain in the community. The majority of convicted felons, approximately, are granted probation.

Types of Probation

The definition of probation given above refers to supervision by the probation officer. This is known as **formal probation** because the person is formally supervised by an officer of the court (the enforcement arm of the court) in those states that operate probation at the county level or is supervised by a state agent in those states that operate probation at the state level. In either case the PO wears two hats. He or she is responsible to supervise and help the defendant while at the same time enforcing all the judge's orders.

In granting probation the judge may order what is called **straight probation**, which is probation straight out of the courtroom and into the community, or **shock probation**, which is probation with some time in jail as a condition of probation. In felony cases this time may be up to one year, and it still is not considered a sentence. Frequently, the jail time ordered is 30, 60, or 90 days. It is done either to shock the defendant out of a criminal lifestyle or to add a little punishment to the probation.

In reporting these cases, the media often confuses the issue by reporting them inaccurately. In the press it usually will say, "John Doe was sentenced to 90 days' jail, followed by three years on probation." Of course that is not what happened. Actually, the judge suspended the sentence and granted probation for a term of three years, subject to the condition that the defendant serve 90 days' jail time. If John Doe's probation is later revoked, he will be given whatever the sentence is for his crime. He will, however, be given credit for the 90 days served, as he would for any days served after the initial arrest.

Not all probationers are supervised, particularly those granted misdemeanor probation. Unsupervised probation is called *court probation* because he or she is on probation directly to the court. A *conditional sentence* is another phrase meaning court probation.

Who Receives Probation?   It is a common misconception that once a person is convicted of a felony, he or she automatically goes to prison. According to the Bureau of Justice statistics in 2004, nearly 7,000,000 people were under some form of correctional control. Of that number, more than 4,000,000 were adults on probation.

Generally speaking, the southern states made more use of probation as an alternative to sentencing, with Texas leading the way. California was second. There are 2,000 probation agencies in the nation, and probation is sometimes operated at the individual county level and sometimes at the state level, depending on the state in question.

Conditions of Probation

The conditions ordered with any grant of probation are of two types: standard and special. **Standard conditions** are the requirements that every probationer must follow, such as report to the probation officer, obey all laws, avoid evil associates, and advise the PO of any change in address or employment. **Special conditions** are the requirements uniquely chosen for a particular defendant or class of defendants.

These conditions must be constitutional, reasonably related to the crime or criminality of the defendant, and must be possible to complete within the term of probation. For example, a bad-check writer might be ordered not to possess any checks except payroll checks on which he or she is named as payee.

A credit card offender might be ordered not to possess any credit cards or open any time payment accounts. A drug offender undoubtedly will be ordered to submit to random chemical testing for the continued use of drugs. Both adult and juvenile probationers associated with gang offenses will be prohibited from possessing gang paraphernalia, or associating with other known gang members.

Special conditions that are frequently ordered include community service work; psychiatric treatment; electronic monitoring, with or without house arrest (confinement); and restitution. Many conditions are required, depending on the nature of the case.

Probation Searches

The most controversial special condition is one that allows the probation officer to search the probationer and his or her possessions. States vary in the authority given probation officers to search, and they vary also in the grounds needed by the officer to initiate a search. And the procedural guidance has come from the legislatures and/or the state appellate courts, rather than from the U.S. Supreme Court. The traditional search condition is termed a **three-way search clause** because the probationer is ordered and agrees to submit his or her person, automobile, or place of residence to search by any peace officer at any time of the day or night without a warrant.

Not all states go this far in allowing probation officers to search their clients. In Wisconsin, for example, where probation comes under the authority of the State Department of Health and Services, a probation officer may search a probationer's home as long as the officer has approval from his or her supervisor and has reasonable grounds to believe that contraband exists. Wisconsin law also makes it a probation violation for refusing to submit to the search of one's home.

This **reasonable grounds** standard satisfied the thinking of the U.S. Supreme Court in one of the few such search cases taken before it. In 1983 a probationer named Griffin was on probation in Wisconsin for resisting arrest, disorderly conduct, and obstructing an officer. One day while Griffin was on probation, Michael Lew, the supervisor of Griffin's probation officer, received information from a detective on the Beloit Police Department that there were or might be guns in Griffin's apartment. Unable to secure the assistance of Griffin's own probation officer, Lew, accompanied by another probation officer and three plainclothes policemen, went to the apartment. When Griffin answered the door, Lew told him who they were and informed him that they were going to search his home. During the subsequent search, they found a handgun.

Griffin was charged with possession of a firearm by a convicted felon, a felony in Wisconsin. He moved to suppress the evidence seized during the search. The trial court denied the motion, concluding that no warrant was necessary and that the search was reasonable. A jury convicted Griffin of the firearms violation, and he was sentenced to two years' imprisonment. The conviction was affirmed by the Wisconsin Court of Appeals.

On further appeal the Wisconsin Supreme Court also affirmed. It found denial of the suppression motion proper because probation diminishes a probationer's reasonable expectation of privacy so that a probation officer may, consistent with the Fourth Amendment, search a probationer's home without a warrant and with only reasonable grounds, not probable cause, to believe that contraband is present. It held that the "reasonable grounds" standard of Wisconsin's search regulation satisfied this "reasonable grounds" standard of the federal Constitution and that the detective's tip established "reasonable grounds" within the meaning of the regulation since it came from someone who had no reason to supply inaccurate information, specifically identified Griffin, and suggested a need to verify Griffin's compliance with state law.

On further appeal the U.S. Supreme Court agreed and concluded that this warrantless search did not violate the Fourth Amendment. In his opinion, Justice J. Scalia stated that:

> To reach that result, however, we find it unnecessary to embrace a new principle of law, as the Wisconsin court evidently did, that any search of a probationer's home by a probation officer satisfies the Fourth Amendment as long as the information possessed by the officer satisfies a federal "reasonable grounds" standard. As his sentence for the commission of a crime, Griffin was committed to the legal custody of the Wisconsin State Department of Health and Social Services (the agency under which probation is operated), and thereby made subject to that Department's rules and regulations. The search of Griffin's

home satisfied the demands of the Fourth Amendment because it was carried out pursuant to a regulation that itself satisfies the Fourth Amendment's reasonableness requirement under well-established principles.

In searching a probationer's house, the PO may search the rooms under the control of the probationer, such as the bedroom, and any common areas shared with others in the house, such as the kitchen, living room, etc. And if the probation officer is at the residence to make a search, giving him or her a legal right to be there, any evidence or contraband of other people, in plain view, may be seized. The same requirement applies to juvenile probationers, whether the parents like it or not.

Police Searches of Probationers

Using the *Griffin* case cited above as the standard, one would conclude that any probation search must be based on reasonable grounds, which is the same standard as reasonable suspicion discussed in Chapter 2. However, that case did not set national precedent, and states must then rely on their own procedures.

The wording used in the probation search clause includes ". . . any peace officer," which means any probation officer, police officer, deputy sheriff, etc. Consequently, if a police officer on patrol stops a person and detains him or her for any lawful purpose and runs a record check that comes back showing that the person is on probation with a **three-way search clause**, the officer may conduct the search, without having any reason, as long as it is for some legitimate law enforcement purpose (a broadly worded caution). The probationer has **no standing** to object to the search because he or she willingly accepted it as a condition of probation.

On the other hand, the U.S. Ninth Circuit Court of Appeals held that ". . . probation searches must be conducted for probation purposes and not [by police] as a mere subterfuge for the pursuit of criminal investigation" (*U.S. v. Knights*, 2000). In some circles this court tends to go against the wind in its decisions, and this one was appealed to the U.S. Supreme Court by the prosecution. By a unanimous decision in 2001, the U.S. Supreme Court upheld the warrantless search of Knights by law enforcement officers because any such search was authorized by the probation three-way search clause (*U.S. v. Knights*, 2001).

As another example, probationers in Arizona are required to submit to a search of their person or possessions by a probation officer if the officer has reasonable suspicion of a violation. Police officers may not stop and search a probationer, although probation officers often have a police officer accompany them on house searches because police officers are better trained in the enforcement and restraint techniques that might be necessary to complete the search.

One note of caution needs to be included. Any search, whether by a police or probation officer, may not exceed the scope of the search clause. If the search order limits the search to a search for stolen property, for example, officers may not search for drugs, or if it is limited to searching the person, they may not search the car or residence. Therefore, it is always better to know of the probation status and of the wording used in the search clause before effecting any search.

If the suspect is on federal probation, police officers probably will not be able to search him or her at all because the scope of the search clause is usually limited to " . . . search by any federal probation officer. . . ."

Modification of Probation Orders

The conditions of probation are the orders of the court, and as stated above, it is the responsibility of the probation officer to enforce those orders. However, any of the conditions may be modified or deleted, and others may be added at any time during the period of probation. If the modification favors the probationer by removing some restraints, it can be done easily and often without a formal hearing.

Examples of this would include deleting a curfew order or an order for drug testing, vacating a fine or restitution order, or changing the time given in shock probation from 90 days to time served. The PO merely will submit a brief report to the court explaining the change wanted and a copy of the new order for the judge to sign. The appearance of the probationer might be a mere formality. However, if the modification will impose more restraint on the probationer, a formal hearing will be required. And a copy of the report recommending these changes will be sent to the defense attorney of record.

Violations of Probation

A probationer may be found in violation of probation for two reasons. If he or she violates one of the conditions of probation but is not arrested for a new crime, it is called a **technical violation**. As an example, if the probationer is on probation for drug use, and a drug test comes back from the lab showing the use of some drug or narcotic, the PO may discuss it with him or her and reinforce what the judge said about not using drugs, or he or she may arrest the probationer for violating that condition against using drugs and return the probationer to court. If the probationer is arrested and charged with a new crime, it is called a **formal violation**.

In either type of violation matter, the PO will recommend the probation be modified to add restraints, such as 30 days in jail to dry out, or to revoke probation and have the probationer sentenced. The judge usually will agree with the recommendation.

A probation violation hearing is a very formal proceeding. It actually requires a **two-stage hearing process**:

1. An initial probable cause hearing
2. A revocation hearing

During these hearings, most of the due process afforded in the original proceedings is required, short of a jury trial (*Gagnon v. Scarpelli*, 1973). In an earlier decision, the Supreme Court granted probationers the right to be represented by an attorney in a probation violation hearing where the judge might revoke probation and impose or execute a sentence (*Mempa v. Rhea*, 1967). That right was made retroactive in another case the following year (*McConnell v. Rhay*, 1968).

Record Expungement

In any case where the probationer has completed the period of probation and fulfilled all the conditions or has been discharged from probation prior to its full completion, many states provide for a process known as **expungement**, the reversal of the conviction. He or she is allowed to withdraw his or her plea of guilty or no contest entered at the time of conviction and to enter a new plea of not guilty. The judge will then dismiss the original complaint, information, or indictment, and the probationer no longer has a criminal conviction.

The probationer has proven him- or herself worthy not only to remain in the community, but to have his or her criminal record reversed. Any rights lost because of the conviction are restored. Except that he or she is told that he or she still must reveal the facts of the conviction when applying for any public office or with any public agency.

There was a time when a person could have his or her record expunged and become a peace officer. However, most states have modified their laws to prohibit a felon from possessing a firearm, regardless of any expungement. A federal law has had the same effect within all the states. In addition, a recent opinion by the Ninth U.S. Circuit Court of Appeals (*United States v. Hayden*, 2001) held that expunged convictions of a state may still be considered as enhancements under the U.S. Sentencing Guidelines when calculating the time for a convicted federal offender to serve.

Most state laws require sex offenders to continue to register as a sex offender even after receiving an expungement. Consequently, once an offender is required to register as a sex offender, the requirement lasts for a lifetime unless a full pardon is granted, which does not happen often. This registration requirement alone will limit the type of employment available to former sex offenders. And new federal law prohibits anyone from possessing a firearm who has been convicted of domestic battery. This law is beginning to have sweeping implications for those currently employed in law enforcement or corrections.

FEDERAL SENTENCING PROCEDURES

Until about 15 years ago, the federal version of the penal code, Title 18 United States Code, provided the maximum prison time a felon could serve, but the sentencing judges had the discretion to choose the actual time up to that limit. Disparity was a serious problem. A simple drug possession offender might be granted probation from a federal judge in San Francisco, whereas the sentence for a similar offense in a Texas district might be 10 years in a penitentiary. Finally, after decades of research and debate about this disparity, Congress established the U.S. Sentencing Commission as a part of the Comprehensive Crime Control Act of 1984.

The Federal Sentencing Commission

The commission was an independent agency in the judicial branch of the federal government. Its purpose was to create sentencing policies and practices and uniform detailed guidelines for all the federal courts. These guidelines became effective on November 1, 1987, as a part of the Sentencing Reform Act. Almost immediately this act was appealed by federal defendants across the country. In fact, the judges of the federal district court in San Francisco declared the act unconstitutional, citing the separation of powers doctrine, because of the way Congress had constituted the membership of the commission. The judges did not want to follow the mandatory guidelines and give up their cherished discretion. However, on January 18, 1989, the U.S. Supreme Court upheld the constitutionality of the act and the commission, making the sentencing guidelines binding on all federal courts. In 2004, however, the same Court held that the guidelines were advisory only, not mandatory.

Federal Sentencing Guidelines

The complete guidelines take up a large volume in book form, and determining a sentence in an involved case can be very complex. It is hoped the following explanation can be understood without providing any complex examples. The guidelines consider the offender's instant offense (crime of conviction) and the nature of the criminal conduct by assigning a base level number to each crime that serves as a starting point. This base level can be increased or decreased depending on the particular circumstances of the case. Factors that can modify it are called **specific offense characteristics** (aka **harms**) which are prescribed in the guidelines.

The base level has a range from one (least serious) to 43 (most serious) that forms one axis (list down the side of a page). A second axis is laid out across the top of the page in six categories to reflect the offender's prior record. In the box at the point where these two axes intersect is the prison time range from which the judge must choose to impose. The sentencing judge has a narrow window to exercise some discretion within that range.

Results of the Guidelines

The use of these guidelines has accomplished one of the commission's primary goals by reducing disparity in the time people serve for the same crime. However, it also has resulted in very long and harsh sentences for most crimes. For example, consider the sentence for the least serious crime of transporting drugs for a defendant with no prior record. Prior to the guidelines, the defendant could receive probation. Now the offense carries a minimum of 10 years in prison. Consequently, the federal prison population has nearly tripled since the guidelines were implemented. By the end of 1997, the Bureau of Prisons housed 101,845 inmates in its 92 facilities nationwide. More than 70 percent of these were serving five years or longer, and more than 40 percent were serving more than 10 years. The cost of running the federal prison system in 2004 ran about $32 billion.

Prison inmates can earn up to 53 days off of their sentence a year, which means that they will serve most of their sentence time. The federal government abolished parole shortly after the guidelines were initiated because it did not think it was necessary. Federal officials soon learned, however, that it was a mistake to abolish parole, so they replaced it with a procedure called supervised release (which is parole). The use of the guidelines, with its many mandatory prison sentences, also has reduced the use of federal probation.

Federal judges sentence approximately 60,000 criminal defendants a year, and they have continued to find the guidelines unsatisfactory and unfair in their efforts to administer justice. The guidelines received several legal challenges over the past 16 years, and finally, in twin majority opinions, the U.S. Supreme Court reversed its own precedent on January 13, 2005, and ruled that the guidelines could no longer be mandatory because it required the sentencing judge to consider factors in sentencing that were not found to be true by a jury. Thereafter, the guidelines have been used as an advisory reference (*United States v. Booker*, 2005, and *United States v. Fanfan*, 2005).

SUMMARY

This chapter presented many of the postconviction procedures associated with sentencing and the primary alternative to sentencing, probation. It began with a list of the possible goals of sentencing, followed by the types of sentencing laws used over the years to achieve one or more of those goals.

Sentencing options in both misdemeanor and felony cases were summarized. Probation, as the primary alternative to sentencing, was presented in some detail, including the roles of a probation officer in the sentencing process, as well as in the procedural aspects of supervision, revocation, honorable termination, and expungement. Also included was an examination of the legal aspects and requirements in some states of probation searches by probation officers and by police officers.

ISSUES FOR DISCUSSION

1. How did the indeterminate sentence law create disparity?
2. Which of the goals of sentencing discussed in this chapter should have priority?
3. How can the system accomplish any of the goals of sentencing?
4. Which is the most effective type of prison sentence, the ISL or the DSA?
5. Who should be granted probation?
6. Should probationers be required to submit to the three-way search, or does that requirement conflict with their Fourth Amendment protections?

REFERENCES

Abadinski, Howard. *Probation and Parole: Theory and Practice*, 9th ed. Prentice Hall, 2005.

Bowman III, Frank O. "The Failure of the Federal Sentencing Guidelines: A Structural Analysis," *Columbia Law Review*, v. 105, May 2005, No. 4, p. 1315.

Champion, Dean J. *Probation, Parole, and Community Corrections*, 4th ed. Prentice Hall, 2001.

Cohen, Neil P., and James J. Gobert. *The Law of Probation and Parole*. New York: McGraw-Hill, 1983.

Ferdico, John N. *Criminal Procedure for the Criminal Justice Professional*, 7th ed. Belmont, CA: Wadsworth, 1999.

Frase, Richard S. "State Sentencing Guidelines: Diversity, Consensus, and Unresolved Policy Issues," *Columbia Law Review*, v. 105, May 2005, No. 4, p. 119.

Morris, Norval, and David J. Rothman. *Oxford History of the Prison: The Practice of Punishment in Western Society*. New York: Oxford University Press, 1995.

Reity, Kevin R. "The New Sentencing Conundrum: Policy & Constitutional Law at the Cross-Roads," *Columbia Law Review*, v. 105, May 2005, No. 4, p. 1082.

INTERNET REFERENCES

http://ojjdp.ncjrs.org/

http://www.probation.homeoffice.gov.uk/output/Page1.asp

http://www.appa-net.org/
http://www.aca.org/
http://www.19thcircuitcourt.state.il.us/links/1_prob_off.htm
http://www.ojp.usdoj.gov/bjs/sent.htm

Case Decisions

Gagnon v. Scarpelli, 411 U.S. 778 (1973)
Griffin v. Wisconsin, 483 U.S. 868 (1987)
McConnell v. Rhay, 393 U.S. 2 (1968)
Mempa v. Rhea, 389 U.S. 128 (1967)
People v. Bravo, 43 Cal. 3d 600 (1987)
United States v. Booker, No. 04-104 (2005)
United States v. Fanfan, No. 04-105 (2005)
United States v. Hayden, No. 00-6042 (2000)
United States v. Knight, No. 99-10538 (2000)

chapter 13

Post-Sentencing Procedures

Amnesty	Parole
Board of parole	Reasonable suspicion
Commutation	Reprieve
County parole	Sexually violent predator law
Discretionary release	Void-for-Vagueness Doctrine
Executive clemency	Writ of *certiorari*
Indemnification	Writ of *habeas corpus*
Mandatory release	Writ of *mandamus*
Morrissey Hearing	Writ of prohibition
Pardon	

INTRODUCTION

This chapter describes a variety of procedures that occur after the formal sentencing of a defendant has been completed. In misdemeanor cases this includes county parole and, later, reversing the conviction. In felony cases it includes the role of the parole board in granting parole and/or setting its conditions or revoking parole. This portion of the chapter also will explain the legal conditions and requirements by which a peace officer may stop, detain, and search a parolee. It also presents the procedures for the honorable termination of parole and an application for pardon.

This is followed by a historical overview of the death penalty, along with a short review of selected appellate cases that have affected death penalty procedures. The law gives the executive branch of government, the governor or president, the discretion to effect criminal procedures through the exercise of four acts of clemency (leniency): a pardon, reprieve, commutation, and amnesty. These discretionary acts are described, along with the regular appellate process and four writs. The chapter concludes with a description of a procedure known as indemnification, paying back a person who has been wrongly convicted and imprisoned.

MISDEMEANOR CASES

The procedures described in this section refer only to those cases in which a misdemeanant is sentenced and not granted probation or given a conditional sentence, such as court probation. Those matters were described in Chapter 12. In the grand scheme of things, this does not amount to many individuals. Of all the individuals convicted of crimes, only about 5 percent are misdemeanants sentenced to jail. And of that small amount, about 10 percent are wobblers, sentenced to jail after receiving felony convictions, automatically changing their crimes to misdemeanors.

The Misdemeanor Sentence

When a person is sentenced to jail, the term will be up to one year. In some cases the person might be serving multiple-year sentences with an order to serve them consecutively, which means that he or she could remain in jail for one year on each sentence. However, when a person is sentenced to jail, in most states he or she is eligible for release on county parole after serving some portion of the sentence, usually half.

County Parole

In many states misdemeanant parole operates at the county level. The county parole board or commission usually is composed of representatives from county justice agencies, such as the sheriff and probation officers, a deputy district attorney, and sometimes a local defense attorney.

County parole boards or commissions meet from time to time during the month to consider applications for parole. They operate as independent bodies with the authority to grant or deny parole.

County parole is defined as:

the conditional and revocable release from county jail of a sentenced misdemeanant into the community under the supervision of an agent of the county parole commission.

As such, it has conditions similar to those imposed on probationers. **Standard conditions** for the parolee might include not leaving the county, obeying all laws, seeking employment, and keeping the parole commission informed of his or her residence. **Special conditions** also might be added, similar to probation cases, such as drug testing and a three-way search clause.

County parole supervision often is provided by a public officer who works with limited peace officer powers under the direction of the county parole commission. Usually, this is a deputy probation officer, designated as the county parole agent, who supervises the parole caseload instead of, or in addition to, a probation caseload. Any violation of the parole conditions may result in the parolee being returned to jail to complete the remaining portion of his or her jail sentence.

FELONY CASES

Reviewing Felony Prison Sentences

In the discussion of felony sentencing in the previous chapter, the elimination of disparity was one of the goals of sentencing under the Determinate Sentencing Law. *Disparity* means the wide and discriminatory terms that individuals serve for the same crime. Under the old ISL, inmates often were kept in suspense for years, not knowing when they would be paroled or what they had to do to win parole. Parole was granted at the discretion of one or two parole board members who heard the case. In many cases, parole came at the whim of a board member. This practice was eliminated under the DSL because discretion as to the length of a sentence is limited, and the sentencing judge must state on the record the factors considered in choosing the time given.

Regardless of this caution, the legislatures in many states have provided additional checks on sentencing so as to further minimize disparity. First, the sentencing judge often retains jurisdiction for a short period of time. This allows him or her time to reflect on and reconsider the sentence chosen and gives him or her the opportunity to recall the individual back to court for resentencing, as long as the new sentence is no greater than the original one.

THE BOARDS OF PAROLE

The second check on the existence of disparity in sentencing often is given to the state's **board of parole**, hereinafter called the **Board**, although the specific names given to these agencies do vary among the states. One of their responsibilities often is to review each prison sentence given within the first year of the sentence to determine the existence of any unreasonable differences in time individuals receive for similar crimes from courts around the state. One way to assess this is to be certain that each judge follows the rules provided by the state's court administrative body as to how sentences are to be determined and what factors are to be considered in mitigation and aggravation.

In some states the Board has the authority to return the inmate to the court for resentencing. Any new sentence may not be longer than the original one.

State parole boards are composed of individuals usually appointed by the governor, with the advice and consent of the senate. Their terms are staggered so that they do not all coincide with any one governor's term. Some states have separate boards for men and women and separate ones for juveniles.

Membership on the Board is the result of a political appointment and not necessarily any professional qualifications. Consequently, the membership often reflects the political philosophies of the governors who appointed them. In addition to reviewing the sentences of inmates, a parole board has several other significant responsibilities. For one, it considers applications for parole from any inmate sentenced under the ISL in those states that use that type of sentencing law. It sets the conditions of parole for all parolees upon release.

Another responsibility of the Board usually is to hear all allegations of parole violations and to decide on whether to revoke parole. The Board also reviews each case in which the person was given life without the possibility of parole for a possible recommendation to the governor to change the sentence, allowing for parole. When a person has been discharged from parole and is crime free for several years, the person may apply to the governor for a **pardon**. All such applications are reviewed by the Board, with a recommendation to the governor about granting the application.

PAROLE PROCEDURES

Parole is defined as:

> the conditional and revocable release of a prison inmate into the community after serving some portion of a sentence, under the supervision of a parole agent.

The parole agent is an agent of the executive branch of state government, as opposed to a probation officer, who might be under the judicial branch of government in those states that operate probation at the individual county level. He or she has peace officer powers that are limited to his or her occupational needs and conditions.

Anyone sentenced to prison with a maximum term of life often will be on parole, if parole is granted, for the remainder of his or her life. The length of regular parole runs from one to five years, depending on the state and the parolee's adjustment within the community.

Discretionary Release

As stated above in the discussion of the DSL, parole in many states is automatic. It cannot be denied by any authority. However, an inmate sentenced to any life term, such as 25 years to life or 15 years to life, is sentenced under the ISL and might be considered for parole after serving some portion of the minimum term. The grant of parole under the ISL is known as **discretionary release** because it is at the discretion of the Board.

Mandatory Release

The parole of all other inmates sentenced under the DSL is called **mandatory release** because their parole is mandatory. The Board cannot deny parole. And the inmate cannot refuse parole. The Board can only set the conditions that the parolee must follow. This can pose a risk to the community if a violent inmate is paroled and has not changed his or her behavior.

A classic example of this situation is the *Singleton* case, which made the news all the way from California to Florida in 1998. In 1978 a 15-year-old California girl accepted a ride in a van from a 50-year-old man named Larry Singleton. He drove her to an isolated place, raped her, hacked off her forearms with an ax, and left her lying beside the road to bleed to death. Fortunately, she lived. He was caught and convicted of mayhem, for which he received the relatively short determinate sentence of seven years instead of a life sentence that he could have received under the ISL. He was paroled early because of good time/work time credits. However, state parole authorities had to hide him and move him from town to town because of the public outrage over his parole.

The public did not understand that under the DSL the law required his parole. He was discharged from parole two or three years later and moved to Florida. On February 20, 1998, he was convicted of murdering a women in Tampa, Florida, who had taken a ride in his van. The jury voted 10 to 2 on February 25 to recommend the death penalty (only a majority vote is required in Florida in death penalty phases of a trial). Singleton was sentenced to death on March 30, 1998. Incidentally, Singleton's 15-year-old California victim, who was then a 35-year-old mother of two and doing well with prosthetic forearms, went to Florida to give dramatic testimony to the jury during the penalty phase of the trial.

Parole Conditions

When a person is released from prison on parole, the Board will set the parole conditions, which are similar to those granted a probationer, **standard** and **special conditions**. Standard conditions usually include reporting to the parole agent within 72 hours of release, not leaving the state or parole district without permission, and not possessing any weapons. Special conditions might include drug testing, mandatory mental health treatment, a three-way search clause, mandatory attendance at AA or Narcotics Anonymous meetings, electronic monitoring, or registering as a sex offender, as required under the state's registration statute.

SEXUALLY VIOLENT PREDATOR LAWS

On July 29, 1994, a seven-year-old New Jersey girl named Megan was kidnapped and killed by a paroled sex offender named Jesse Timmendquas, who had moved into her neighborhood. Soon after, the New Jersey legislature enacted a law that requires all convicted sex offenders to register with the law enforcement agency having jurisdiction in the area where they live. After registration, the danger potential the risk poses by the offender is rated. If the risk is moderate, the police are required to notify the local schools, day-care facilities, and youth organizations of the offender's identity. If the risk is high, police may publicly post the identity of the offender and may even make door-to-door identifications in the offender's neighborhood. This New Jersey law is now known as **Megan's Law**. Now all states and the federal government have some form of Megan's Law, designed to protect the public from sexual predators.

After the passage of Megan's Law, officials in many states began questioning why their sentencing laws allowed the parole of these offenders in the first place. They thought that if an offender posed a risk of reoffending against another child, he should not be released. Consequently, many states enacted **sexually violent predator laws**, which allow state officials to detain sex offenders in locked hospital facilities after the completion of their determinate sentence.

A jury trial and a burden of proof beyond a reasonable doubt is required to certify a person as a **sexually violent predator** and to be so confined. However, almost immediately defense attorneys and civil rights attorneys contested these laws, claiming that they punished the offender twice for the same offense, constituting double jeopardy. Attorneys also claimed that the new laws could not be applied to offenders whose original offense was committed prior to the enactment of the law.

In a test case in 1996, the state of California filed petitions against a sex offender named Rasmuson and 14 others convicted of sexual assault, whose prior acts were committed before the enactment of this law. They appealed, claiming the law could not be applied to them retroactively, that it could not use offenses committed before the "predatory" (SVP) law was enacted. The trial court agreed because the *ex post facto* law does prohibit the imposition of punishment on crimes committed before the new "predatory" law was enacted. However, the second DCA reversed and upheld the application of the SVP law because the law was enacted under a civil code and predatory proceedings are civil and not subject to the *ex post facto* clause (*Garcetti v. Superior Court*, 1997).

In another case a Kansas court held that a similar practice was unfair and unconstitutional. That case went before the U.S. Supreme Court (*Kansas v. Hendricks*) during the 1997 session. By a vote of 5 to 4 on June 24, 1997, the Court upheld the Kansas law, ruling that extended confinement was a civil commitment for treatment, not a criminal punishment. Justice Clarence Thomas wrote the opinion for the conservative majority, stating, "Even though they may be confined against their will [in mental hospitals], they are not being punished."

In Arizona the Department of Corrections has referred the cases of 19 sex offender prison inmates to local prosecutors for civil commitment proceedings. On March 16, 1998, attorneys for nine of the inmates appealed to the Arizona Supreme Court for relief, claiming that the state's sexual predator law that allows a civil commitment after completion of a criminal sentence is unconstitutional because it constitutes double jeopardy. The court agreed to hear arguments in the cases, after which it declined to accept jurisdiction of the case.

In 1990 the state of Washington passed the Community Protection Act, which authorizes the civil commitment of "sexually violent predators." That exercise of law was appealed by a Washington inmate named Andre Brigham Young, who was confined to a hospital for treatment after his last prison sentence was completed. He had been convicted of six rapes over three decades.

The Washington Supreme Court upheld the act as a legal civil proceeding (*In re Young*, 1993), but the case found its way to the U.S. Supreme Court after a lower federal court reversed the Washington court's decision. The case was heard during the 2000–2001 session. On January 17, 2001, that Court held by a vote of 8 to 1 (with Justice John Paul Stevens dissenting) that the Washington law was not unconstitutional (*Seling v. Young*, 2001). It created a civil procedure whose purpose was rehabilitative rather than punitive and did not amount to double jeopardy.

According to the *New York Times*, by the end of the year 2000, approximately 900 SVPs were confined nationwide in a civil treatment facility after the expiration of their prison sentences. This might be keeping certain violent sexual predators out of mainstream society, but the cost of doing so is getting prohibitive. Washington state, for example, estimates that it costs up to $110,000 per year to hold and treat, plus up to $70,000 for the legal costs of the civil trial and appeal process. California is planning to build a prison treatment center to house 1,500 SVPs at a cost of $360 million, whereas Washington expects to pay about $81 million for a 400-bed center.

POLICE SEARCHES OF PAROLEES

Interesting legal issues surround the three-way search condition for parolees. One issue centers on requiring the parolee to waive his or her Fourth Amendment protection against unreasonable search and seizure when he or she cannot refuse parole. Also at issue is whether the standard of reasonable suspicion of a parole violation is required before an officer may search a parolee. States differ in their procedures. In 1986 in California, the state supreme court held that:

> The conditional nature of a parolee's freedom may result in some diminution of his reasonable expectation of privacy and, thus, may render some intrusion by parole officers "reasonable" even when the information relied on by the parole officer does not reach the traditional level of "probable cause." However, the search must be related to the proper purpose of parole supervision and requires a standard of "reasonable suspicion" of criminal activity (*People v. Burgener*, 1986).

A majority of states agreed with the view of parole in this context. This distinguished a probation search from a parole search as to the cause required by police. Parole searches had to meet the standard of **reasonable suspicion** of criminal activity. States such as Colorado, Massachusetts, Michigan, Montana, Nevada, South Dakota, Utah, and Wisconsin have either administrative directives or state court decisions that require a similar standard.

However, California enacted a law effective on January 2, 1998, that requires a prison inmate who is granted parole to sign parole orders that allow for the search of his or her person, place of residence, or automobile without any cause or suspicion.

Pennsylvania already had a similar parole law, requiring an inmate to sign parole orders accepting a search clause that does not require reasonable suspicion (or any suspicion, for that matter) by a peace officer before that officer may conduct a search. In 1997 a prison inmate named Scott came up for parole but objected to signing his parole orders allowing the three-way search. However, if he refused to sign, he would have had to serve 10 more years of his sentence. He signed the orders and was granted parole. He also agreed to a parole condition that prohibited him from possessing any weapons.

In a subsequent search of Scott's home, police and parole officers found firearms and a bow and arrows. He was arrested on a parole violation. At his parole revocation hearing, he objected to the admission of the evidence based on grounds that the search violated his Fourth Amendment rights. The parole board rejected his challenge, revoked his parole, and recommitted him to prison. He appealed to the Commonwealth Court of Pennsylvania, which agreed that his rights had been violated and reversed the parole board's decision. The State appealed to the Pennsylvania Supreme Court, but it agreed with the lower court, so the State appealed Scott's case to the U.S. Supreme Court.

The U.S. Supreme Court had already ruled that the Fourth Amendment does not allow the search of a probationer's home without reasonable suspicion (*Griffin v. Wisconsin*, 1987). It was hoped that the Scott case would provide a federal precedent for states to follow in parole searches. The case was argued in March 1998 and decided in June 1998. The U.S. Supreme Court held that **the Exclusionary Rule does not apply to parole searches** (*Pennsylvania Board of Probation and Parole v. Scott*, 1998), and it reversed the Pennsylvania Supreme Court's decision that had overturned Scott's parole revocation.

This case set a national standard for parole searches: **a parolee has no Fourth Amendment protections and no standing to object to any search**. It threw open the door for states to allow parole searches without any cause.

Almost immediately the California Supreme Court decided a case (*People v. Reyes*, 1998) that had been on hold, so to speak, pending the *Scott* decision. A California prison inmate named Rudolfo Reyes was released on parole after signing his parole orders that included a three-way search clause as a condition. In a subsequent search of a shed on his property, Woodlake police officers found a small amount of methamphetamine. He was charged with a new crime of possession, and the evidence obtained by police was admitted at his trial over his objections, and he was convicted.

The court of appeals reversed his conviction because the state's *Burgener* decision, cited previously, required reasonable suspicion of criminal activity before police could search. The state supreme court, however, reversed the lower appeals court and its own precedent, and upheld Reyes's conviction. In a 4-to-3 decision, the court majority dismissed its own argument in *Burgener* and referred to a juvenile probation search case (*In re Tyrell*, 1994) as precedent and stated that:

> . . . the search here appears to be for a proper purpose and we hold that in the absence of particularized suspicion [reasonable suspicion], the search did not intrude on any expectation of privacy society is prepared to recognize as legitimate.

Consequently, in California and Pennsylvania, at least, parolees do not have any Fourth Amendment protection and may be searched by any peace officer without cause. Other states might follow this lead, balancing the scales (the social contract) in favor of social protection rather than individual liberty.

PAROLE REVOCATION PROCEDURES

A parolee may violate his or her parole by either committing a new offense or breaking one of the conditions of parole, a technical violation. There was a time when parole was considered to be a mere extension of an inmate's cell out into the community, rather than a release from confinement. As such, one did not get back any freedoms, and any revocation of parole simply moved the person's cell back behind the prison walls. All this was done without any due process.

In 1972, however, a paroled robber named Morrissey, had his parole revoked and was returned to prison to serve the remaining portion of his sentence. He claimed that he had been deprived of his freedom without due process, using the Fourteenth Amendment as the basis of his appeal. The U.S. Supreme Court agreed (*Morrissey v. Brewer*, 1972) and established a **two-stage hearing process** as a requirement in all parole revocation cases.

The first stage is actually called a **Morrissey Hearing** and is a probable cause hearing before a representative of the parole board in which the parole agent must establish probable cause to believe that a violation occurred. The second stage is similar to a trial, only without a jury and before a parole board member or panel of three members. The parolee has the right to discovery, to cross-examine witnesses against him or her, and to present witnesses on his or her own behalf. The Board must state its reason for revoking parole, with its decision based on a preponderance of the evidence. It was these same procedures that the Supreme Court extended to probation revocation hearings in its *Gagnon* decision in 1973.

SEX OFFENDER REGISTRATION

As part of the 1994 Violent Crime Control and Law Enforcement Act, Congress passed the Jacob Wetterling Crimes against Children and Sexually Violent Offender Registration Act, requiring states to enact laws mandating that certain sex offenders register with the local law enforcement agency having jurisdiction where the offender lives. It included any offender who, on or after July 1, 1995, was convicted of a sex offense (or minors adjudicated of having committed such acts) against a minor, sexual exploitation, or a sexually violent crime. In 1995 the Wetterling Act was amended by subsequent legislation, Megan's Law, requiring states to make the identities and residences of certain sex offenders available to the public. These registration laws were designed to control all convicted sex offenders, whether the victim is an adult or a child.

Most states' laws require that the offender must register if convicted and released into the community on probation, released from jail, prison, a youth facility, or a mental hospital. Each convicted offender is informed of this requirement before release and must sign a form acknowledging that he or she understands the law. The form contains the offender's intended address upon release, and is sent to the state's department of justice (DOJ) for the purpose of tracking the offenders. The appropriate law enforcement agency is notified of the offender's pending release and address.

If a sex offender relocates, he or she must not only register with the law enforcement agency in the new jurisdiction, he or she must notify the present agency of the move and new address. DOJ is also notified of each new registered address. In many states anyone convicted of failing to register is guilty of a felony, punishable by a prison term. However, if he or she has two prior violent felonies that count as strikes, this might count as the third strike in those three-strike states. Also, any person on probation or parole who fails to register will have his or her probation or parole revoked.

In many states anyone required to register shall, at the time of release into the community, be required to provide two samples of blood and a saliva sample for DNA analysis by DOJ. These sex offender registration laws are designed to keep the identities and presence of sex offenders visible within the law enforcement community. In those states with their own version of Megan's Law, local law enforcement agencies have a list of sex offenders registered within their jurisdiction on file on a computer CD. The list is divided into three categories: the serious risks, the average risks, and others. Officials may circulate or cause to be published the names and pictures of those in the serious risk category.

Any person from the public may go to a law enforcement facility and use the CD on a computer to scan the average risk category to determine if anyone lives within their area, within the area where they work, or within the area where their children attend school. It is a criminal offense, however, for anyone to take any action against the person or property of a sex offender based on the information learned from such a public inquiry. The reader may research his or her own state registration requirements and offender list at one of several Internet Web sites, including www.sexcriminals.com or www.parents formeganslaw.com.

Apparently, most offenders do register when first required but, for many reasons, do not reregister upon relocation. This makes tracking and/or locating sex offenders within a community very difficult. It is particularly difficult in large urban areas with a large transient population. However, some states have formed sexual predator apprehension teams to assist local law enforcement in locating unregistered offenders and arresting them individually or in sweeps within a jurisdiction. Some jurisdictions now report that unregistered sex offenders who have heard about the sweeps are voluntarily reregistering to avoid a third-strike arrest.

In recent years at least 16 states have increased the scope of their registration laws to include broad residency restrictions. In the state of Iowa, these residency restrictions, commonly known as the 2,000 feet law, have been taken one step further by many city governments. These laws usually restrict any registered sex offender from living within 2,000 feet of any school or child-care facility. Civil rights advocates have challenged these restrictions in Iowa, and in one instance filed a class-action case, calling the law cruel and unusual punishment (*John Doe v. Miller*, 2005). In April 2005 the U.S. Eighth District Court of Appeals ruled against the challenge and upheld such a law. This decision has been appealed to the U.S. Supreme Court, but as of this writing a decision has not been reached as to an acceptance of the appeal. In July 2005 the Iowa Supreme Court upheld a similar law from another city (*State v. Seering*, 2005).

In June 2005 Iowa's Jackson Township Committee enacted an ordinance prohibiting sex offenders over the age of 18 years from living within 2,500 feet of any school, park, playground, or day-care center. In July the committee extended its restricted zone to include roller rinks, movie theaters, and amusement parks (*Asbury Park Press*, July 29, 2005). This was a significant restriction in that the Six Flags Great Adventure amusement park is within the Jackson Township.

The city of Des Moines enacted a similar ordinance in October 2005 and extended its restriction to include swimming pools, libraries, and recreational trails. Polk County's chief deputy sheriff, Bill Vaughn, noted that since that enactment, the number of registered sex offenders within the county jumped from 76 to 114 as sex offenders moved out of Des Moines (*DesMoinesRegister.com*, November 2, 2005). Vaughn also expressed concern about the cost of helping to enforce the ordinance and of jailing the violators who refused to move. In October 2005 the city of Ely, Iowa, with a population of 1,500, and without having any school or day-care center, passed an ordinance restricting sex offenders from living near parks, playgrounds, and libraries, in effect making the entire city a sex offender–free zone.

Similar moves are being made in Florida and New Jersey, however, ordinances there have not gone so far beyond state law as they have in Iowa. Although in Florida the city of Miami Beach passed an ordinance creating a 2,500-feet sex offender–free zone around schools, parks, and day-care centers, making nearly the entire city off limits to sex offenders. Whether city or county governments have the authority to enact ordinances that exceed what is required in state laws is an interesting question that has yet to be decided. In any event, the eyes of city governments across the nation are on the U.S. Supreme Court and if and how it might rule on the constitutionality of such ordinances.

THE DEATH PENALTY

The use of the death penalty is one of the most controversial issues in the field of criminal justice. Feelings about it run high, and it is seldom that one person can convince another to change his or her views through an argument. The reasons for and against it have remained the same for many years, and are detailed in much of the literature on the death penalty as an issue (Noll, a). The scope of this text is not issue oriented, and there is no intention here to argue the merits of the death penalty.

A Brief History of the Death Penalty

Executions have been carried out by a number of gruesome methods throughout history. In early America the methods included hanging, burning, stoning, and the swallowing of pins. As society allegedly became more sensitive about how it carried out its executions, hanging became the predominate method, although the firing squad remained in common use in Utah. Hangings used to be a public display, and the last public hanging was carried out in Owensboro, Kentucky, in 1939.

The uses of the electric chair, firing squad, and gas chamber replaced hanging, and now the use of a lethal injection is replacing those other methods in many states. Since 1608, when execution records first became available (Schmalleger, p. 305), approximately 19,000 have been executed. And the controversy over its use has been argued at length in recent years (Noll, b).

During the past 34 years, the U.S. Supreme Court has decided a number of death penalty cases that created significant precedent. The case that led the way is *Furman v. Georgia* (1972). Georgia's death penalty law gave the jury complete discretion as to whether to impose death or life in prison. Furman, a 26-year-old black man, killed a homeowner during the commission of an attempted burglary and was sentenced to death. His attorney appealed on the grounds that the penalty constituted cruel and unusual punishment, in violation of the Eighth Amendment.

Four Supreme Court justices believed that Georgia's law was legal. Justices Thurgood Marshall and William J. Brennen, Jr., thought that the death penalty in any form was cruel and unusual, and three remaining justices believed that the death penalty, per se, was legal, but that the procedure used in Georgia, giving full discretion to the jury, was unlawful. Consequently, by a vote of 5 to 4, Furman's sentence was disallowed, and Georgia's death penalty law was declared unconstitutional. The death penalty laws in most other states were similar to Georgia's and were also found to be unconstitutional.

The *Furman* decision meant that the death penalty of all inmates who had been sentenced using these unconstitutional procedures had his or her sentence reduced to life. They were removed from death rows and placed in the prison system's regular populations. The decision also created a moratorium on imposing the death penalty until the states enacted new laws that met the constitutional test. The new laws had to provide for the presentation to a jury of both mitigating and aggravating factors, and the sentences had to receive mandatory appellate review.

By 1976 many states had enacted new and lawful death penalty statutes in cases of homicide with special circumstances. In 1976 the U.S. Supreme Court approved of a death penalty law that provided a two-stage hearing process: the trial and a sentencing hearing in which evidence could be provided as to the appropriate sentence in a case (*Gregg v. Georgia*). In 1977 the Supreme Court ruled that the death penalty could not be imposed on persons convicted of rape (*Coker v. Georgia*). The case also implied that the death penalty could be used only in homicide cases.

By 1988 the 37 states that had reinstated the death penalty had condemned 2,124 persons to death and had actually executed 100. By the end of 1998, more than 570 had be executed. The popular mood today seems to favor the death penalty, and most politicians would not risk their careers by opposing it. Also, there are efforts at both the federal and state levels to expedite the appellate process so as to avoid the long delays, often between nine and 14 years, from sentencing to execution.

An increasing number of executions are being carried out by lethal injection and, in time, that method probably will replace the other ways of administering capital punishment, according to an AP news story by David Crary in August 2001. It will even replace the electric chair, sometimes referred to in cruel terms as Old Smokey, Yellow Mama, and Old Sparky.

According to Crary, the first condemned man to be electrocuted was William Kemmler, convicted of the ax-murder of his lover. He was electrocuted in New York's Auburn State Prison on August 6, 1890. Since that date, more than 4,300 people in 26 states have gone to the electric chair, one in 2003. However, human rights concerns have supported the change to lethal injection.

As of August 2001, only Nebraska and Alabama use the electric chair as the sole method of execution. Florida switched to lethal injection in 2000 to avert a U.S. Supreme Court review of whether electrocution was cruel and unusual punishment. Georgia's legislature changed to lethal injection for those inmates condemned after May 1, 2000. Condemned prisoners convicted prior to that date still face electrocution. As of November 2005, 37 of the 38 states with death penalty laws allow juries to consider life without the possibility of parole as an alternative.

In 2003, according to the Bureau of Justice Statistics, 65 persons were executed in 11 states: 24 in Texas; 14 in Oklahoma; 7 in North

Carolina; 3 each in Alabama, Florida, Georgia, and Ohio; 2 each in Indiana, Missouri, and Virginia; and 1 each in Arkansas and the federal prison system. Statistics for 2004 show a decline in both death sentences and executions. As of December 31, 2004, there were 3,315 people on death row, with California, Florida, and Texas accounting for 44 percent of the total. In 2004 57 inmates were executed in 12 states: 23 in Texas; 7 in Ohio; 6 in Oklahoma; 5 in Virginia; 4 each in North Carolina and South Carolina; 2 each in Alabama, Florida, and Nevada; and 1 each in Maryland and Arkansas.

WRITS AND THE APPELLATE PROCESS

A convicted person may appeal his or her conviction based on a denial of procedural rights guaranteed in the state or federal constitutions or on the question of the legality of the law itself. An appeal usually questions some procedural aspect of the arrest, trial, or sentencing and rarely questions the legality of the substantive law that the person was convicted of violating.

An appeal that questions the law itself is made on the basis of one of three claims: that the wording of the law is too vague for an ordinary person to understand what behavior is prohibited and is declared to be invalid by the **Void-for-Vagueness Doctrine** (*Maillard v. Gonzales,* 1974, and *Kolendar v. Lawson,* 1983); that the law is unconstitutional in that it prohibits some right or freedom otherwise guaranteed; or that the law criminalizes some behavior that was either not a crime or not a separate crime but a part of another crime.

The first two situations in which the law would be questioned need no explanation. The latter situation requires clarification. As an example, the mere act of forcibly moving a person from room to room in order to complete a robbery used to be sufficient to meet a legal definition of kidnapping. In one case a man attempted a robbery one night of a local hofbrau, during which he forced the cook, a waiter, and the manager to move from room to room to open the safe and collect all the available cash. He was charged with attempted robbery and kidnap. The kidnap portion of the charge was reversed because it was not a separate crime but was a necessary part of the crime of robbery.

A conviction in municipal court, or other lower court, may be appealed to superior court, then to the courts of appeal, then to the state supreme court if the appeal involves some state constitutional question. A felony conviction in superior court may be appealed in the same manner. If either appeal is based on some issue that arises out of the U.S. Constitution, it may be appealed up the federal appellate ladder, from the district court, to the federal courts of appeal, and finally, to the U.S. Supreme Court.

Very few cases reach the top level. The Supreme Court has discretion in accepting cases on appeal and will select only those that have a

significant constitutional question. More than 5,000 cases are appealed to the Supreme Court in a year, and it agrees to hear fewer than 200. Nevertheless, it maintains a full schedule and will hear those cases that undoubtedly will establish procedural precedents that all the states must follow.

Writ of *Certiorari*

A **writ of *certiorari*** is the basic document used to appeal a conviction. A writ is a legal request, when filed. It is a legal order when granted, permitting the review by the higher court of the decision of the lower court. The purpose of appealing any conviction is to have it overturned, regardless of whether the case will be retried. At the U.S. Supreme Court level, it takes a vote of four to grant *cert*—to agree to hear the case.

Writ of *Habeas Corpus*

A **writ of *habeas corpus*** is a writ filed by a person who claims to be held in custody without due process or by the denial of some constitutional right. If a person wants to appeal a conviction, and he or she is already in custody because of it, he or she will file both a writ of *certiorari* and a writ of *habeas corpus*. In this latter writ, the person filing the writ is named first and the person who has custody of him or her is named second. For example, in the *Gideon* case described in Chapter 7, Gideon was in custody in a prison in Florida and he wanted to have his conviction reviewed because of his claim that he should have been appointed an attorney.

The writ cited, when discussing his case, is the writ of *habeas corpus,* naming Wainwright as the second party because he was the director of the Florida Department of Corrections.

Writ of *Mandamus*

A **writ of *mandamus*** is a request made to compel a lower court to perform some action or duty. It might be used when a person requests some lower court to do something and it refuses. The matter is appealed to a higher court on the hope that the higher court will order the lower court to comply with the request. For example, it might be used to mandate the return of some evidence that is no longer relevant, that an agency otherwise will not return.

Writ of Prohibition

A **writ of prohibition** is a writ, or request, that is the opposite of the *mandamus*. It is a request to prohibit some lower court or justice agency from taking some action or performing some duty. For example, it might be used to ask a higher court to prohibit a lower court from admitting certain evidence at trial.

EXECUTIVE CLEMENCY

The executive of a state is the governor, and of the United States it is the president. Each has the authority to exercise **executive clemency**, or leniency, in only one of four ways: pardon, reprieve, commutation, and amnesty, as described below. Their authority in these areas is without question or accountability.

Pardon

This is an act of forgiveness in which the offense is erased as if it never happened. To qualify, a person must have been crime free for some extended period of time, depending on their offense and the state. Most states provide that an application for a pardon will be filed with and reviewed by some board, often the parole board or board of prison terms. If the pardon is granted by the executive, most of the civil rights lost as a result of the conviction are restored. The right to possess or carry a firearm is excluded from this restoration in many states.

At the federal level, the president has sole authority in granting pardons, and no justification need be given to grant or deny an applicant a pardon. For example, just hours before leaving office in January 2001, President Clinton granted 140 pardons. Those pardoned included Patty Hearst Shaw, granddaughter of the famed William Randolf Hearst, founder of the Hearst media empire, who had served 21 months in federal prison for her role in the SLA bank robbery in 1973; Roger Clinton, the President's half-brother; Whitewater scandal figure and partner of Clinton in the ill-fated Whitewater real estate deal, Susan McDougal; former Clinton Housing and Urban Development Secretary Henry Cisneros; retired CIA Director John Deutch; and Fife Symington, former Arizona governor. Those denied a pardon included Michael Milken, the junk-bond king of Wall Street, and the American Indian Leonard Peltier.

Reprieve

This is a temporary delay or postponement in carrying out a sentence, pending some final decision. For example, the governor might grant a **reprieve** to a person who has been given an execution date and faces immediate execution. However, the person also has an appeal pending before some court that could affect his death sentence.

Commutation

This is a lessening or shortening of a sentence. The usual grants of **commutation** are to time served or from life without parole to life with parole. As mentioned above under the discussion of the board of parole, one of their responsibilities is to review all sentences of life without the possibility of parole and to recommend to the governor the desirability of commuting it to life with the possibility of parole. The governor also may commute any death sentence to life. This is one reason that political opponents in a governor's race for election question each other as to their stand on the death penalty.

In his last hours of office, President Clinton commuted the sentences of 36 individuals, including those of the 1970s radicals, Susan Rosenberg and Linda Sue Evans, both serving long terms for terrorist activities. In the previous administration of Jimmy Carter, he had commuted the five-year prison sentence of Patty Hearst to time served, 21 months, and was influential in Clinton's decision to pardon her.

Amnesty

This is an executive act of freeing a person, and usually a group of people, from prosecution. People might be pending trial or prosecution and, because of some political or other reasons, the governor or president thinks that they deserve not to be prosecuted. This writer equates it with the childhood game of hide-and-seek and the use of the phase of (phonetically) **olly-olly-oxen-free**. The executive is calling the game over, either to forgive the players or because he cannot find them. All the players are safe from capture and can return home to start a new game.

An example is the act of President Carter granting **amnesty** to all those who did not register for the draft and instead fled the country. It was as if he stood at the border of Canada and yelled, "Olly-olly-oxen-free," and they all came home, all free from prosecution.

INDEMNIFICATION

Indemnification is money paid as compensation to a person who was convicted of a felony and imprisoned then later pardoned by the governor either because no crime was ever committed or if it was, the convicted person was not the one who committed it. If a person thinks that he or she qualifies, he or she files a claim with the state board designated to hear such matters, with evidence presented by the claimant and by the attorney general, if the claim is disputed. If the Board finds in favor of the claimant, it will award compensation. The amount varies between the states.

SUMMARY

This chapter described many of the procedures that occur after the formal sentencing of a defendant. In misdemeanor cases this included county parole and reversing the conviction. In felony cases it included the role of the parole board in granting parole to ISL inmates and setting the conditions of parole for both the ISL and DSL inmates, along with hearing all parole violation matters and revoking parole.

This portion of the chapter also explained the legal conditions by which a peace officer may stop, detain, and search a parolee. The chapter included a discussion of sex offender registration laws and their recent extension by cities to establish sex offender–free zones, a summary of the death penalty, and a discussion of the procedures by which a governor or a president may exercise four acts of clemency (leniency). The meaning of these acts were described, as were the writs used in the appellate process.

The chapter concluded with a review of the act of indemnification, the compensation to a person who has been wrongly convicted and imprisoned then pardoned for a felony that either never occurred or, if it did, he or she actually was innocent of the charge.

ISSUES FOR DISCUSSION

1. Discuss the advantages and disadvantages of using mandatory and discretionary parole release.
2. How are the Fourth Amendment rights of a parolee diminished from those guaranteed the average citizen?
3. Should the executive of a state or nation have the authority to grant clemency in criminal cases?
4. Discuss the pros and cons of using capital punishment, as well as the most humane way to carry it out.
5. Discuss the pros and cons of having sex offender registration laws, including those with residency restrictions.

REFERENCES

Abadinski, Howard. *Probation and Parole: Theory and Practice*, 9th ed. Prentice Hall, 2005.

Champion, Dean J. *Probation, Parole, and Community Corrections*, 4th ed. Prentice Hall, 2001.

Cohen, Neil P., and James J. Gobert. *The Law of Probation and Parole*. New York: McGraw-Hill, 1983.

Noll, James. *Taking Sides: Clashing Views on Controversial Legal Issues*, 12th ed., Guilford, CT: Dushkin, 2003.

Schmalleger, Frank. *Criminal Justice Today: An Introductory Text for the 21st Century*, 5th ed. Prentice Hall.

Asbury Park (Iowa) Press, July 29, 2005.

Press Democrat, November 11, 2005, p. A5.

INTERNET REFERENCES

http://ccadp.org/electricchair.htm

http://www.desmoinesregister.com

http://www.geocities.com/trctl11/chan.html

http://www.iowasexoffender.com

The following site gives access to every state parole board in the United States: http://www.crimelynx.com/stateparole.html

The following site gives access to the department of corrections for every state: http://www.corrections.com/links/viewlinks.asp?Cat=5

The following site gives access to the U.S. Parole Commission: http://www. usdoj.gov/uspc/questions.htm

http://www.usdoj.gov/uspc/

http://www.appa-net.org/

http://en.wikipedia.org/wiki/Parole

http://www.shurhire.com/

http://www.usdoj.gov/pardon/clemency.htm

http://www.deathpenalty.org/

http://www.deathpenaltyinfo.org/

CASE DECISIONS

Coker v. Georgia, 433 U.S. 584 (1977)

Doe v. Miller, 405 F.3d 700 (8th Cir. 2005)

Furman v. Georgia, 408 U.S. 238 (1972)

Garcetti v. Superior Court (Rasmuson), 49 CA 4th 1533 (1997)

Gregg v. Georgia, 428 U.S. 153 (1976)

Griffin v. Wisconsin, 483 U.S. 868 (1987)

Kansas v. Hendricks, 521 U.S. 346 (1997)

Kolendar v. Lawson, 461 U.S. 352 (1983)

Mailliard v. Gonzales, 416 U.S. 918 (1974)

Morrissey v. Brewer, 408 U.S. 471 (1972)

Pennsylvania Board of Probation and Parole v. Scott (1998) 97-581

People v. Burgener, 41 CA 3d 505 (1986)

People v. Reyes (1997) 52 Cal App. 4th 975

Seling, Superintendent, Special Commitment Center v. Young, No. 99-1185 (2001)

State (Iowa) v. Seering, No. 34/03-0776 (July 2005)

United States v. Knights, 534 U.S. 112 (2001)

Subject Index

Case Index